4/06

2

AMAZING STORIES®

CANADIAN CHRISTMAS TRADITIONS

Altitude Publishing

AMAZING STORIES®

CANADIAN CHRISTMAS TRADITIONS

by DeeAnn Mandryk

with traditional Canadian
Christmas recipes
by Jeff O'Neill

PUBLISHED BY ALTITUDE PUBLISHING CANADA LTD.
1500 Railway Avenue, Canmore, Alberta T1W 1P6
www.amazingstories.ca
1-800-957-6888

Extreme care has been taken to ensure that all information presented in
this book is accurate and up to date. Neither the author nor the
publisher can be held responsible for any errors.

Publisher	Stephen Hutchings
Associate Publisher	Kara Turner
Editors	Melanie Jones & Margaret F. Sadler
Layout and design	Scott Manktelow

We acknowledge the financial support of the Government
of Canada through the Book Publishing Industry Development
Program (BPIDP) for our publishing activities.

Altitude GreenTree Program
Altitude Publishing will plant twice as many trees as were used
in the manufacturing of this product.

Library and Archives Canada Cataloguing in Publication Data

Canadian Christmas Traditions / DeeAnn Mandryk.

Mandryk, DeeAnn
Canadian Christmas traditions / DeeAnn Mandryk.

(Amazing stories)
ISBN 1-55439-098-2

1. Christmas--Canada. I. Title. II. Series: Amazing stories
(Calgary, Alta.)

GT4987.15.M35 2005   394.2663'0971 C2005-904915-4

Printed and bound in Canada by Friesens
2 4 6 8 9 7 5 3 1

To my niece and nephews: Eleni, Turner, and Peter.
Keep asking "why?"   D.M.

Contents

A traditional Christmas greeting.
For more on the origin of Christmas cards, see page 322.

Introduction

"I will honour Christmas in my heart,
and try to keep it all the year.
I will live in the Past, the Present, and the Future.
The Spirits of all Three shall strive within me.
I will not shut out the lessons that they teach."
Ebenezer Scrooge
Charles Dickens, *A Christmas Carol*, 1843

Holidays and Holy Days are fascinating. All kinds of exciting stories can be found in their history. The month of December holds one of the most celebrated and cherished holidays in the world, Christmas. Many people, however, celebrate this holiday without really knowing its true heritage or the origins of its traditions, customs, and rituals. Like all holidays, Christmas was an invented, or rather re-invented, tradition from the beginning and one that continues to change and evolve over time in accordance with cultural and political shifts.

Canadian Christmas celebrations represent a rich tapestry of multi-cultural customs and traditions imported by European explorers, traders, pioneers, and settlers. Arriving on Canada's eastern shores, they made their way west, building homes and communities, creating memories and planting roots that would nurture and sustain generations to come. Part of the legacy these pioneers left behind for future generations is the customs, the recipes, the songs, and the stories that make up this season called Christmas. The Christmas tree, Advent wreath, and gingerbread houses are a few of the traditions that the German pioneers brought; carolling and mummering came with the British, Irish and Slavic settlers; the Scottish brought their delectable shortbread; the custom of setting up a nativity crèche was introduced by the French settlers; Santa Claus came from Canada's southern neighbours where he had evolved from Dutch, German, and Scandinavian folklore....and on it goes.

Regardless of the country or nationality of origin, virtually every tradition associated with the Christmas season has its roots in long-ago times and long before the birth of Christ. Knowing how and why these ancient traditions, customs, rituals, and symbols came to be associated with Christmas sheds a lot of light on the true spirit of the holidays.

The Origin of Christmas Day

On the surface, the origins of Christmas Day seem simple. Everyone knows that Christmas is the celebration of the birth of Jesus Christ who was born on December 25. Surprisingly, that's far from correct.

The Bible doesn't specify what day Jesus was born, nor does it say anything about celebrating his birthday. It does however give clues, and biblical scholars have developed several arguments. Most scholars agree that Christ's birth most likely occurred in autumn, not December. One of the reasons is that John the Baptist was believed to have been born at Passover, which takes place in the spring, and Jesus was said to have been born six months later. Others believe Jesus may have been born in the spring or summer, but the winter is highly unlikely based on the fact that there would have been no shepherds watching their flocks in December. Palestinian winters are too wet and cold to keep the sheep in the fields, let alone stay out all night watching over them. Flocks were either brought inside or slaughtered just before this time of year due to the hardships of feeding and sheltering them.

On another tack, Mary and Joseph were said to be in Bethlehem for a census. But, historians agree it is unlikely that Cæsar would have forced Jews to make a trek to their home cities for this purpose. Roman Emperor Augustus Caesar (Publius Sulpicius Quirinius) held a census in the years 28 BC, 8 BC, and AD 14, and these were only for Roman citizens. Even if there had been a census at the time Jesus was born, it surely would not have been held during the rainy season when travel to Judea was nearly impossible.

There is quite a wide consensus of scholarly opinion that Jesus was born at some time during the High Holy Days of Rosh Hashanah (New Year), Yom Kippur (Day of Atonement), or most likely, Succoth (Tabernacles — also known as "The Season of our Joy"). These festivals normally occur in the autumn, about September or October, but it varies from year to year because the Jewish calendar is based on the cycles of the moon and doesn't track with the Gregorian calendar.

Bible analysis aside, early Christians simply did not celebrate Christ's birth. Not only was the actual date unknown, but they were more concerned with preparing for the Lord's return, which they felt would occur in their lifetimes. In the early years of Christianity, Easter was the most important holiday. It wasn't until the fourth century that church officials, under the leadership of Emperor Constantine, decided to institute the birth of Christ as a holiday on December 25. The sole reason for choosing this specific date was to effectively replace the cherished winter holidays and festivities of the pagans whom they were trying to convert. Ironically, the celebration of the birth of the Son of God began as the celebration of the birth of the Sun God.

Winter Solstice Celebrations

Myths and stories about the sun are among the earliest known to humankind and can be found in cultures throughout the world. The word "solstice" is derived from Latin *solstitium*, from *sol* meaning "sun," and *-stit-*, *-stes* meaning "standing." For three days in late December and again in late June, the sun appears to rise and set in virtually the exact position. Winter solstice in the northern hemisphere occurs when the North Pole is at its furthest point from the sun, between December 20 and 22, when the night is longest and the day is shortest.

Ancient man recognized that the sun makes an annual descent southward, stops moving southerly for three days and then starts to move northward again. For ancient peoples, the winter solstice was a fearsome, mysterious, and powerful phenomenon. Harsh winter conditions rendered food sources scarce and survival uncertain. Vegetation was dormant, migratory birds had long since flown south to warmer regions, and many animals had disappeared into hibernation. As the weeks drew closer to the solstice, anxiety rose over increasingly darker days. These conditions were even more extreme for tribes living in the Arctic where the sun would disappear altogether from November 11 until mid-day on winter solstice, December 21.

The mythologies of these indigenous peoples reflect their spiritual relationship with the natural environment upon which their survival was dependent. The sun, moon, rain, wind, plants, and animals were all part of a complex governing body of powerful deities. Primitive civilizations struggled to understand how to appease and supplicate these gods; they watched and learned how to decipher the clues of what was right and what was wrong; they learned what taboos should never be broken to ensure a good hunt or bountiful harvest; they learned what sacrifices should be made to lure the sun back; what part fire played in enticing the sun god and what plants had the power to ward off the evil that lurked in the dark. Communities and tribes learned that they needed to work together and take care of each other in order to ensure survival.

The return of the sun at mid-winter was great cause for celebration and virtually universal among human cultures, and for a good reason. Whether hunter-gatherers or agri-culturalists, the hard work of the hunt, the harvest and the slaughter were now completed with all the supplies collected and preparations made for the coldest, darkest period of the year. It is quite understandable that these people would want to relieve some tension, reap the rewards of the hard work, and pay homage to the gods for their bounty and blessings.

Ancient Egypt

Scientists have calculated that in 10,500 BC on the day of winter solstice the sun would have risen exactly between the paws of the Great Sphinx of Egypt and have theorized that the Sphinx was possibly built to commemorate this event. Additionally, the shadows of all three of the Great Pyramids of Egypt align perfectly at the the moment of the winter solstice. Throughout known history, the winter solstice signified the victory of day over night, light over darkness, life over death, order over chaos, good over evil. From this moment, darkness began to wane ending the cycle of death and decay while light began to rise beginning the cycle of birth and growth. The association between the fewer hours of sunlight with the end of the old year and the return of the sun as the birth of the new year was natural. Many ancient cultures extended this metaphor to include the death and rebirth of a deity. To the ancient Egyptians, Osiris was the god whose annual death and resurrection personified the self-renewing vitality and fertility of nature. In his resurrected form, Osiris became the judge and ruler of the dead. About 7,000 years ago Egyptians began celebrating his demise and subsequent return on the day when the sun started regaining its power.

Another popular myth of the winter solstice was that

of a great earth mother giving birth to a celestial boy child. Again since the time of the Egyptians, humans have set aside the shortest day of the year to celebrate the birth of a lord of light. Among the Egyptians, this was manifested in the mother and child cult of Isis as the goddess of nature giving birth to the sun god, Horus, posthumous son of the god Osiris. At midnight on the solstice priests would emerge from shrines crying out "The Virgin has brought forth! The light is waxing!" Other winter solstice divine births include the Greek god Apollo, the Roman gods Bacchus (Dionysus in Greek) and Saturn, Balder, Krishna, Mithras, and Buddha to name a few.

Mesopotamia

The Mesopotamians were a polytheistic people, living in what is now the Middle East around 4,000 years ago. Out of their pantheon of gods, Marduk the sun god was their chief god. Each year as winter arrived it was believed that Marduk would do battle with the monsters of chaos. To assist Marduk in his battle, the Mesopotamians held a 12-day festival, called Zagmuk, for the new year. During the festival they re-enacted Marduk's epic battle with chaos, and his creation of the world. At the end of the festival the Mesopotamian king would return to the temple of Marduk and swear his loyalty to the god.

The traditions called for the king to die at the end of the year and to return with Marduk to battle at his side. In order to spare their king, the Mesopotamians devised the idea of using a "mock" king. A convicted criminal was chosen and dressed in royal attire. For 12 days he was given all the esteem and privileges of a real king. At the end of the celebration the mock king was stripped of the royal accoutrements and ceremoniously beheaded, thus sparing the life of the real king. The ancient Persians and the Babylonians celebrated a similar festival called the Sacaea, part of which included the exchanging of places between slaves and masters.

Through trade routes and conquests the Mesopotamian traditions and beliefs travelled to other parts of the world including Greece and Rome as well as central and northern Europe.

Ancient Greece

In ancient Greece, the Winter Solstice ritual was called Lenaea, the Festival of the Wild Women. In very ancient times, a man representing the god Dionysus was torn to pieces and eaten by a gang of women on this day. Later in the ritual, Dionysus would be symbolically reborn as an infant. By classical times, a goat was sacrificed instead of a man, with women acting only as funeral mourners and observers of the symbolic rebirth of Dionysus on December 25. Dionysus is best known as the god of wine whose dismemberment by the Titans and return to life was symbolically echoed in tending vines, where the vines must be pruned back sharply, and then become dormant in winter, for them to bear fruit.

The ancient Greeks also held a festival similar to that of

the Zagmuk and Sacaea festivals to assist their god Kronos who would battle his son Zeus and his Titans. According to later Roman mythology, Zeus (renamed Jupiter by the Romans) defeated Kronos who fled to Latium (Italy) where he became their god known as Saturn. Having first demonstrated his leadership abilities, he became a ruler in Latium. As a king of Latium, Saturn was responsible for the remarkable achievements of this legendary time. According to the myth, Saturn introduced agriculture to his people by teaching them how to farm the land. For this reason, Saturn was thought of as a god of fertility and agriculture also representing death and rebirth; the end of the old year and beginning of the new.

Ancient Rome

In ancient Rome, these celebrations merged with a Bacchanalian festival where the Romans would feast, gamble, exchange gifts, and drink themselves into a state of intoxicated revelry. The Romans celebrated the winter solstice with a festival called *Saturnalia* in honour of Saturn. Beginning in the middle of December and ending with the first of January, Romans celebrated Saturnalia by parading in the streets wearing masks and began a tradition which continues today in the form of "mummers" and other similar end-of-winter carnivals throughout Europe and North America (like *Fasching* and *Mardi Gras*). With cries of "Jo Saturnalia!" the celebration, in addition to masquerading, included indulging in lavish festive meals, visiting friends, and exchanging good-luck gifts called *Strenae* (lucky fruits). They decorated their houses with garlands of laurel and evergreen trees decorated with candles and small pieces of metal.

The Saturnalia was a special time of peace, equality, and goodwill towards fellow men when wars could not be declared, when slaves and masters could share a meal at the same table, and when gifts were exchanged as a symbol of affection and brotherhood. The gifts they gave included coins for prosperity, pastries for happiness, and lamps to light one's journey through the darkness. Another common gift was to give dolls made of wax or clay as effigies hearkening back to the days when humans were sacrificed to gods.

In reminiscence of the Mesopotamian mock king, one slave from each household was chosen by his compatriots to serve as the Lord of the Misrule, although, to his good fortune, he was not beheaded at the end of the festival. The inversion of the social structure provided a kind of release whereby the tensions between the rich and poor could be eased. This tradition, with its macabre beginnings nearly 4,000 years ago, continued on as a common practice throughout the Middle Ages during the Feast of Fools or Festival of Madmen. The festive practice of role reversal was also passed down and developed into a parlour game in the Victorian era whereby the family of the house would serve Christmas dinner to its servants. This tradition even continues today in Canada where many businesses will host a Christmas party with the company executives or board of directors acting as the waiters serving dinner to the employees. In fact, anyone who dons a paper crown from a Christmas cracker is paying homage to this custom of the mock king.

As Rome grew increasingly more corrupt, Saturnalia became a hedonistic time, when food and drink were plentiful. In fact, today the word "saturnalia" has come to mean unrestrained, licentious partying. Peasants were in command of the city; businesses and schools were closed so that everyone could participate in the merriment. Social and moral codes were loosened and once again chaos ruled the land for 12 days.

Celtic

Over 5,000 years ago, the ancient Celts in the Boyne River Valley region of what is now County Meath in eastern Ireland built the complicated tombs of Newgrange. These graves were designed to capture the first sunbeam at the dawn of the winter solstice, harnessing the power to warm the bones of the dead, perchance to revive them. Centuries later the traditions of Roman Saturnalia were incorporated into the Celtic Winter Solstice rituals celebrating the rebirth of the sun and the arrival of the new year. For 12 days, the Celts would feast, party, and play. Passion plays enacting the battle for domination of the year between the Holly King, who ruled winter, and the Young Oak King, who ruled summer, were performed. In some traditions, the ruling king stepped down, went on a symbolic hunt assisting the god of light to regain his power, and upon his return ascended to the throne once more.

Groups of costumed singers and musicians would parade door to door, performing songs and dances in exchange for food and drink. Neighbours would visit each other, exchanging gifts. It was also a time of charity and sharing with those less fortunate or unable to provide for themselves. In a tradition called First Footing, welcoming strangers into the home at midnight on the last day of the year would bring luck to the household.

A King of the Feast or a Lord of Misrule was appointed as the leader of the feasting and the clowning. As in ancient Mesopotamia and Rome, peasants and lords switched places and everything was topsy-turvy symbolizing the impending chaos and the sun god's battle to overcome it. Winter Solstice practices such as these not only restructured the chaos, but also offered a period of atonement and release from previous habits plus an opportunity to rekindle old acquaintances and make amends for the new year. The coming of the light brought forth hope for the future.

In similar fashion to the Romans during Saturnalia, the Celts decorated their homes with sacred evergreens — holly, ivy, and mistletoe — to symbolize the hope for the coming spring, to provide a warm place for the forest spirits to take refuge from the cold, and to protect the home from evil spirits so prevalent during that vulnerable time of year.

Norse

In the colder northern regions, the Scandinavians had even more reason to celebrate the rebirth of the sun god at mid-winter. From Norse mythology and traditions, the Christmas season adopted the burning of the yule log and even the name *Yuletide* for a mid-winter festival when the *Yule* (wheel) turns the *tide* (seasons). Also originating from the Norse tradition is the Christmas ham, which stems from the annual sacrificing of a pig at Winter Solstice in honour of the god Frey.

The Norse god Odin can be found in the evolution of Santa Claus. With the arrival and spread of Christianity, the worship of Odin slowly died out, but many of his characteristics and attributes influenced the legend of Saint Nicholas.

Slavic

The Slavic winter solstice festival is called *Koljada* which probably comes from the Latin word "calendae" meaning the first days of the month, or possibly from the word "kolo" for wheel like the Anglo-Saxon word "yule" representing the circular nature of time and the turning of the season. Like the other pagan winter solstice festivals, Koljada is also a time for revelry where processions of people wearing animal masks and cross-dressers roamed the village.

The origins of Slavic belief, like all cultures and ancient mythologies, were founded in animism and ancestral worship. Food and fires were highly symbolic elements of the festivities. The ancient Slavs had a profound sense of reverence for the four elements. Fire was personified by the god, Svarozhich and it was considered taboo to spit into a fire. Mati Syra Zemlja, or Mother Earth, however, was given the greatest amount of respect as the fertility goddess. Trees were also highly symbolic to the Slavs as sacred places where the Sky Father and Earth Mother met. It is likely that this Slavic reverence for trees developed from their exposure to Siberian natives who were in the habit of keeping a tree near their home as a conduit to other realms.

Bonfires would be lit and the spirits of ancestors were invited inside to warm themselves. Mock funerals were staged where a person pretending to be dead was carried into the house amidst both laughter and wailing. A young girl would then be chosen to kiss the "corpse" on the lips, symbolically bringing the dead back to life and representing the cycle of rebirth. Apparently sometimes even a real corpse was used, but it's doubtful the kiss did anything other than spook the poor young girl! A place was customarily set at the dinner table as well for the ancestors to join in the festive meal. This custom is still honoured today in many Slavic homes.

Even today many cultures, including some in Canada, believe that on Christmas Eve the dead ascend from their graves to receive mass. The parish priest, dressed in white surplice and golden stole, kneels at the graveyard cross where he recites the prayers for the Nativity to the spirits. The dead are then said to rise and look longingly at the village and houses where they were born and then return silently to their resting place. In many areas of Europe, the relatives of the deceased place candles in red glass votives on the graves and the entire cemetery glows red all night long on Christmas Eve. These rituals have been carried forward from ancient times when it was believed that a portal between the worlds of the living and the dead opened up on the longest night of the year.

North American Aboriginal

To the ancient peoples of the North American Arctic, the longest night of the year was a sacred time to gather, share food and drink, light the candles, and burn the fires. It was a time for Inuit families to wait together for the return of Sister Sun. They would not see the sun the next day, or for many days, in fact. Their celebration was an act of faith that the sun would return, bringing light and life back into the land.

"The traditional Inuit rite of solstice was the Bladder Festival, during which the men, the hunters, undergo a purification ritual in the *kashim* hut, which is filled with the inflated bladders of all the animals they've killed that year. After five days, they cast the bladders into a hole cut in the sea ice, then leap through a bonfire, engage in contests of strength, and take a final sweat bath."[1] To the Inuit, the animal bladders represented the souls of the dead that would be reborn by the power of the returning sun. The bonfire symbolized the sun; the contests of strength were a tug of war between the old year and the new year, chaos and order;

and the sweat bath purified, purged, and cleansed the soul in preparation for salvation. Many of the winter solstice practices of First Nations people continue to be practiced today much as they were tens of thousands of years ago.

Early Christianity

All of these winter solstice traditions developed long before the birth of Christ. By the time the Romans began to spread the new Christian religion, mid-winter festivities were so deeply ensconced in the pagan psyche that nothing short of mass lobotomy could have erased the ancient memories or quelled the instinctual need to play out the cycle of death and rebirth. Pagan traditions and stories taught that sharing the bounty, taking care of each other, and welcoming the stranger are the best creative responses to the chaos of the world. But the church had a problem with the hedonistic revelry and idolatry that drove the festival.

Not only could the Church Fathers not stop the newly converted pagans from celebrating their 12 days of feasting and misrule, but the deeply rooted ancient traditions also made it difficult to convert them in the first place. It was, however, possible to Christianize the festival.

So instead of abolishing these winter solstice festivities, the Church appropriated them. In AD 320, Pope Julius I declared December 25 as the official date of the birth of Jesus Christ (winter solstice occurred on December 25 by the Julian calendar in the fourth century AD). In AD 325, at the

First Ecumenical Council of Nicaea, Constantine the Great, the first Christian Roman emperor decreed Christmas as an immovable feast on December 25. And, in AD 354, Bishop Liberius of Rome officially ordered his members to celebrate December 25 as the birth date of Jesus.

The 12 holy Roman days (or rather nights, there are 13 days) established in 47 BC between the end of the Saturnalia (December 19) and the kalends (the first) of January eventually became the 12 holy days of the Christian Christmas celebration. The Romans transferred Saturnalia to the beginning of the year in the fourth century. The 12 holy days were officially adapted to the Christmas-Epiphany period at the Council of Tours, 567 AD. January 6 became known variously as the Epiphany, the Twelfth Day of Christmas, Twelfth Night, Three Kings Day, and the Theophany.

This day is observed as a church festival in commemoration of the arrival of the Magi as the first manifestation of Christ to the Gentiles; in the Eastern Church the festival commemorates the baptism of Christ. The word "epiphany" means the appearance or manifestation especially of a divine being; an illuminating discovery, a revealing scene, event, or moment, and is used to describe how the Magi illuminated the divinity of the Christ child with their worship and gifts. Even though Jesus was much older when the Wise Men made their visit, the arrival is celebrated 12 days after Christmas.

Much of the symbolism and revelry of the winter

solstice celebrations naturally carried over to the Christian adaptation. Although it was instituted by the Church as a solemn period to commemorate the birth of Jesus Christ, in a world where most people engaged in agriculture and remained tied to the cycles of nature, December remained a symbolically charged time for very non-religious reasons. Therefore the Church reinterpreted the 12 days and gave new meaning to all their traditions to fit the story of the birth of Jesus thus making conversion and the transition easier for the pagans to accept. Hence the reason why there are so many legends of miracles associated with Christmas; holly, mistletoe, evergreen trees, the partridge in the pear tree, yule logs and all the other trappings of Saturnalia and Yuletide had to be made to figure in the nativity. The agricultural celebration was replaced with the celebration of salvation for mankind; rejoicing in the light of the sun god was traded for rejoicing in the light of the saviour; and the feasting and merry-making remained for the most part the same.

"By holding Christmas at the same time as traditional winter solstice festivals, Church leaders increased the chances that Christmas would be popularly embraced, but gave up the ability to dictate how it was celebrated. By the Middle Ages, Christianity had, for the most part, replaced pagan religion. On Christmas [Eve], believers attended church, then celebrated raucously in a drunken, carnival-like atmosphere similar to today's Mardi Gras."[2]

Mithraism versus Christianity

The popularity of the pagan Winter Solstice festival of Saturnalia and its ancient roots were just one reason for Emperor Constantine to choose December 25 as Christ's birthday. Many scholars, historians, and theologians have theorized that perhaps the most plausible reason for choosing December 25 as the date to celebrate Christ's birth was that the Church leaders of the Roman Empire were attempting to compete with another growing religion, Mithraism — the worship of the sun god Mithras — whose holy day was also December 25 and was celebrated as *Natalis Solis Invicti*, the festival of the "Birth of the Invincible Sun," or "Unconquerable Sun." There exists much controversy and debate over the role of Mithraism in the development of Christianity and with much of the "hard evidence" having been destroyed and history being re-written by the victors, so to speak, it is difficult, but not impossible, to ascertain what actually occurred.

Iconographic evidence and remnants of this religion can be found in monuments scattered throughout the countries of Europe. The cult is believed to have originated in the Near East, dating back to about 1400 BC, and spread east through India to China and west throughout the Roman Empire. Grotto temples to the faith have been found in Italy, Britain, Germany, Hungary, Romania, Bulgaria, Turkey, Persia, Armenia, Syria, Israel, and North Africa.

For a while, Mithraism and Christianity were serious

rivals with many resemblances in their respective doctrines and practices. By the beginning of the first century, Mithraism had become the largest sun god worship cult of the western world. Within the next 200 years, it had become the largest monotheistic religion in the Roman Empire.

The first Roman emperor to be initiated into Mithraism was Commodus in the latter part of the second century AD. In 270 AD, Emperor Aurelia, a professional army officer, succeeded in reuniting the Roman Empire through military might. In 274 AD he attempted to unite the religions of the empire under the state religion of *Sol Invictus* by erecting a temple to the sun god and proclaiming the winter solstice date of December 25 as *Natalis Solis Invicti.* Although Mithras was not formally acknowledged in the new temple, Romans began calling him *Sol Invictus.* Essentially Aurelia's proclamation served to harmonize the cult of Mithras with the worship of other Babylonian sun gods, such as Marduk/ Baal and Astarte, into one monotheistic sun god encompassing the sum attributes of all other gods or potential rivals.

Emperor Diocletian, also a worshipper of Mithras, is thought to have burned much of the Christian scriptures in AD 307, thus enabling Emperor Constantine to later merge the cult of Mithras with that of Christianity. Emperor Constantine considered himself to be the supreme spiritual leader of both the sun cult of *Sol Invictus* and of Christianity. The big turning point was brought about by Constantine's assembly of the First Ecumenical Council of Nicaea in AD 325, which he called to resolve controversy and establish Christian orthodoxy in an effort to consolidate the empire. A cult or state religion that could encompass all other cults within it obviously helped to achieve this objective. And it was under the auspices of the *Sol Invictus* cult that Christianity consolidated its position.

The Council established December 25 as the official date of Christ's birth and declared that date to be an Immovable Feast for the whole Roman Empire. It also replaced the Jewish principle day of worship, the Sabbath, from Saturday to the Mithraic Sun Day as the Christian holy day, and established the date of Easter. It was out of this assembly that Jesus was formally declared to be the Son of God, and Saviour of Mankind and the Holy Trinity was affirmed as an essential tenet of Christianity.

"Had [Emperor] Constantine decided to retain Mithraism as the official state religion, instead of putting Christianity in its place, it would have been the latter that would have been obliterated. To Constantine, however, Christianity had one great advantage, it preached that repentant sinners would be forgiven their sins, provided that they were converted Christians at the time of their Passing, and Constantine had much to be forgiven for."[3] He personally did not convert to the new religion until he was on his deathbed, since only sins committed following conversion were accountable not those committed prior. "Mithraism could not offer the same comfort to a man like Constantine, who was regarded as being one of the worst mass-murderers of his time."[4] Had history gone a little differently all those centuries ago, modern mid-winter celebrants might be wishing each other a "Merry Mithrasmas!"

Tens of thousands of years ago, pre-historic man peered out of his cave and noticed the sun was getting weaker. From the very beginning of time, the fear of death has sparked a quest and fuelled the collective imagination. "Fear of the dark is the fear of death and fear of death is a primordial fear woven into every human being. The customs of Christmas are all about overcoming the darkness. In the world of botany, the tendency of a plant to turn its tendrils towards the sun is called phototropism. Human beings also turn towards the light. It is part of their genetic remembrance. We do not call it phototropism. We call it Christmas!"[5]

Christmas
and Xmas

The word Christ is derived from the Greek word *Christo (Xristo)* which means "the anointed one." It is also common to find the Hebrew word *meshiyach* ("messiah") translated in English to "anointed" in the Old Testament. In the ancient Hebrew culture it was customary to pour oil on the head of one being given a position of authority. This practice was called "anointing." King David was anointed as king as was every Jewish king from the house of David. Priests were also anointed to symbolize consecration to their office. Originally the term "messiah" did not have a divine connotation. When Jesus began his ministry, he was known as "Jesus the Anointed" and in Hebrew, "Jesus the Messiah." When translated into Greek this became "Jesus the Christ" which was later altered, incorrectly, to the name Jesus Christ.

Christmas and Xmas

The word Christmas comes from Middle English *Christemasse,* from Old English *Cristes* (Christ's) and *maesse* (celebration), meaning literally Christ's Mass, or the celebration of Christ.

The familiar abbreviation Xmas is of Greek origin. As mentioned, the word for Christ in Greek is *Xristos.* During the 16th century, Europeans began using the first initial of Christ's name, "X" in place of the word Christ in Christmas as shorthand for the word. Although the early Christians understood that X stood for Christ's name, and the equivalent of "CH," later Christians who did not understand the Greek language mistook "Xmas" as a sign of disrespect and an attempt by heathens to rid Christmas of its central meaning. Although it was never meant in disrespect, many Christians still object to the use of the shortened version.

The Christmas Tree

O Tannenbaum, O Tannenbaum
(*O Christmas Tree, O Christmas Tree*) from
a German folk song by August Zarnack, 1820

he Christmas tree is one of the most recognized symbols of Christmas, yet its origins are far more pagan than Christian and directly tied to Winter Solstice. Many pagan pre-Christian cultures cut down evergreen trees in December and moved them into the home or temple in recognition of the winter solstice. These cultures believed evergreen trees had magical powers that enabled them to withstand the life-threatening powers of darkness and cold. The co-opting of pagan customs by the Christian Church, in order to facilitate the conversion to Christianity, has a long, well-documented history. The Christmas tree is a case in point. The Christmas tree has nothing to do with the birth of Christ. It is merely the continuation of the ancient custom of bringing evergreens indoors at mid-winter.

The Christmas Tree

Pre-Christian

The ancient Egyptians worshipped a sun god called Ra, whom they pictured as having the head of a hawk with the sun as a blazing disc in his crown. At the winter solstice, when Ra began to regain his strength, the Egyptians filled their homes with green palm rushes, which, for them, symbolized the triumph of life over death. The Egyptians were part of a long line of cultures that treasured and worshipped evergreens.

In northern Europe and in ancient Great Britain, the Druids, the priests of the ancient Celts, decorated oak trees with fruit and candles to honour their gods of harvest and sun during winter solstice. The Druids decorated their trees with symbols of prosperity such as fruit to ensure a bountiful harvest, coins for wealth, as well as charms for love or fertility. The ancient Norse people of Europe also revered the sacred oak tree. The connection they drew between the tree and their sky/sun-god, Thor, may have been derived from the much greater frequency with which the oak tree appears to be struck by lightning than any other tree of the European forests. One of the symbols associated with Thor was the lightning bolt. An Old Norse saying goes: "Beware the Oak. It draws the stroke" (of lightning).

The Norse pagans and Celtic Druids revered evergreens as manifestations of gods because they stayed green and alive when other plants died in the winter or appeared bare.

Scandinavian nature-based religions brought their decorated trees indoors to give shelter to woodland fairies that they thought could ward off evil beings. The Saxons, a Germanic pagan tribe, are believed to have been the first to place lights on their trees in the form of candles. Living trees were also brought into homes during the old Germanic feast of Yule, which originally was a two-month feast beginning in November.

Ancient Romans decorated their homes with evergreens at their Winter Solstice Festival of Saturnalia and exchanged evergreen branches with friends as a symbol of good luck and good health. These gifts were called *strenae* after Strenia, the goddess of health. It became popular to bend these evergreen branches into a ring and display them on entranceways. The modern Christmas practice of displaying a wreath on the front door of the house hails from this ancient Roman custom.

According to Virgil, early Romans decorated pine trees with little masks of the fertility god, Bacchus, in the hopes that as the wind blew these trinkets around, Bacchus would grant fertility to every part of the tree the masks faced. To the ancient Persian/Roman Mithraic religion the "Tree of Life" was a pine in which lived birds and other creatures symbolic of the souls of the dead or unborn.

European Christian

Many credit an eighth century English missionary with creating the first Christmas tree. In AD 719, on the blessing of Pope Gregory II, Father Boniface (born Winfred, or Wynfrith and later known as Saint Boniface) set out to teach the gospel to the heathens of Germany. He is renowned for his work in Germany and is now the patron saint of brewers, tailors, and file-cutters, as well as several German cities. Much of his time was spent in Thuringia, a region in Germany that is well-known today for its production of Christmas decorations. In AD 722, he was consecrated by the Pope as Bishop of the whole of Germany to the east of the Rhine.

According to legend, in order to show the Old Saxon heathens how utterly powerless their gods were, Boniface chopped down the oak tree sacred to their thunder-god Thor. He proclaimed a tiny fir tree growing at its roots as the new Christian symbol to replace the pagan oak. Some legends claim that when he felled the oak tree, it knocked down everything in its path except one small fir tree. He then had a chapel built out of the oak wood and dedicated it to the prince of the Apostles. The heathens were so astonished that no thunderbolt from the hand of Thor struck down this blatant offender that many converted to Christianity. The fall of this oak is said to be responsible for the fall of heathenism.

Legend also has it that St. Boniface used the triangular shape of the fir tree to describe the Holy Trinity of God the Father, Son, and Holy Spirit. The converted people began to revere the fir tree as God's Tree, as they had previously revered the oak tree. By the 12th century, central European Christians were hanging fir trees upside-down from ceilings at Christmas time, as a symbol of their faith.

The modern custom of the Christmas tree is also thought to have derived its origins from the Paradise tree, which was common in medieval religious plays throughout Europe, which in turn derived from the pagan customs. The "Paradise Play" was one of the "Mystery Plays" that enacted the story of the creation of Adam and Eve, their sin and subsequent banishment from Paradise. The play ended with the prophecy of a coming Saviour and therefore was often enacted during Advent.

The Garden of Eden was represented by a fir tree hung with apples. It represented both the Tree of Life and the Tree of Discernment of Good and Evil that stood in the centre of Paradise. Eve would eat of the fruit and give it to Adam. The Church considered these plays to contain immoral behaviour and therefore forbade them during the 15th century. By this time the Paradise tree had become so deeply entrenched a tradition that people began erecting their own Paradise tree in their homes annually on December 24 to commemorate the feast day of Adam and Eve. Since the tree represented not only humanity's fall from Paradise, but also the promise of salvation, people tended to decorate their trees with not only apples, but also with bread or wafers (Holy Eucharist), and often sweets (symbolizing the sweetness of redemption). In sections of Bavaria, fir branches and little trees, decorated with lights, apples, and tinsel are still called Paradies. The Paradise tree subsequently became the symbol of the Saviour and evolved into the Christmas tree, as it is known today.

Thus the evergreen tree went from representing life over death to good over evil to Christian salvation.

Martin Luther, the 16th century German leader of the Protestant Reformation, has also been credited with originating the concept of the Christmas tree. So the story goes, as he was walking home one starry Christmas Eve, contemplating his Christmas sermon, he paused to gaze upon the sky in reverent meditation. He was so inspired by the scene of the night stars flickering through the forest trees that he proceeded to cut down a tiny pine tree and bring it home. To recreate the awesome image for his family, he put up the tree in his home and wired its branches with small lighted candles in metal holders. Some people credit Luther with inventing the Christmas tree to show his young children the beauty of the forest and the night sky. The glittering tree is said to have become a tradition in the many Christmases to come for his family as well as for families around the world. Sceptics claim, however, that the earliest verifiable reference to a Christmas tree appears almost 60 years after Luther's death, and therefore consider this legend highly implausible.

The city of Riga in Latvia claims to have the first documented use of a decorated evergreen tree in 1510. Legend goes that the tree was decorated with paper ornaments and similar to a yule log was ceremonially set on fire. Some stories also say that the Riga tree was Martin Luther's tree.

The recorded history of the modern Christmas tree goes back to 16th century Germany where a 1561 Alsatian statute declares that "no burgher [citizen] shall have for Christmas more than one bush of more than eight shoe' length." The decorations hung on a tree in that time were multi-coloured paper roses (representing Rose of Sharon), apples, and wafers (representing the Eucharist). Later other fruits and nuts were added and sweet treats replaced the wafers. By the 1700s the *Christbaum*, or "Christ tree," (also known as the *Tannenbaum* which means "fir tree") was a firmly established tradition in Germany. The tradition of the Christmas tree spread from Germany to other parts of the Christian world.

The first Christmas trees were adorned with fruits, nuts, and flowers, but only the strongest trees could support the weight without drooping. To solve this problem, German glassblowers began producing lightweight glass balls to replace heavier, natural decorations. These lights and decorations were symbols of the joy and light of the birth of Christ. The star that tops the tree is symbolic of the Star of Bethlehem.

The earliest traceable written reference to a lighted tree is found in a letter written by Lieselotte von der Pfalz, Comtesse d'Orleans in 1660. She wrote that it was the custom in Hanover, Germany, to decorate trees with candles at Christmastide.

There are documented cases of Christmas trees being present in England as early as 1789, however it was not until the late 1820s that they became fashionable. The tradition of the Christmas tree first came to England from Germany with the Georgian Kings and also by German merchants living in England who decorated their homes with a Christmas tree. The British people, who were not fond of the German monarchy, chose not to copy the fashions at court, which is why the Christmas tree did not take root in Britain at that time. A few English families did have Christmas trees, however probably more from the influence of their German neighbours than from the royal court.

Prince Albert, Queen Victoria's German husband, is often credited with popularizing the tradition of the Christmas tree in England. As the son of the duke of Saxe-Coburg-Gotha (a duchy in central Germany), Albert had grown up decorating Christmas trees, and when he married Victoria, in 1840, he requested that she adopt the German tradition.

Queen Victoria, however, was already familiar with the custom, which had been introduced by her grandmother, Queen Charlotte, the wife of George III, in 1800. According to her diary entries, the decorating and lighting of the Christmas tree was a central feature of Princess Victoria's childhood Christmases.

The first Christmas tree that Prince Albert provided his family in 1841 at Windsor Castle was decorated with the finest of German hand blown glass ornaments, plus candles, and a variety of sweets, fruits, and gingerbread. Prince Albert was known to carry on the annual tradition of decorating the trees himself with sweets, wax dolls, strings of almonds and raisins, and candles. For Victorians, a good Christmas tree had to be six branches tall and be placed on a table covered with a white damask tablecloth.

The custom of the time was to light the tree candles on Christmas Eve for the distribution of presents, and again on Christmas Day. Traditionally, gifts were laid out on linen-covered tables beside the tree, not under the tree as is the custom today. The tree was then moved to another room where it would remain until Twelfth Night, at which time the decorations were to be removed. To do so before or after this day was considered bad luck.

Around this time, the Christmas tree was also spreading into other parts of Europe. It was only the Mediterranean countries that were not too interested in the tree custom, preferring to display only a crèche scene. Italy adopted a wooden triangle platform tree called a *ceppo* that contained a crèche scene as well as decorations.

After Charles Dickens' publication of his short story, *A Chrismas Tree* in 1850, the popularity of the custom exploded.

North America

The Christmas tree made its first recorded appearance in Canada on Christmas Eve 1781, in Sorel, Quebec. The Baroness Riedesel hosted a party of British and German officers. She served an English pudding, but the sensation of the evening was a fir tree in the corner of the dining room, its branches decorated with fruits and lit with candles.

The Christmas Tree

The German and English immigrants further popularized the Christmas tree in Canada. In fact, it is highly likely
that many Nova Scotians were displaying Christmas trees
in their homes long before the Baroness's infamous party,
since many of them immigrated to Canada from Germany in
the 1700s. Lunenburg County, Nova Scotia, according to its
municipal website "has produced the best and most popular Balsam Fir Christmas trees in the world for more than a
century. In 1996, the County was designated as the Balsam Fir
Christmas Tree Capital of the World. There are approximately
600 growers in Lunenburg County ranging from very large
growers to those who have a small plot in their backyard.
The province exports over two million trees and one-half
million wreaths annually. More than 50% of the annual harvest comes from Lunenburg County."[6]

The earliest known Christmas tree of sorts in North
America was in Bethlehem, Pennsylvania, in 1747 when a
"wooden pyramid of green brush wood" was decorated with
candles. The German immigrants had brought the Christmas
tree to America in the 17th century, however, like many other
festive Christmas customs the tree was adopted rather late
in America. To the New England Puritans, Christmas was a
sacred observance with no tolerance for the so-called "pagan
mockery." Influential Puritans like Oliver Cromwell preached
against "the heathen traditions" of Christmas carols, decorated trees, and any joyful expression that desecrated the
sanctity of Christmas.

The first retail Christmas tree stand was set up by Mark Carr in New York City in 1851. The first time a Christmas tree was lit by electricity was in 1882 in New York. Edward Johnson, a colleague of Thomas Edison, lit a Christmas tree with a self-made string of 80 small electric light bulbs. These strings of light began to be produced around 1890. One of the first electrically lit Christmas trees was erected in Westmount, Quebec, in 1896. In 1900, some large stores put up illuminated trees to attract customers.

Tree Fashion

The High Victorian tree of the 1890s was a joy to behold. It was as tall as the room, and jam-packed with glitter and tinsel and toys galore. Trees were over-decorated in an "anything goes" style. Virtually everything that could possibly go on a tree went onto it.

By the 20th century, themed Christmas trees were *de rigueur* in upscale Victorian homes. Themes included colour coordinated trees with monochromatic ribbons or balls, or exotic cultural themes inspired by Asia or Egypt. Queen Victoria's death in 1901, however, brought a period of mourning in Britain and ornate trees became a thing of the past. While some families and community groups still displayed large tinsel-laden trees, many opted for the more understated tabletop tree. These were available in a variety of sizes. The artificial tree, particularly the Goose Feather Tree, became a popular choice.

The Christmas Tree

Although artificial trees first originated in Germany in the late 1800s, they did not make an appearance in North America until around the middle of the 20th century. The Addis Brush Company created the first brush trees in the 1930s, using the same machinery which made their toilet brushes. As artificial trees improved, becoming more realistic looking and durable, their use has continued to rise. Most recently, artificial trees have come pre-wired with hundreds of tiny clear or coloured lights. Fibre optic trees with a range of special effects are also available.

The 1930s saw a revival of Dickensian nostalgia, particularly in Britain. Christmas cards depicted 1840s-style crinoline-clad ladies with muffs and bonnets. Christmas trees were large and real again, decorated with bells, balls and tinsel, as well as ethereal golden-haired angel tree-toppers. But, World War II brought minimalism back once again. It was forbidden to cut down trees for decorative purposes, and with so many air-raids, most people preferred to keep their most precious heirloom Christmas ornaments carefully stored away in protective metal boxes. They usually decorated only a small tabletop tree with homemade ornaments, which could be carried down into the shelters for a little Christmas ambience, when the air-raid sirens blared.

Post-war Britain saw another revival of nostalgia. People craved the security associated with Christmas and the comfort of tradition in a rapidly changing world. Trees became one such comfort that they could afford. As well, huge public and communal trees became a way of bringing people together in an atmosphere of friendship to share the joy of the season. One of the most famous community trees in England is the one placed every year in Trafalgar Square, London, as a gift of gratitude from the people of Norway for the help they received from Britain during World War II. Similarly, since 1971, the Province of Nova Scotia has annually presented the "Boston Christmas Tree" to the people of Boston in memory and gratitude for the relief supplies received from the citizens of Boston in 1917 following the collision and explosion of a ship in Halifax harbour. The explosion levelled part of the city and injured thousands.

The late 1990s witnessed a revival of the Victorian concept of themed trees (the "Victorian Tree" was even one such theme). Variety was limited only by imagination.

Today the Christmas tree is a firmly rooted tradition throughout Canada, where the fresh fragrance of the evergreen combined with the colourful decorations contrast with the dark nights and bleak winter landscape. Beyond its pagan and Christian origins, the Christmas tree has become a universal symbol of hope, peace on earth, rebirth, and of light in the darkest time of the year.

Christmas Ornaments and Decorations

Decorating the tree is an especially cherished custom that in many cultures is shared by the entire family. Each special ornament evokes memories of Christmases past: some are family heirlooms, others are travel mementos, and some proudly crafted by the tiny hands of a child long since grown up. Just as Christmas has evolved over millennia, so have the objects and decorations used to adorn the tree. Today, glittering glass, resin, and plastic ornaments, electric lights, and fibre optic motion angels have replaced the gilded fruits, pine cones, sweets, apples, and candles that were once used as decorations.

Druids decorated sacred oak and pine trees with apples, candles, and cakes in the form of various animals and birds as an offering of gratitude to their gods of fertility and sun. Ancient Greeks and Romans decorated the trees sacrosanct to their gods and goddesses with garlands of flowers and cloth. The Chinese draped their hallowed trees with red banners bearing prayers of thanksgiving and praise. In Finland, Lapps filled little boats with bits of food and placed them in a pine tree marked with sacred symbols. Then they sacrificed a reindeer and placed its internal organs in another tree which they smeared with the animal's blood — not a very pleasant way to decorate a tree but symbolic nonetheless.

Christian legend states that on the night of Christ's birth all the trees of the earth blossomed for joy, and bore fruit. In addition, all earth's rivers ran happily with wine. In honour of this legend, Austrians brought boughs of cherry, hawthorn, and pear trees into their homes at the beginning of December and placed them in jars of water so they might blossom in time for Christmas.

The Paradise tree is another very old and charming European custom of decorating a fir tree with apples, representing the Garden of Eden, and small white wafers representing the Holy Eucharist. These wafers were later replaced by small pastries cut in the shapes of stars, angels, hearts, flowers, and bells. Eventually other cookies were introduced in the shapes of men, birds, roosters, and other animals. Originally these cookies were shaped by hand, but later wooden moulds and tin cookie cutters were created to aid the baker. Round glass ball ornaments eventually replaced the apples and came to symbolize the fruit of redemption.

After Prince Albert made Christmas trees fashionable by decorating the first English Christmas tree at Windsor Castle in 1841, other well-to-do English families soon followed suit, using all kinds of extravagant items as decorations. In 1850, Charles Dickens described such a tree as being covered with dolls, miniature furniture, tiny musical instruments, costume jewellery, toy guns and swords, fruit, and candy. At one time, horns and bells were used to decorate the trees, the purpose of which was to frighten away evil spirits. Later, these ornaments took on a Christian message such as heralding the birth of Christ. In some parts of Europe, fairy-like figures were used on the trees, as it was believed fairies lived in the evergreen trees, but later these became angels. The Victorian tree was typically decorated with garlands, candies, cookies, and paper flowers. Young ladies spent hours making Christmas crafts: quilling snowflakes and stars, sewing little pouches for secret gifts, and folding paper baskets containing sugared almonds, as well as stringing garlands of coloured popcorn and dried fruit. Small bead decorations, fine drawn out silver tinsel and beautiful angel tree-toppers were imported from Germany. Candles were often placed into wooden hoops or metal cups for safety.

Most of the 19th century Americans found Christmas trees an oddity. The first record of one being on display was in the 1830s by the German settlers of Pennsylvania who used it to raise money for a local church. Later in 1851 a tree was set up outside a church but the people of the parish thought it such an outrage and a return to paganism that they demanded the minister take it down.

By the 1890s Christmas ornaments were arriving from Germany and Christmas tree popularity was on the rise throughout North America. Up until that time, Canadians and Americans were decorating their trees mainly with homemade ornaments including garlands of brightly dyed popcorn interlaced with berries and nuts.

In 1880, F.W. Woolworth brought the German glass ornament tradition to North America. By 1890 he was importing upwards of 200,000 ornaments annually. Initially, the only ornaments offered were simple glass balls, but soon there were everything from fairytale characters to fruit and vegetables, flags, crosses, butterflies, birds, dolls and soldiers. From the 1870s to 1930s, Germans made the finest moulds for mercury glass ornaments with nearly 5,000 different shapes at the time. As the years turned into the 20th century there were over 100 small cottage glass-blowing workshops in Europe. Today the Germans continue the tradition of fine craftsmanship not only for glass ornaments, but traditional nutcrackers, smokers, pyramids, wood cutouts, and many more fine Christmas collectibles.

A new type of ornament hit the market in the 1890s. These were constructed of cotton batting folded and glued over wire or cardboard figures depicting Santa Claus or angels. These shapes were then covered with shiny powdered glass. At the same time, Czechoslovakian glass-bead makers introduced a new style of glass ornament consisting of geometric beads and hollow glass tubing strung on wire in a wide variety of shapes, colours, and designs.

With all these new ornaments available and the increasing popularity of decorating Christmas trees, a simple device was needed to secure these lovely baubles to the branches. And so it was in 1892 that the wire hook for hanging tree ornaments was patented in the United States.

To facilitate ease of obtaining ornaments, Sears began advertising and selling glass ornaments by mail in 1910.

During the turn into the 20th century almost all ornaments were made in Lauscha, a small town nestled in the Thuringian mountains of Germany. After 1918, restrictions made exporting difficult for Germany and so Japan and America quickly took up the slack left in the ornament and lighting market.

In 1939, Corning became the first company to mass-produce Christmas tree glass ornaments by machine; before this, all glass ornaments were hand-blown. During World War II, Corning was unable to continue to add the silver coating to the interiors of their ornaments. Instead they manufactured clear glass bulbs painted with stripes, which later became popular collectibles.

After World War II, glass ornament production in East Germany declined under Communist management philosophies. Some of the original glass ornament moulds that managed to survive the war fell into disrepair or were lost. Many of the craftsmen left for West Germany, where fine lines of high quality glass ornaments are still created today.

The Legend of the Christmas Spider
There is a legend that tells how tinsel originated. A poor family, unable to afford decorations for their tree, woke one morning to find that spiders had covered their tree in webs during the night. Some traditions add that either the Christ child or the rising sun turned the webs to silver.

Other legends tell the tale of the spiders being banished to the attic on Christmas Eve to escape the mother's broom as she cleaned the house in preparation for the visit by the Christ child. The tree was decorated and waiting for the children to see it. But the poor spiders desperately wanted to behold the special tree, and share in the Christ child's visit. So when all was quiet in the house once again, the spiders crept back down from the attic to witness the beautiful tree. They were filled with awe and joy as they crawled along each and every branch, admiring the glittering beauty and glorious colours of the ornaments. But alas, by the time they had finished admiring the tree, it was completely draped with their sticky cobwebs. When the Christ child arrived, he smiled as he looked upon the happy little spiders. He knew, however, that the mother would be heartbroken when she saw the web-shrouded tree. So he reached out and touched the webs and, blessing them, turned them into silver and gold. Now the Christmas tree sparkled and shimmered and was even more splendid than before. Thus the custom to have tinsel of silver and gold and a spider ornament amongst the other decorations on the Christmas tree was born.

Superstition also dictates it is bad luck to destroy a spider's web until the spider is safe. Symbolism of the spider includes creativity, pattern of life, connecting the past with the future, creating possibilities. Spiders, especially a Spider Woman, feature prominently in the creation myths of aboriginal peoples.

Tinsel or "icicles" for Christmas trees have been made and sold in Germany since 1878. The manufacturing process was initially a secret one, first developed by the French to decorate military uniforms. The Germans obtained the formula in 1610. Silver-plated copper wire is drawn through a series of spools rendering it very fine, after which it is rolled and flattened.

The Legend of the Christmas Pickle Ornament

Supposedly there is a very old Christmas Eve tradition in Germany of hiding a pickle (*saure Gurke*) deep in the branches of the family Christmas tree. The story can be found on tags attached to glass pickle ornaments for sale in North America. The "legend" claims that German parents would hang a pickle on the Christmas tree as the finishing touch after all the other ornaments were in place. The first child to find the pickle would receive an extra gift. The first adult to find the pickle traditionally receives good luck for the whole year.

Nice story but the problem with the German pickle tradition is that apparently no one in Germany has ever heard of it, let alone participated in it.

North Americans, however, often tell a different "story" regarding the origins of this peculiar custom. Some people claim the pickle tradition is a regional custom — from a very small region in Germany that manages to remain anonymous; perhaps the inhabitants are too embarrassed to claim the custom as theirs. Apparently, the claimants say, the practice of hiding the pickle originated as a stall tactic whereby parents, who had just spent hours decorating the tree on Christmas Eve, could get their children to spend some time looking at the tree, and presumably admiring it, before tearing into their presents. In Germany the custom is for the parents to decorate the tree on Christmas Eve while the children impatiently wait in another room for the annual visit from *Christkindle* (the Christ child) or the *Weihnachtsmann* (Christmas Man), who, like the American Santa Claus, brings them gifts and also gets the credit for decorating the tree. When the tree is done the parents fetch the children to admire the tree and receive their gifts. So hiding the pickle somewhere on the tree for the children to find, and then be rewarded, was really a diversion.

Another version of the pickle ornament story is the

"Victorian Christmas Pickle Legend." In this account, the tradition of hiding a pickle inside the Christmas tree comes from a medieval folktale of a miracle performed by Saint Nicholas. The story tells of three students travelling home from university for the holidays. They were tired from their travels so they stopped at an inn to spend the night. The innkeeper was a mean and evil man who stole their possessions, murdered the three boys, then cut up and stuffed their bodies into a pickle barrel (some versions refer to the murderer as a butcher who intended to sell the boys as meat). That evening, Saint Nicholas stopped at the inn for a rest and discovered that the boys were inside the pickle barrel. Saint Nicholas tapped the pickle barrel with his staff and the boys were magically restored.

Through time, the celebration of this miracle developed into the Victorian tradition of hiding a hand-blown glass pickle on the Christmas tree. The person who finds the pickle first on Christmas morning receives a special gift.

There are other related stories such as the German immigrant in the U.S. who was captured and imprisoned while fighting in the American Civil War. One Christmas Eve as he lay on his deathbed he begged a guard for "just one pickle" before he died. The guard acquiesced and the sustenance from that pickle saved the man's life. When he was reunited with his family he supposedly began the tradition of hiding a pickle in the Christmas tree.

According to Hyde Flippo, the German guide on

About.com, the one possible connection to Germany is that in 1847 craftsmen in the small German town of Lauscha began producing glass ornaments in the shape of fruits and nuts using a unique hand-blown process combined with moulds. Today Lauscha exports pickle ornaments to the U.S. — where they are sold along with the dubious German story (written in English only). The pickle ornaments are not marketed in Germany. One thing is certain: the "German" Christmas pickle is neither of German origin nor a tradition in Germany.

So the next time you see a Christmas ornament with a legend tag attached, by all means, buy the ornament if you like it, but take the legend with a pinch of salt.

Christmas Tree Lights

In the days when candles were used to adorn Christmas trees, it was necessary to keep buckets of water close at hand to douse the inevitable fires. On many occasions, disaster befell not only a single home, but entire neighbourhoods. In 1882, just three years after the invention of the incandescent bulb, Edward Johnson invented the first Christmas tree lights. He was Thomas Edison's friend and partner in the Edison Illumination Company in New York City. Johnson hand-wired 80 red, white, and blue bulbs and wound them around a rotating evergreen tree in his home then invited the New York press to witness the spectacle. Only one reporter attended, but the event did make the news in the *Detroit Post and Tribune*.

It wasn't until 1895, when President Grover Cleveland commissioned a White House tree illuminated with over 100 multi-coloured Edison bulbs, that the average American heard of electric Christmas tree lights. Shortly thereafter, members of high society began hosting elaborate and costly Christmas tree parties employing the services of a wireman to set up the lights and a generator to run them.

In 1903, the General Electric Company began selling pre-assembled lighting packages, called festoons, for about US $12. The package consisted of eight green pre-wired porcelain sockets, eight Edison miniature coloured glass lamps and a screw-in plug. Many department stores would rent a festoon for the season at a cost of $1.50. General Electric was unable to obtain a patent for the festoon design and hence the market was open for anyone to replicate the design.

But, the person credited with popularizing electric Christmas tree lights was Albert Sadacca. In 1917, Sadacca's family owned a novelty business selling wicker cages with imitation birds that lit up. Fifteen-year-old Albert suggested that his parents try making electric lights for Christmas trees to replace the commonly used, but dangerous candles. They tried the idea, but only 100 strings of electric Christmas tree lights sold in the first year. Albert tried colouring the clear bulbs and business boomed. Albert Sadacca founded NOMA Electric Company with his brothers Henri and Leon. Their multi-million dollar business grew to become the largest Christmas lighting company in the world prior to 1965.

Many of the earliest electric Christmas lights generated so much heat that they were about as dangerous as the candles they were intended to replace. Genuine outdoor Christmas lights were not introduced to the public until 1927 — nearly half a century after the first electric tree lights were demonstrated.

Christmas Straw Decorations
In some European countries, straw was traditionally spread on the floor on Christmas Day to symbolize the stable and manger where Jesus was born. But this custom can also be traced further back to its pagan origins of ensuring a good crop in the coming season. Today, it is still an integral part of Ukrainian and Polish Christmas feast traditions that straw be placed under the table or under the table cloth. Some say it symbolizes Christ's manger and others say it symbolizes the importance of the crop. Many Christmas decorations were (and still are) made from straw, too.

The Finnish people make an intricate straw mobile called the *himmeli*. It is difficult and time-consuming to construct; the straw used to make the *himmeli* must be straight and of good quality and the first preparations are made during the harvest season. The strong rye straws are first peeled and cleaned by removing the tough outer layer and then softened in the warmth of a Finnish sauna or by soaking in warm water to render them workable. The straw is then cut into equal lengths. Cutting is an exact job and according to some Finnish stories, the Santa Claus Office bookkeeper elf with his measuring tape is called to help with the cutting. When the straws are cut into suitable lengths, they are dried again. Next, the straw is threaded into triangles, squares and octagonal shapes. These various shapes are then combined to produce larger and more intricate shapes. A finished straw mobile is a beautiful, complicated, symmetrical work of art glimmering and swaying as it hangs from the ceiling.

In Norse mythology, the goat was an important folk figure often representing the embodiment of evil. Going by the name of *Joulupukki* in Finland and *Julbocken* in Sweden, literally meaning "yule buck," these characters evolved into a Christmas Goat, often used to scare children into good behaviour. Today, they are portrayed in a much nicer light and have even become Christmas gift-givers. Handmade straw goats bound with red ribbons are a very common Christmas decoration in Europe, especially Scandinavian countries, and sold at every Christmas market. Originally people used to make these straw goats and leave them on a neighbour's porch as a prank.

Preparing the House for Christmas

In many rural areas of Great Britain there existed an old mid-winter custom of whitewashing all the buildings and structures including the outhouses. At one time it was the whole farm, inside and out, that would be scrupulously cleaned. The women would scrub and polish until everything shone, and the men would take buckets of whitewash, or lime-wash, and purify everything in honour of the coming of the Christ child.

This custom goes back long before Christianity or even Celtic civilization. It originated as a purifying ceremony from the ancient Mesopotamians, 4000 BC, who would cleanse their homes and sweep the streets in an attempt to assist their god in his battle against the powers of chaos. And in central European lore, it was believed that the deity, Frigga (Odin's wife), would check the threshold of each house to make sure it was swept clean. From this ancient custom come the modern traditions of decorating with fresh, festive curtains, special Christmas bedcovers, cushions, table linens, and so on.

The Christmas Star

*"I am a star which goes with thee
and shines out of the depths."*
Mithraic saying

Throughout history man has been mystified and inspired by stars. As beacons shining in the darkness, stars have represented the divine, heavens, the spirit, guidance, wisdom, truth, and hope. By virtue of their nocturnal nature, stars came to represent the struggle against the forces of darkness and the unknown, while their fixed nature ties them to order and destiny. It was upon this framework that astrology and astronomy were founded over 5,000 years ago.

The history of western astrology can be traced as far back as the Mesopotamian civilizations (ancient Babylon, approximately 3000 BC), but it did not begin to flourish until the influence of the ancient Greeks during the Hellenistic period (323–330 BC) reaching Rome before the beginning of the Christian era. Astrology underwent further developments in Islamic culture, which in turn later influenced western astrology during the Middle Ages when Islamic science had a powerful influence on Europe. Astronomy did not begin to be separated from astrology until the 16th century, when the system of Copernicus established that the earth itself is one of the heavenly bodies.

Legend tells that on the night Christ was born, a brilliant star appeared in the sky and it was this star that guided the Wise Men to the Baby Jesus. The Wise Men from the East may also have been astrologers of their time and as such they would have believed in the indisputable link between phenomena observed in the heavens and occurrences on earth.

The star of Bethlehem has been the subject of scholarly examination, debate and discussion for centuries. Some believed it was a supernova explosion, others a comet or a conjunction of the planets Saturn and Jupiter, associated with specific constellations that heralded the birth of a king in Israel. The greatest obstacle in trying to pinpoint what exactly caused the strange astronomical phenomenon is that the exact date of Christ's birth is unknown, although modern scholars now date his birth between 7 BC and 4 BC.

Stars are also said to have signalled the birth of Krishna, Lao-Tze, Moses, and Abraham. Babylonians used three stars to represent a god. The Egyptians believed that certain gods controlled particular stars and constellations. Most of the ancient world believed stars represented their gods. The six-pointed Star of David became the symbol of the Hebrew nation.

The eight-pointed star that has since come to symbolize the Star of Bethlehem was also an ancient symbol for the planet Venus, and her namesake, the Roman goddess of fertility. Venus is usually only visible a few hours before sunrise or a few hours after sunset. When at its brightest, however, Venus may be seen during the daytime, making it one of only two heavenly bodies that can be seen both day and night (the other being the moon). It is sometimes referred to as the Morning Star or the Evening Star. In dark skies, it is by far the brightest star and so it is not unusual that these two heavenly bodies, the Star of Bethlehem and the Star of Venus, would come to share the same symbol — a symbol that already had a long-standing association with a goddess and the birth of her celestial son many millenia before the birth of Jesus.

In the 14th century, astronomer Albert Magnus noted that the constellation Virgo rose above the horizon at midnight on December 24 at the reputed time of Christ's birth.

The eight-pointed star became a popular manufactured Christmas ornament around the 1840s and many people place a star on the top of their Christmas tree to represent the Star of Bethlehem. The first star ornaments were handmade of straw or paper.

Holiday Flora

Oh, by gosh, by golly
it's time for mistletoe and holly ...
Frank Sinatra

t one time just about any plant that retained its greenness in winter was revered and held a place of honour, including holly, ivy, mistletoe, and even rosemary and bay laurel. The practice of bringing evergreens indoors at mid-winter was a widespread custom among the ancient Jews, Mesopotamians, Persians, Babylonians, Egyptians, Greeks, Romans, Celts of Gaul and Britain, and Scandinavians. But the greenery was not used merely for its decorative capabilities. The evergreens were used as defence against evil spirits thought to be especially prevalent around the winter solstice. Evergreens were believed to hold magical powers because they stayed green all year and did not perish; therefore, they had power over the winter demons. Ancient temples were decorated with evergreen boughs as a symbol of everlasting life.

Holiday Flora

Many early Europeans believed in the existence of evil spirits, witches, ghosts, and trolls and that all elements of nature possessed supernatural powers — good as well as evil. The pre-Christian Celts of Gaul and Britain brought green plants into their homes during the winter supposedly to provide a safe haven for fairies, and other friendly spirits, from the ravages of winter. The Druids, priests of the ancient Celts, used holly and mistletoe as symbols of eternal life, and placed evergreen branches over doors to keep away evil spirits.

Ancient Roman houses and public places were decorated with evergreens during the Saturnalia at Winter Solstice and Kalends (the first) of January. Bay laurel was associated with Apollo, god of light, and served as a reminder that the long winter would soon melt into spring. These deep-rooted customs held fast as paganism slowly began to give way to Christianity. In the Christian sect, bay laurel came to symbolize the triumph of humanity as represented by the Son of God. As the bay tree — the true laurel of the ancient Romans — is scarce in England, substitutions such the common cherry laurel came to be used.

At first the early Church objected to this intrusion of paganism into the sacred season due to their inherent superstitious sentiments. But these pagan customs were too entrenched for prohibitions to have permanent effect, and in due course they became absorbed into Christianity. Instead of banning these practices, the Church tended to permit their continuance, directing their efforts toward investing the symbols with a new sanctity and meaning. While they were often made to represent higher and holier notions, the original connotations were not always discarded; hence, the mixture of ideas, pagan and Christian, became entangled with the greenery of the season.

Holly (*Ilex, Aquifoliaceae* family)
There are many varieties of holly. The most well known is a type that has red berries and dark, shiny, thorny green leaves. Holly flourishes in almost every kind of soil and extreme temperatures, but does not do well in the shade. The berries are poisonous to human beings. Holly was revered by the Druids, who believed that its evergreen leaves attested to the fact that the sun never deserted it, and since the sun was held in worship, holly was holy. Holly was thought to be despised by witches, and was therefore placed on doors and windows to keep out evil spirits. The plant's sharp points were presumed to snag the evil beings and prevent their entering while at the same time harbouring congenial wandering spirits. Holly was associated with masculinity and was thought to protect the home from thunder and lightning as well as bringing good fortune.

Holly had been the subject of myth, legends, and customary observances for centuries before Christianity. Under the influence of Christian thought and sentiment, holly remained very sacred. Holly's red berries, in Norse mythology, represented the blood drops of the beautiful Balder (see "Mistletoe"). In its new Christian meaning, the berries came to represent the blood drops drawn by Jesus' crown of thorns and holly is even called *Christdorn* in Germany. According to legend, a painful crown of thorns woven with holly branches was placed on Christ's head while the soldiers mockingly cried, "Hail, King of the Jews." The legend claims that holly berries used to be white, but Christ's blood stained them crimson.

Another Christian legend says one winter's eve, the holly miraculously grew leaves out of season in order to hide the Holy Family as they fled from Herod's soldiers. Since then, it has been an evergreen as a token of Christ's gratitude.

The plant has come to stand for tranquillity, joy, and merriment. People often settle disputes under a holly tree. In England it is believed that twigs of holly around a young girl's bed on Christmas Eve would keep away naughty little goblins. In England, the thorny holly variety was referred to as male, and the smooth variety as female. The belief used to be that the first type brought into the house would determine who would dominate the household in the following year, the husband or the wife. For the sake of marital harmony, couples sometimes brought both varieties in at the same time. Other beliefs included the practice of putting a sprig of holly on the bedpost to bring sweet dreams and that making a tonic from holly could cure coughs.

Ivy on the other hand was usually considered to be a bad

luck magnet when brought into the home although growing it on the outside of the home was believed to offer protection to the inhabitants. Christmas time was an exception to this "rule" and it was acceptable to have holly and ivy together under one roof as a symbolic representation of male and female united in harmony. According to superstition, ivy should never be presented as a gift to someone ill, and in fact all ivy should be removed from the home of an ailing person. Some cultures practised the tradition of placing an ivy leaf in a bowl of water on New Year's Eve or on Twelfth Night Eve to predict the state of a person's health in the coming year. If the ivy was still fresh and green in the morning then the person could expect a good year. If the leaf developed black spots overnight, however, it was believed to signify poor or declining health ahead.

The Holly and the Ivy

The holly and the ivy,
When they are both full grown,
Of all the trees that are in the wood,
The holly bears the crown.
The rising of the sun
And the running of the deer,
The playing of the merry organ,
Sweet singing in the choir.
The holly bears a blossom
As white as the lily flower,

Holiday Flora

And Mary bore sweet Jesus Christ
To be our sweet saviour.
The holly bears a berry
As red as any blood,
And Mary bore sweet Jesus Christ
To do poor sinners good.
The holly bears a prickle
As sharp as any thorn
And Mary bore sweet Jesus Christ
On Christmas day in the morn.
The holly bears a bark
As bitter as any gall,
And Mary bore sweet Jesus Christ
For to redeem us all.
The holly and the ivy,
When they are both full grown,
Of all the trees that are in the wood
The holly bears the crown.

Old English Christmas Carol

Mistletoe (*Viscum album, Loranthaceae* and *Santalaceae* families)

The European variety of mistletoe is a green shrub with small yellow flowers and white sticky berries that are considered poisonous. Mistletoe is a parasitic plant that grows on the branches or trunk of a host tree leaching nutrients from the tree; although mistletoe is also capable of producing its own food by photosynthesis and surviving on its own. Mistletoe is most commonly found on apple trees and on rare occasion on oak trees. This rarer oak mistletoe was greatly venerated by the ancient Celts and used as a ceremonial plant by early Europeans.

The common name "mistletoe" originates from the ancient belief that the plant was propagated from bird droppings left on a branch and that life could spring spontaneously from dung. Derived from the Old English word *Misteltan,* whereby *Mistel* meant "dung" and *tan* meant "twig," mistletoe literally means "dung-on-a-twig." As it turns out, this ancient belief was partially accurate. Sixteenth century scientists discovered that the bird droppings did contain seeds and therefore the mistletoe was spread through the digestive tract of birds.

Mistletoe has a long and illustrious history as a magical plant. Despite its toxicity, Druids called this plant *Ull-ice* or "all-heal." It was used in various potions as a cure-all remedy, a fertility drug, and an aphrodisiac. It was used to give strength to the athlete, the hunter, and the swordsman. Norse warriors often dubbed their swords *Mistelsteinn* because of the mistletoe's reputation for magical and strengthening powers. By 1682, French herbalists prescribed it for epilepsy and nervous disorders, and in other countries it was being used as a treatment for apoplexy, giddiness, to stimulate glandular activities, as a heart tonic, and digestive aid.

Holiday Flora

Ancient Druids believed mistletoe was of divine origin brought to earth by a stroke of lightning and sharing in the strength of the sacred oaks they worshipped. After the winter solstice, white-robed priests gathered the plant with great ceremony in a sacred fertility ritual. The mistletoe was cut with a golden sickle and caught in a purified cloth to avoid contamination by contact with iron or the earth and risk losing its powers. It was then offered to their gods along with two sacrificial bulls amid prayers that the recipients of the mistletoe would prosper. The Druids elevated mistletoe to sacred status and even used it in ceremonies of human sacrifice.

In the Middle Ages and later, branches of mistletoe were hung from ceilings and over doors to ward off evil spirits and keep out witches. The custom of using mistletoe to decorate houses at Christmas is a survival of the Druid and other pre-Christian traditions. Mistletoe is used for protection from lightning, diseases, fires, and general misfortunes. If placed in a cradle it was believed to protect the child from being stolen by fairies and replaced with a changeling. Wearing a ring carved of its wood was said to ward off illness and people often carried a piece of mistletoe on them to quickly cure fresh wounds and prevent poisoning or fits. It was also carried or worn to bring good luck during hunting expeditions. Women used mistletoe to aid in conception. If placed beneath the pillow, hung on the bedpost, or by the door, it was reputed to promote restful sleep and wonderful dreams.

People would burn it to banish evil, and in extreme cases some even believed that mistletoe worn around the neck could render its wearer invisible. English and Welsh farmers often gave the Christmas mistletoe to the first cow that calved in the new year in order to bestow good luck upon the entire herd. According to some English apple growers, mistletoe should only be cut at midnight on Christmas Eve, and if preserved throughout the following year, fortunate times will follow.

Originally the Church banned the use of mistletoe in Christmas celebrations because of its pagan origins and Church officials suggested the use of holly as an appropriate substitute for Christmas greenery. Nevertheless, it remained a popular Christmas symbol of love and eternal life. It was called *Herbe de la Croix* and *Lignum Sanctae Crucis* or "the Wood of the Sacred Cross" because it was reputed to have been the tree from which the wood for Christ's cross came. For its part in the Crucifixion, legend says, it was condemned to the life of a parasitic vine, in the same way the serpent was said to be condemned to crawl upon its belly for its part in the Fall. The legend says that as an additional penance, mistletoe was required to bestow good fortune and blessings upon everyone who walked beneath it.

Mistletoe has since become a romantic symbol representing happiness, peace, and welcome. Today, kissing under the mistletoe is a popular Christmas custom. According to tradition, a berry of the plant is to be plucked off for each kiss and when the last berry is gone, there should be no more kissing. Also by tradition, any unmarried woman who is not kissed under the Christmas mistletoe will remain single for yet another year. In some parts of England, the Christmas mistletoe is burned on the Twelfth Night to ensure the marriages of all the boys and girls who have kissed under it.

Kissing under mistletoe hails from the Norse myth of Frigga, the goddess of love and beauty, and her son Balder, god of sunlight and vegetation (the Norse equivalent of Apollo the sun god). According to this myth, Balder was fraught with disturbing dreams about his death, so Frigga set about extracting a solemn promise from every creature, object, and force in nature that they would never harm Balder. All agreed that none of their kind would ever hurt or assist in hurting Balder. Thinking him invincible, the gods enjoyed themselves thereafter by using Balder as a target for knife-throwing and archery. Frigga's efforts ensured Balder could not be hurt by anything on earth or under the earth. Unfortunately, Frigga overlooked the mistletoe that grew neither on the earth nor under the earth, but instead attached itself to apple and oak trees. Balder's enemy Loki, the god of evil, tricked his blind brother, Hoder, the god of winter, into throwing a mistletoe spear at Balder and inadvertently killing him. The death of Balder brought winter into the world and caused Frigga to cry so woefully that her tears turned into the plant's white berries. The other gods took pity upon Frigga and restored Balder to life. The grateful Frigga declared that from then on the mistletoe must bring love rather that death into the world. Every couple passing under mistletoe was enjoined to embrace as Frigga planted a kiss of gratitude upon them for the resurrection of her son.

In Scandinavia, mistletoe was considered a plant of peace, under which enemies could embrace and declare a truce or sparring spouses would kiss and make-up. The Romans adopted mistletoe as a symbol of peace and kissing under the mistletoe became a Roman custom. Notwithstanding the mythological explanation, kissing under the mistletoe more likely hearkens back to mistletoe's long association with fertility. Infusions made from mistletoe were given both to women attempting to conceive and to those in labour, to relax childbearing muscles.

Poinsettia (*Euphorbia pulcherrima,* *Euphorbiaceae* family)

Poinsettias are native to Mexico and South America where they can grow to heights of three metres (10 feet). The Mexicans call this beautiful flower *Flor de la Noche Buena,* which means "Flower of the Holy Night." The flowers were given their common name in honour of the first U.S. Ambassador to Mexico, Joel Robert Poinsett. In 1828 or 1829, Poinsett sent some of these flowers from Mexico to his home in South Carolina, where they thrived in his greenhouse. Even though Poinsett had an illustrious career as a United States congressman and as an ambassador, he is primarily remembered for introducing the poinsettia into the United States. In 1833, the first red poinsettias were sold in Philadelphia and the first pink poinsettias were produced in 1923. The actual flower of the poinsettia is small and yellow. But the large, bright red leaves surrounding the flower are often mistaken for petals.

Flowering is induced in the poinsettia when the nights are longer than the days thus making it a good candidate for a Winter Solstice and Christmas season flower. Without long nights, this plant will continue to produce leaves and will grow but will not flower. Contrary to popular belief, the poinsettia is non-toxic. According to the Society of American Florists, no other consumer plant has been as widely tested. Like other non-food items, if ingested, the poinsettia may cause some stomach discomfort or mild irritation due to the latex in the sap — but nothing more.

There are several legends concerning the origin of the poinsettia. One legend tells the story of two poor Mexican children, siblings Pablo and Maria, who were on their way to church one Christmas Eve but had no gift for the Christ child so they gathered some weeds and fashioned them into a small bouquet. The other children teased Pablo and Maria making fun of their gift. When they placed their modest bouquet at the manger in the church, the weeds miraculously transformed into brilliant red and white leaves.

In another version of the legend, the poor children prayed for a gift to present to the Christ child and as they knelt at the altar praying, bright red and green plants grew up at their feet. There are many similar legends, but all with the same message that the simplest gifts, when given with love, are the most beautiful.

A third legend says that as the Star of Bethlehem shone on the earth, the earth responded by producing a plant that mirrored the star's beauty. The flower's star-shaped leaves were originally white with a golden star centre. The legend says that the leaves turned red on the day Christ died on the cross as a reminder to people of the blood of Jesus. Some leaves however remained white as a reminder of the purity of his sacrifice.

The Christmas Rose (*Hellebarus niger, Rosa* family)

The Christmas rose is regarded as a true Christmas flower because it blooms in the depths of winter in the snowy mountains of central Europe during the holiday season. It is also sometimes called the Snow Rose or the Winter Rose. While a variety of plants over time have come to be called "Christmas Rose," they all are steeped in a legend that dates back centuries. The legend is of a young girl named Madelon who wanted to come to Bethlehem and worship the Christ child. She saw that others had brought gold, frankincense, and myrrh to the humble manger, and she despaired that she had no gift to bring because she was very poor. She searched all over the countryside for a flower that she might bring, but the winter had been cold and harsh and no flowers were to be found. As she began to cry, an angel passing over her stopped to provide comfort and when he brushed back the snow where Madelon's tears had fallen, a bush of white roses appeared. Madelon picked a rose and presented it as her gift to the Christ child. It has become a tradition in some countries to place a rose by the front door on Christmas Eve.

Rosemary (*Rosmarinus officinalis, Larniaceae* family)
Rosemary was another revered ceremonial plant symbolizing remembrance, friendship, and fidelity. At medieval weddings it was woven into a bride's wreath, used to decorate the church, and was presented, tied with ribbons, to the bridesmaids and guests. The floor of the church was strewn with it at Christmas as were homes and, as a poor man's incense, it was burnt in place of the real thing. During exams, Greek students wore rosemary in their hair in the belief that it would aid their memories. It was cultivated in monastery gardens as both a medicinal plant and an edible herb.

There are many legends surrounding rosemary, but perhaps the best known is that the humble rosemary will never grow taller than Jesus. Even if it outlives Jesus' 33 years of life, it will grow outwards rather than upwards.

According to another legend, rosemary was originally a white-flowered plant until it got its colour from Mary's blue cloak. As Mary, Joseph, and the baby Jesus were fleeing to Egypt, Mary laid her cloak on a rosemary bush and its colour changed to blue.

Yule Logs

I n the northern latitudes of Scandinavia, the sun disappears for many days during the winter months. In ancient times, scouts would be sent to the mountaintops to look for the return of the sun god after 35 days of darkness. When the first rays of light were seen, the team would return bearing the good news. This news launched a great festival, called the Yuletide, and a special feast would be served around a great fire burning with a sacred yule log. In some areas, people would tie apples to branches of trees as a reminder that spring and summer would once again return and the sun god had not forsaken them.

The word "yule" is derived from the Anglo-Saxon word *geol* for feast, and is akin to the Old Norse word *jol* (the "j" is pronounced like the English "y") for a midwinter festival.

Yule is also believed to be related to an ancient Indo-European word meaning "wheel" or "to go around" as in the turning or cycles of the year. The word "tide" as in "Yuletide" may come from the Old English *tid* meaning "division of time" and in the case of "yuletide" means "time or season." These ancient peoples did not see time as linear; they viewed time as an eternally turning circle. They were acutely attuned to the cycles of nature, of life and death and rebirth. Nature died every winter and was reborn again every spring. The wheel of time continued to go around and it was cause to celebrate. And fire was an important ritual of the celebration bringing forward its sacred flame of hope and enlightenment into the new year ahead.

Celts, Norse, and Teutons believed that trees were the earthly representatives of the gods. Sacrificing a yule log to the dying sun was a universal practice although local customs varied. The yule log was ceremonially decorated with evergreens and ribbons, and a libation poured over it before the lighting. The magical attributes of the sacred oak were so significant that each year a firebrand was rescued from the flames and reserved to kindle next year's yule log. During the interim, it served as a talisman to protect the home from a variety of evils, including lightning.

Fortunes were told by the burning of the yule log and its light was considered sacred and powerful enough to keep evil spirits at bay. The Norse believed that each spark from the fire represented new livestock that would be born during the coming year. The yule log would be kept burning for 12 days with a different sacrifice being offered on each of the 12 days. Afterwards the ashes were carefully gathered and preserved to impart a magical efficacy to a variety of spells and cures.

The English custom of "Bringing in the Yule Log" is derived from the Scandinavian tradition, brought over the North Sea by invading forces to Great Britain and then spread throughout Europe, eventually reaching North America. As Christianity spread, the custom become more closely associated with Christmas, especially in England where Father Christmas was often seen carrying the yule log. The blaze of the fire was made to symbolize Christ as the Light of the World. The Church incorporated the lights and fires into the Nativity celebration to symbolize the fact that the darkness of the world was past and true light now shone. At one time, the burning of the yule log was also one of the most staunchly rooted customs of the Christmas season. Echoing its pagan origins, all aspects of the yule log custom continued to be fraught with ritual and superstition to prevent bad luck and ensure good fortune in the coming year.

It was considered unlucky to purchase a yule log. Lucky logs were found on one's own property or obtained from a neighbour's woodpile. The mass of wood could also be a tree stump or trunk instead of an actual log but, whatever the form, it was brought home on Christmas Eve and ceremonially placed in the family's hearth. Choices about the type of wood, the method of lighting, and the length of time it took to burn constituted a genuine ritual varying from region to region. The master of the house would then make libations by sprinkling the trunk with oil, salt, and mulled wine, and reciting certain prayers. Sometimes this privilege went to a young daughter or the mother.

The first step towards lighting the yule log was to retrieve the carefully-preserved scrap of the previous year's log from under the homeowner's bed where it had remained throughout the year to keep the house safe from fire, lightning, and the malevolent powers of the devil. This remnant of the previous log was then used to light the new log, which had to catch fire during the first attempt at lighting it; failure to do so was an omen of misfortune befalling the family. This important task with such serious consequences had to be undertaken gravely and with clean hands only; which often proved to be a difficult achievement in itself considering the source of ignition. Any attempt to light the log with dirty hands would have been a devastating sign of disrespect. There also existed a belief that it was extremely unlucky if the yule log was touched by a barefooted woman or a squint-eyed man. A flat-footed visitor to the house whilst the log was burning was also considered to be a bad omen.

Once lit, the log had to be kept burning for 12 hrs. This was not always an easy task either, since the embers could not be stoked during the lengthy Christmas Eve supper. While any part of the meal remained on the table, or while anyone was still eating, the log was not supposed to be tended.

After dinner, and while the log continued to burn, the family and their guests sipped hot cider and took turns telling ghost stories and legends of old. Shadows that were cast upon the wall were carefully examined, for it was believed that a bodily shadow showing no head foretold the death of the person casting it within the year. In some regions the yule log was called The Mock and children were allowed to stay up until midnight on that special night to "drink to the Mock."

As the yule log tradition spread through Europe it acquired many new rituals and different names. The Irish called it *bloc na Nodleg* or Christmas block. In Spain, children followed the log as it was dragged through the village, beating it with sticks to drive out the evil spirits and people who lived along the way would give gifts of nuts and chocolates to the children. In the Balkan areas of Europe, women decorated the log with red silk, gold wire, needles, and flowers before its ritual burning. In Italy the yule log was called a *ceppo*. The tradition also dates back to the 12th century in France and was brought to Quebec by the French.

In some parts of the Scottish highlands, the head of the household would search out a withered stump and carve it into the likeness of an old woman, the *Cailleach Nollaich* or Christmas Old Wife. She was considered a sinister being representing the evils of winter and death. She was the goddess of winter, the hag of night, and the old one who brings death. Burning her likeness was meant to drive away the winter and protect the occupants of the household from death.

If a neighbour's fire had gone out, one was never to give fire from his own house to the neighbour. This was regarded as one of the most unlucky things that could be done as it was believed to ensure a death within the donating family during the coming year.

In Newfoundland, a slightly new variation was added to the yule log ritual: the Newfoundlanders threw a piece of the flaming log over the roof of their homes in the belief that this would protect the home and its inhabitants from fire during the coming year. Of course it was considered very bad luck if the flaming log landed on the roof.

Similar to the yule log was the Christmas candle. It too was lit on Christmas Eve, usually at sun down. Care was taken to keep the Christmas candle burning all night long or at least as long as the hosts were awake. Like the yule log, a proper Christmas candle could not be purchased, so merchants made a practice of handing them out to customers. A piece of the burnt-down candle was also preserved from one year to the next as a lucky talisman for the household.

The yule log traditions persisted up until the last quarter of the 19th century. Its disappearance coincides with loss of huge central family hearths, which were gradually replaced by cast-iron stoves and smaller fireplaces. The traditional yule log was subsequently replaced by a smaller one, often adorned with candles and greenery, taking a place of honour as a centrepiece on the Christmas dinner table.

A different version of the yule log is available today, still known as the *buche de noel*. It is an edible variety in the form of a rich chocolate roll, covered with chocolate icing that looks like tree bark and is decorated with frosted berries and holly leaves. This delicious yule log is served as part of the Christmas Eve meal in France called *réveillon*, which occurs after midnight mass. The *buche de noel* can be bought and no part of last year's cake need be preserved to make the next year's cake. Traditionally, a piece was often retained to protect the home from storms. The Slavic people still practice a similar ritual but with a special bread called "kulach."

Christmas Candles and the Festival of Lights

Because Saturnalia took place at the solstice, it was also known as the Festival of Lights. Often the presents given were candles, used to summon the sun back to life. Several hundred years later, the Celts celebrated a winter festival, which later became known as "Candlemas." In part, it was a midwinter house-cleaning day wherein people would light candles and clean everything. The burning of candles also often accompanied the burning of the yule log. The lights and fires, incorporated into the Nativity celebration, were made to symbolize the fact that the darkness of the world was past and with the arrival of Christ, the Saviour, true light now shone and he was the Light of the World. The followers of the Jewish and

Hindu faiths also celebrate mid-winter Festivals of Lights, known respectively as Hanukkah and Diwali.

Many Christians throughout Europe still place Christmas candles in their windows and use candles in holders on their trees instead of lights. This tradition of placing candles in windows is believed to have originated in Ireland as a way of lighting the way for a stranger in the dark, dating back to ancient times when the laws of hospitality were stronger. To have a light in the window on Christmas Eve to welcome the stranger meant that the household was welcoming the Holy Family, too. During the years of religious suppression, candles were put in windows as a signal to fugitive priests of safe harbour within that household and that the saying of mass was welcome there.

There is a lot of folklore involving candles and by their very nature candles and flame throughout history have been rife with superstition. All one need do is light a candle in the dark to get a sense of the mystique and eeriness that emanates from the flickering flame and the dancing shadows cast by the light.

The following are some of the ancient superstitions associated with candles:

- A Christmas candle should be left to burn all night on Christmas Eve to light the way for the Holy Family and also to ensure light, warmth, and a prosperous year ahead.

- It is considered unlucky to light three candles with a single match, as well as to burn three candles at the same time.
- An ancient rhyme says: "If a candle falls and breaks in two, double trouble will come to you!"
- A candle left to burn itself out will bring misfortune.
- A candle suddenly going out by itself is an omen of a death in the family.
- To dream of a white candle foretells true love.
- If a single woman sees two white candles in a dream, it is a sign that she will soon receive a proposal of marriage.
- To dream of five candles is an omen of love and marriage.
- To dream of a candle in a holder is an omen of a happy and prosperous future.
- To dream of a candleholder without a candle in it foretells sorrow and misfortune.
- A blue light emanating from a candle is a sign that good spirits are nearby.
- Always light candles at moments of birth, marriage, and death to ensure evil spirits are kept at bay during these crucial moments.
- Light a brown candle on the eve of Candlemas for protection against evil spirits and ghosts.
- In Sicily, fishermen burn ornate candles to their

patron saint to obtain blessings and protection.
- Place a burning candle in a window to ensure the safe return of a lover.
- Accidentally knocking a candle out is a sign that there will be a wedding in the near future.
- Light a white candle on your wedding day to ensure a long happy marriage.
- Light a new white candle in a new house to bring good luck and happiness to the home.
- If a candle suddenly goes out by itself during a wedding ceremony, the marriage will surely end in sorrow.
- Light a green candle on the night of a new moon to attract money.
- Lighting a candle from the fire will prevent wealth.
- If a candle will not light, a storm is on its way.
- A wavering flame where there is no draft is a harbinger of bad weather; if the flame of a candle burns blue, it is a sign of frost.
- A blessed candle from a Candlemas ceremony can be used to conjure storms.
- A candle with a tall straight flame indicates the arrival of a stranger.
- A candle showing a bright spark indicates that the person sitting opposite will receive an unexpected letter.

Christmas Candles and the Festival of Lights

Hanukkah

The eight-day Jewish festival of Hanukkah, (also known as Feast of Lights, Festival of Lights, Feast of Dedication, or alternatively spelled Chanukah, Chanukkah, or Hanukah) was once a minor festival, but it has recently grown in importance mainly due to the popularity of Christmas.

Hanukkah celebrates the retaking of the Temple at Jerusalem by the Maccabees in 166 BC from Antiochus Epiphanies IV, King of Syria, who had rededicated it to a pagan deity at the time of the winter solstice and extinguished the flame of the sacred menorah (candelabrum/oil lamp). Judah, the Maccabee leader, in winning for the cause of religious freedom, restored the temple and relit the menorah. The flame was said to have miraculously burned for eight straight days on consecrated oil deemed sufficient for only 24 hours. As a result, Hanukkah is more commonly celebrated to give thanks for the ancient miracle, with a nine branch menorah holding a candle lit for each of the eight days plus a servant light, called a *shammus*, used to ignite the others.

Traditional Hanukkah foods are usually fried in oil to commemorate the miracle of the sacred oil. Potato pancakes called *latkes* are a popular Hanukkah dish. Contemporary celebrants also exchange gifts, although this was not a traditional part of the holiday, and play *dreidel* (spinning top) games. The traditional explanation of the dreidel games is that during the time of Antiochus' oppression, it was forbidden to study Torah (Jewish teachings) and those who wanted to do so would conceal their activity by appearing to be play-ing legal gambling games with a four-sided top. If they were at risk of getting caught studying, they could claim they were merely playing games.

What the Maccabees saw as desecration by the Syrian Greeks was a winter solstice celebration honouring the Greek sun god and involving the ritual sacrifice of pigs at the Temple altar. According to Jewish scholars, Hellenized Jews (those who accepted Greek culture) had adopted many of the pagan ways for themselves. So the Maccabees set out to conquer the Greeks not only for the Temple, but also for the hearts and minds of their own people. The Maccabees re-established Jewish holiness at the Temple by dedicating Hanukkah at the same time as the winter solstice. The Jewish calendar places Hanukkah "at the moment of the darkest sun and darkest moon," assuring the highest contrast for a festi-val of lights. In this way the Maccabees succeeded not only in recovering the Temple, but also in luring back wayward Jews, reaffirming Jewish identity, and competing successfully with other solstice rituals. Although this war ended in the fall, around October, the Maccabees waited to rededicate the Temple until the Jewish winter solstice festival called Nayrot (meaning "lights") which was an eight-day agricultural cel-ebration of the rebirth of the sun. They changed the name of Nayrot to Hanukkah, which means "dedication" thereby concealing the original meaning of the Nayrot festival.

As in other ancient civilizations, the Israel nomads

celebrated Winter Solstice. Most Jewish holidays likely originated as celebrations of the annual cycles of the sun and were later assigned new religious significance. The three major holidays of the First Temple Israelites (1000 BCE (before the Common Era)) were Succoth (at the autumn equinox), Passover, (at the spring equinox), and Shavuot, 49 days after Passover (derived from the mystical number of 7 x 7). Rosh Hashanah and Yom Kippur came later, most probably adopted after the Jewish exile in Babylon (586 BCE).

Nearly 300 years after the Maccabeen uprising, rabbis developed a story that served to downplay the responsibility that humans have for their own lives and to emphasize, instead, reliance on God. The new story, written in the Talmud hundreds of years after the military victory, dismissed the political uprising and added the story of the menorah oil. According to the rabbis, the menorah flame in the Temple was supposed to burn throughout the night every night but there was only enough oil to burn for one day, yet miraculously, it burned for eight days, giving enough time to prepare a fresh supply of consecrated oil. The rabbis declared an eight-day festival to commemorate this miracle. Based on this explanation, Hanukkah celebrates the miracle of the oil, not the military victory.

Diwali
Diwali, the most pan-Indian of all Hindu festivals, is a Festival of Lights symbolizing the victory of righteousness and the

lifting of spiritual darkness. This festival is also known as *Deepawali,* a Sanskrit word literally meaning rows of *diyas* (clay oil lamps). People traditionally light small oil lamps and place them around the home, both indoors and out. Like other aspects of Hinduism—the world's oldest religion—the origins of Diwali are remote. The celebration probably has its roots in ancient harvest festivals. And like Hinduism, observance of Diwali is richly varied among the faith's 800 million adherents.

There are two mythological legends associated with Diwali. The first Diwali was held to celebrate the return of the Rama, King of Ayodhya, his wife Sita, and brother Lakshmana to Koshala after a war in which he killed the demon Ravana. According to legend, as it grew darker, people along the way lit oil lamps to light the path for their return. According to the second legend, Diwali commemorates the killing of the evil demon, Narakasura, by Lord Krishna. Thus Diwali is a festival which has come to symbolize the destruction of evil forces.

Diwali is by far the most popular festival of the year in India and it features the exchange of sweets and other gifts, decorating houses, festive meals, and huge fireworks displays. Diwali is a harvest festival and a celebration of the lunar new year which, like other similar festivals the world over, has strong astrological associations. Basically, this is a seasonal, astrological festival marking the transition from the old lunar year to the new in Hindu India, though it has lost some of this emphasis with the rise of modern urban civilization. The celebration takes different forms in different parts of India, but it generally means as much to Hindus as Christmas does to Christians.

The Diwali festival takes place over five days, beginning on the 15th day of the Hindu calendar month of Kartika (Ashwin), each day having its own significance, rituals, and myths. The Hindu calendar is a lunar calendar, with most years consisting of 12 lunar cycles and an extra month inserted approximately every seven years to resynchronize the calendar with the seasons. Diwali falls in the Gregorian month of October or November, and always on the day of a new moon. Since the precise moment of the new moon falls on different Gregorian dates depending on geographical location, the date of Diwali also depends on one's location.

Origin of Advent

dvent represents the beginning of the church year for most churches in the western tradition. It is a period beginning on the fourth Sunday before Christmas Day and ending on Christmas Eve, December 24. In the event that Christmas Eve falls on a Sunday, it will be counted as the fourth Sunday of Advent and Christmas Eve will technically begin at sundown (as it would have traditionally when days began at sunset, not after midnight). Historians believe Advent has probably been observed as far back as the fourth century. Originally, it was a time when converts to Christianity prepared themselves for baptism. The word "advent" is derived from Latin for "coming towards."

During the Middle Ages, Advent lasted from November 11, the feast of St. Martin, until Christmas Day as was proclaimed by the Council of Tours in AD 567. Advent was considered a pre-Christmas season of Lent when Christians devoted themselves to prayer and fasting. The faithful were also forbidden from being absent from regular church attendance during this period. The Orthodox Eastern Church observes a similar Lenten season, from November 15 until Christmas, rather than Advent.

Although many Christians still view Advent as a season to prepare for the Second Coming, in the last half century, it has become more a time of anticipating Christmas Day.

Advent Calendars

One of the most widely celebrated Advent traditions is the Advent calendar. The origin of the calendar, like so many of our Christmas traditions, started in Germany back in the 19th century. Various methods of counting down the days to the celebration of Christmas were used such as drawing a chalk line to mark off the days, lighting a candle every night, or putting up small religious pictures. Before long, commercial entrepreneurs started replacing the ephemeral chalk lines and other markers with printed calendars.

On the first Sunday of Advent, German children write their Christmas letter to *Christkindle* (Christ child) who, along with his angel helpers, brings the decorated Christmas tree and the presents on Christmas Eve. In Denmark, the Christmas season begins on December 1, with the lighting of the calendar candle. This special Advent candle is marked with 24 lines, one for each day before Christmas; the burning of the candle signifies the waiting and preparing for Christ's coming.

The first printed Advent calendar was made by Gerhard Lang (1881–1974) of Maulbronn, Germany. When he was a child, his mother made him an Advent calendar with 24 candies attached to a cardboard sheet, one for each day. In 1908, Lang published miniature coloured pictures that could be affixed on a cardboard calendar of December. This was the first printed Advent calendar and it was dubbed "Christmas-Calendar" or "Munich Christmas-Calendar." Soon Lang was producing the first Advent calendars that had little doors or windows that could be opened for each day of Advent. At this time the Sankt Johannis Printing Company started producing religious Advent calendars that included Bible verses instead of pictures behind the doors.

The celebration of Advent and the associated Advent calendar were extremely popular in the early decades of the 20th century. Despite the great success of Lang's Advent calendars, however, he was forced out of business in the 1930s due to World War II. The observance of Advent subsided for a time in Germany. During the war, cardboard was rationed in Germany and it was forbidden to produce calendars with pictures. After the war, Richard Sellmer resumed the production of printed Advent calendars. In 1958, chocolate treats were added to the Advent calendars and these have become the most popular variety to this day.

Origin of Advent

Advent festivals are observed primarily in the German-speaking areas of Europe and in the Protestant German-settled areas of North America. In Nuremberg, Germany, the season begins with a gala opening of the *Christkindle Markt* (Christ Child shopping market) on the Friday before the first Sunday of Advent. The multi-storey-high Advent calendar on the Sachsenplatz in Leipzig, Germany, is considered by the *Guinness Book of Records* to be the world's largest free-standing Advent calendar. Although Advent has not traditionally been a common observance in Canada, the calendars are becoming increasingly popular as a treat for children to count down the days to Christmas.

A 20th-century ecumenical liturgical revival brought a return of ancient ritual, including colours, to the mainline denominations (Presbyterian, Lutheran, United Church, Roman Catholic, Anglican) in Canada and the USA. Advent practices, reflected in liturgy, music, colours, atmosphere, and the Advent wreath, are common in many churches.

Advent Wreaths
The circular form of the wreath, with no beginning or end, is a Christian symbol of eternity. The evergreens in the wreath can symbolize life, growth, and the immortality of the soul, and green is the colour the Church uses to represent hope and new life. The Advent wreath has developed into a custom that is accepted by both Catholic and Protestant Christians. Many families light Advent wreath candles following the

evening meal and recite specific prayers at the lighting of each candle.

The true origin of the Advent wreath is not known. Some credit Johann Hinrich Wichern, a Protestant parson from Hamburg, Germany, with creating the first Advent wreath in either 1839 or 1848. Others believe that it was inspired by the crown of lights that young Swedish girls wear on Saint Lucia's Day. There are many legends associated with Saint Lucia, but all that is really known for certain is that she was a martyr in Syracuse in Diocletian's persecutions of AD 303. Thus she is also known as Saint Lucy of Syracuse. Her veneration spread to Rome, and by the sixth century the whole Church recognized her courage in defense of the faith.

According to one legend of Saint Lucia, she was a young Christian woman from a wealthy family who rejected an arranged marriage to a pagan and instead used her entire wedding dowry to buy food for the poor. Soon after that, she was martyred for her Christian beliefs. She is depicted as a bride dressed in white. Her halo is symbolized by the crown of lights. Traditionally, the Saint Lucia crown is covered in evergreen boughs, and holds four candles, just like the Advent wreath. Her feast day in the western Church is December 13. She is the patron saint of the blind. Lucy is the only saint celebrated by Lutherans in Sweden and Norway, in celebrations that retain many pre-Christian elements of a midwinter light festival.

The origins of the Advent and Christmas wreaths are

also linked to the folk practices of the pre-Christian Germanic peoples who, during the cold and dark month of December, would light wreaths of evergreen boughs as a symbol of hope in a coming spring and renewed light. The wreaths were round to represent the sun. Likewise, Scandinavians began the tradition of hanging the wreath at Yule, the beginning of their new year, to commemorate new beginnings in the cycle of life. As part of their Winter Solstice celebrations, early Scandinavians decorated cart wheels with evergreens and candles then hung them from the ceiling and spun them to represent the anticipated return of the sun god. A wreath often represented the Wheel of the Year. Its circle has no beginning and no end, symbolizing the cyclical elements of nature and the seasons.

At Christmas time in rural Germany there still exists an ancient custom of setting ablaze a giant four-spoke wheel bound with a human effigy and rolling it down a hill. The effigy probably hearkens back to a time when human sacrifices were made in plea to the sun god to return warmth back to earth.

Christians later claimed it was St. Boniface (apostle of Germany martyred June 5, 755) who first took these wreaths and created the Christian Advent wreath. The Christians, in preparation for their own festival of light and life — Christ's Nativity — found this wheel or wreath an appropriate means to help contemplate the coming of the Lord during the Advent season. They added one candle for each of the four Sundays in Advent, representing a growing hope for salvation. On the first Sunday of Advent a candle is lit and a new one is lit each successive Sunday. The increasing light each Sunday is said to represent the Light of the World (Jesus) approaching.

The colour of the four candles is also significant. Three candles are typically violet, or purple, and one is rose. Purple dyes were at one time extremely rare and costly and therefore associated with royalty. The Roman Catholic Church used purple in the priests' robes and vestments at Christmas and Easter to honour Jesus. The colour purple is associated with penitence in the Catholic church and is said to remind Christians that Advent is the season to spiritually prepare the soul to receive Christ.

The three purple candles in the Advent wreath are meant to symbolize hope, peace, and love. Some also believe these three purple candles are to represent penance, sorrow, and longing expectation. These candles are lit on the first, second, and fourth Sundays of Advent. The rose candle, which symbolizes joy, is usually lit on the third Sunday of the Advent season. This third Sunday is also called "Gaudete" Sunday, which is Latin for "rejoice."

Sometimes a white candle is placed inside the Advent wreath. This candle is lit on Christmas Day and its white colour is associated with angels and the birth of Jesus. Other customs replace the four coloured candles by four white ones all lit on Christmas Day.

Colours of the Season

he traditional colours of Christmas are green, red, and white. Green represents hope, the eternal longing for spring, and all the promises of the future. Green is the symbol for earth, nature, youth, and the hope of eternal life. It is for this reason that Christmas is often considered to be a feast of hope, with a newborn child as its central symbol. Holly, pine trees, ivy, mistletoe and other evergreen plants are closely associated with Christmas with origins in ancient pagan beliefs and rituals.

Red symbolizes love and reflects warmth. It is also associated with passion and the greatest excitement. As a religious symbol, red stands for fire, blood, courage, martyrdom, and charity. The red holly berries and poinsettias are two winter plants traditionally used as Christmas decorations and red is the colour of Eastern Orthodox Bishops' robes.

White symbolizes purity and glory and is represented by the crystalline form of water and the snowflake. As a religious symbol, white also represents light, faith, truth, and eternity. White is seen in the robes of Christmas angels, and in Santa's beard, as well as in Christmas snow.

In AD 325, the Council of Nicaea, which established the Nicene Creed, set forth guidelines for symbolism in Catholic art, including that of specific colours:

Red:	Blood, sacrifice, divine love, courage, martyrdom
Green:	Hope, earth, growth, spring, safety, rest, youth, victory
Purple:	Royalty, riches
Violet:	Justice, penitence, pain, pity, sadness
Gold:	Spiritual riches, achievement, good life
White:	Purity, faith, truth, peace, eternity
Black:	Evil, unknown

Since the 20th-century liturgical revival, some churches now use blue to distinguish the season of Advent from Lent. Blue is the liturgical colour for hope. Royal blue is sometimes used as a symbol of royalty; or bright blue as a symbol of the night sky just before daylight returns, the anticipated announcement of the King's coming, or even to symbolize the waters of Genesis 1, the beginning of a new creation.

Christmas Bells

I heard the bells of Christmas Day,
Their old familiar carols play;
and wild and sweet
the words repeat
of Peace on earth,
good will to men.
Henry Wadsworth Longfellow

any centuries ago, bells and noisemakers of all kinds were used by pagans at festivals during Winter Solstice. These noisemakers were used to frighten away evil spirits in the darkness of winter. It was thought that evil spirits could be driven out by loud noises, and bells often accompanied singing and shouting. They were also used to ward off storms, lightening, and fires.

Later, people believed that bells had holy powers and so they were tolled during funeral processions to ward off evil spirits. During the Middle Ages, bells were rung beginning at dusk on Christmas Eve with increasing frequency until midnight. This practice was meant to warn the devil of the approaching birth of the Christ child. Eventually bells became associated with celebrations and joy rather than protection against demons.

Bells are mentioned in the Old Testament as being worn on the robes of the high priest. The people would have known, by the sound of the bells, that the high priest was offering sacrifices for their sins. Church bells have post-Romanesque Christian ties to Christmas and were rung to announce church services and midnight mass.

Christmas bells have their share of legends associated with them, too. One legend tells the story of a village in England. The villagers had worked hard raising enough money to buy their church bells. They were so happy with their glorious bells that the entire village eagerly gathered every Christmas Eve in the church to rejoice and ring them. Sadly, one Christmas Eve disaster struck when an earthquake buried the church and the bells. It is said, though, that if you truly believe, you can put your head to the ground where the church was buried and still hear the bells ringing on Christmas Eve.

Another legend recalls the tale of a poor blind boy who wanted to visit the Baby Jesus in the manger, but he was unable to find the way until he heard the faint tinkling of a cowbell. He followed that sound, which led him to the cow in the stable and the Baby Jesus.

Bells worn on travelling animals is a practice that dates back to antiquity. But, it wasn't until the early 1900s that the first sleigh bells were made and could be purchased in 20 different sizes. Sleigh bells have a ball shape, distinct from the dome shape with an open bottom. The small, sleek one-horse sleighs were silent and swift, but without brakes they were a potential hazard. Therefore, bells were attached to the horse's harness to jingle merrily with the rhythm of the horse's gait. This merry sound has been immortalized in the song "Jingle Bells" (recorded by J.S. Pierpont, Boston, 1857). "Jingle Bells" has become one of the most popular and well-known Christmas carols in Canada, but oddly enough the lyrics make no reference to Christmas.

Jingle Bells
Original Title: "One-Horse Open Sleigh"
Words and Music: James Lord Pierpont (1822–1893), copyright 1857

> *1. Dashing through the snow*
> *In a one-horse open sleigh*
> *Through the fields we go*
> *Laughing all the way.*
> *Bells on bob-tail ring*
> *Making spirits bright*
> *What joy it is to ride and sing*
> *A sleighing song tonight.*

Christmas Bells

Chorus:
Jingle bells, jingle bells
Jingle all the way,
Oh what fun it is to ride
In a one-horse open sleigh, O
Jingle bells, jingle bells
Jingle all the way,
Oh what fun it is to ride
In a one-horse open sleigh.

2. A day or two ago
I thought I'd take a ride
And soon Miss Fanny Bright
Was seated by my side;
The horse was lean and lank
Misfortune seemed his lot,
We ran into a drifted bank
And there we got upsot. Chorus

3. A day or two ago
The story I must tell
I went out on the snow
And on my back I fell;
A gent was riding by
In a one-horse open sleigh
He laughed at me as I there sprawling laid
But quickly drove away. Chorus

4. Now the ground is white,
Go it while you're young,
Take the girls along
And sing this sleighing song.
Just bet a bob-tailed bay,
Two-forty as his speed,
Hitch him to an open sleigh
and crack! You'll take the lead. Chorus

Feasting Traditions

In the pre-industrial, agrarian societies of our ancestors, the end of December was an ideal time for feasting in most areas of Europe. The extended darkness made the return of the sun a central event in the northern European year, and not solely because of sun worship. At that time of year, most livestock were slaughtered to avoid feeding and sheltering them during the long cold winter months. For many people, it was the only time of year when they had a supply of fresh meat. By December, most of the wine and beer made during the year was finally fermented and potable (the Vikings called their midwinter festival Drinking Yule). The long, hard work of harvest was completed for the year, and there was little else to do until planting began again in the spring. The land may have been in winter slumber, but the conditions were ripe for revelry.

The season of the Winter Solstice was a time of celebration for many ancient religions, and a time of sacrifice to invoke the gods to provide a prosperous year. The Christmas festival, having evolved from these ancient celebrations, adopted, and embellished many of the same customs and traditions, and especially the feast. In fact, the overindulgence in food and drink is one of the major traditions stemming from the Roman feast of Saturn. Although the term "feast" (from Latin *festa*) refers to religious observance, it can also encompass the massive consumption of food as part of an elaborate meal or banquet.

Anthropologist Dr. B.K. Swartz Jr., in his lecture "The Origin of American Christmas Myths and Customs," traces the origins of the "traditional" Christmas meal in North America primarily from two types of feast patterns brought to the new world by European immigrants. The first is the ancient "Winter Festival" feast, with Germanic-Celtic origins and centred on the Winter Solstice celebration. North American Winter Festival food consists of oysters, fish, meat, wild fowl, bread, and eggnog. Traditional Winter Festival food in England was boar, roast, mincemeat pie, goose, plum pudding, and sugarplums, plus a potent beverage in the wassail bowl that was kept full from Christmas Eve until Twelfth Night.

The second food pattern is the "Harvest Bounty" feast, which has a Reformist background with origins from the post-Henry VIII Harvest Home ceremony. Harvest Bounty food consists of turkey, pumpkin, corn, lima beans, and cranberries. By the 19th century, these two basic feast traditions were blending in Europe and North America, with combinations such as turkey stuffed with oysters.

From the early settlement of Canada on into the 19th century, rural inhabitants prepared for Christmas much like their European ancestors had. As soon as the weather turned cold, pigs, cattle, and poultry were slaughtered to supply the household with all kinds of meat. The animals were butchered into different cuts: filets, roasts, hams, and pigs' knuckles, cutlets, chuck steak, ribs, and loins. The meats and poultry were then sealed in containers and buried in the snow, or else stored in the cold root cellar. Some meats were cured in the smokehouse as a method of preserving and flavouring; others were made into sausages, blood pudding, headcheese, meatballs, and patties or the French Canadian specialties of pâté and tourtière from traditional family recipes that had been passed on for generations.

Homemade wines, beers, and spirits were started in the fall from the harvesting of fruits, vegetables, grains, and herbs. They would be ready in time for the Christmas celebrations and were heartily offered to guests as a gesture of hospitality and good cheer.

In the newly settled Prairie provinces, Christmas dinner was like nothing ever seen in Europe. Fish fried in buffalo marrow, boiled buffalo hump, buffalo veal, and beaver tail were just as likely to be the main course of the Christmas feast as roast turkey. These "local specialties" have been long extinct from the Canadian Prairie Christmas menu.

Often dinner ended with an assortment of pastries made from local ingredients: eggs from the henhouse, honey from the beehives, and wild berries.

Christmas Goose, Turkey, and Ham

English setters in Canada preferred to serve stuffed roast goose as the main course of the Christmas dinner, whereas the settlers of French origin leaned more towards turkey. Interestingly, the turkey is indigenous to North America. Before being domesticated, turkeys could be found wild in southern Ontario, some parts of Quebec, several American states, and even in Mexico. At the beginning of the 16th century, the Spanish brought this bird back to Europe from Mexico and it was soon domesticated in Spain, France, and England.

The turkey quickly gained popularity as a Christmas meal in Europe. In fact, it had become so common in western Europe before the active colonization of North America that the first settlers of permanent English and Dutch colonies knew it before they arrived. And although they would propagate the domesticated strains that had originated further south, they would enjoy the turkey as both wild game and tamed barnyard fowl. Once established in early Canadian settlements, turkey was enjoyed in the culinary styles of Old World kitchens.

Throughout the ages, wild boar has also been a popular holiday dish. The ancient Romans ate boar during Saturnalia in honour of the god Adonis who was slain by a boar. Possibly a leftover from the Roman occupation of Britain, the boar's head has figured prominently in English festivities. In medieval British castles, manor houses, and boarding school refectories, boar's head was a traditional Christmas platter, served with all the fanfare of trumpet and procession.

There is a legend that an English schoolboy from Queen's College, Oxford, was walking alone in the forest one Christmas Day when he was attacked by a wild boar. He saved himself by stuffing a manuscript of Aristotle's works he happened to be reading down the throat of the beast, causing its death. He had the boar's head brought to the college to prove the incident to his classmates.

Another explanation says that the tradition of serving a boar's head at the Christmas feast originated because the Old Norse pagan god Freyr/Froh, who was responsible for the well-being of livestock, was symbolized by the boar. Therefore boar was often sacrificed in hopes of a prosperous spring herd. Eventually, the boar's head custom became impractical as a part of European Christmas feasting. Boars were increasingly hard to find and dangerous to catch. It also took a week of preparation to make the boar presentable.

The days of hunting and butchering a wild boar as part of the festive celebrations are gone, but the importance and significance of the custom survives today in the serving of the Christmas ham as a featured holiday dish. Regardless of its form, pork has figured strongly in British holiday feasts for centuries. The most popular Christmas dinner in Elizabethan England was brawn (roast pork) with mustard or roast beef. Also popular were mince pies, frumenty (a dish of wheat boiled in milk and usually sweetened and spiced), plum porridge, and a Christmas pie of tongue, eggs, sugar, spices, lemon, and orange peel.

Christmas Cheer

Good husband and huswife, now chiefly be glad,
Things handsome to have, as they ought to be had.
They both do provide, against Christmas do come,
To welcome their neighbors, good cheer to have some.
Good bread and good drink, a good fire in the hall,
Brawn, pudding, and souse, and good mustard withal.
Beef, mutton, and pork, and good pies of the best,
Pig, veal, goose, and capon, and turkey well drest,
Cheese, apples and nuts, and good carols to hear,
As then in the country is counted good cheer.
What cost to good husband, is any of this?
Good household provision only it is:
Of other the like, I do leave out a many,
That costeth the husband never a penny.

Thomas Tusser (1524?–1580)

Christmas Plum Pudding

"Hallo! A great deal of steam! the pudding was out of the copper [boiler]. A smell like washing-day! That was the cloth [the pudding bag]. A smell like an eating house and a pastrycook's next door to each other, with a laundress's next door to that! That was the pudding! In half a minute Mrs. Cratchit entered—flushed, but smiling proudly— with the pudding, like a speckled cannon-ball, so hard and firm, blazing in half of half-a-quartern of ignited brandy, and bedight with Christmas holly stuck into the top.

"Oh, a wonderful pudding! Bob Cratchit said, and calmly too, that he regarded it as the great-est success achieved by Mrs. Cratchit since their marriage..."

Charles Dickens, *A Christmas Carol*

Christmas pudding as popularized by the Victorian Christmas feast was preceded by a host of versions includ-ing suet pudding, plum pudding, bread pudding, and apple pudding. The common ingredients in these puddings were their dried fruits (commonly raisins), breadcrumbs, beef suet, spice, and often spirits. Most of the ingredients were expensive, denoting wealth and festivity.

But, all of these puddings evolved from a medieval dish called *frumenty*, a spicy, wheat-based dessert. This traditional Christmas dessert was made from dried fruit added to a mixture of boiled beef and mutton meat, cloves, ginger, currants, raisins, ginger, breadcrumbs or oatmeal, butter, butter, rum, brandy, sugar, and eggs. It originated as a porridge or gruel, and was served as the first course at the Christmas feast.

The word "plum" in Victorian times also referred to raisins or dried currants when used in desserts, not strictly plums as in the fruit from a *prunus* tree. Plum puddings were made in large copper kettles and prepared several weeks before Christmas but not eaten until the Christmas feast. Christmas puddings were often made on the first Sunday of Advent. It was called "Stir-Up Sunday" because the prayers recited for that day read, "Stir up, we beseech thee, O Lord, the wills of thy faithful people." The entire household attended the making of the pudding and each family member took turns stirring the thick steaming stew, each making a wish. This activity of stirring up the ingredients was meant to symbolize that the heart must be stirred in preparation for Christ's birth. Specific tokens of a coin, a thimble, a button, and a ring were mixed into the pudding. Later when the pudding was eaten, each object would have significance for the finder. The coin would mean wealth in the new year, the button meant bachelorhood, the thimble spinsterhood, and the ring foretold marriage.

Feasting Traditions

The Christmas puddings made today usually take the shape of the vessel in which they are cooked. But the earliest puddings were quite different. They were long and round and shaped like a thick sausage. This is because the pudding mixture was always tied up in a cloth or bag and then boiled in a large tub, often the same tub that was used to boil the clothes on wash day. Originally, the bag was the intestines of a sheep or pig. As the pudding cooked it would swell out until it became round in shape. Since these puddings were boiled in a bag, they were originally called "bag puddings" and naturally there exists a legend to explain the pudding's origin:

One Christmas Eve an English king and his servant found themselves deep in a forest with only a little food for the remainder of their journey. The King knocked on the door of a woodman's cottage and asked for food and shelter. The occupant had few provisions but was honoured to offer what little he had. So the king's servant mixed together all the food the woodman could offer with the small amount the king had left. The result was a sticky mixture of chopped suet, flour, sugar, eggs, apples, dried plums, brandy, and ale. This mixture was boiled in a cloth and a delicious pudding was invented.

🐦 Plum Pudding

INGREDIENTS

¼ lb	flour	110 g
¼ lb	currants	110 g
1 tsp.	salt	5 ml
¼ lb	sultanas	110 g
1 tsp.	allspice	5 ml
2	cooking apples, peeled, cored and chopped	2
1 tsp.	ground ginger	5 ml
1 oz.	cut mixed citrus peel	30 g
1 tsp.	ground cinnamon	5 ml
1 pinch	fresh grated nutmeg	1 pinch
1	zest and juice of orange	1
1	zest and juice of lemon	1
¼ lb	fresh breadcrumbs	110 g
¼ lb	molasses	110 g
½ lb	shredded suet	225 g
4	large eggs	4
¼ lb	brown sugar	110 g
2 tbsp.	brandy	30 ml
¼ lb	dried chopped apricots	110 g
¼ lb	chopped prunes	110 g
¼ lb	chopped dates	110 g

DIRECTIONS

Sift flour, salt and spices into a large bowl. Stir in breadcrumbs, suet and sugar. Add fruits, citrus peel, and zest. Beat lemon juice, orange juice, molasses, and eggs together and add to other ingredients. Pour mixture into a greased mould or can, cover and seal tight. Steam in a covered kettle or roaster for 5 to 6 hours. After steaming, cover and store in a cool place to mature for approximately 5 weeks. To serve, re-steam for another 3 hours. Remove from mould or tin, pour warm brandy over, and set it ablaze.

Mince Pies

Mince pies, also known as Christmas pies or crib pies, contained minced meat and spices, and were baked in oblong-shapes to represent Jesus' crib. The three spices of cinnamon, clove, and nutmeg are said to have represented the three gifts given to the Christ child by the Magi. Christmas pies at one time were much larger than the tiny mince pies of today. One pie is recorded as having among its ingredients: a hare, a pheasant, a capon, two rabbits, two pigeons, two partridges, the livers of all these animals, as well as eggs, pickled mushrooms, and spices. Sometimes these pies could weigh as much as 220 lbs requiring iron handles to hold them together during baking.

As time went on, mince pies became smaller and smaller, and are most common now as tarts rather than pies. It was believed to bring good fortune to eat one mince pie on each of the 12 days of Christmas. It was, however, bad luck to eat mince pies before Christmas Eve or after Twelfth Night, and they were never cut lest the luck be cut. Another name for them was "wayfarers" pies since they were given to visitors during the Christmas holiday.

Traditional Mincemeat Pie

INGREDIENTS

2 lbs	lean ground beef	900 g
1 lb	ground suet	450 g
2 lbs	sugar	900 g
5 lbs	tart apples, peeled, cored, and chopped	2.25 kg
2 lbs	muscat raisins	900 g
1 lb	currants	450 g
1 lb	sultana raisins	450 g
½ lb	citron, chopped	225 g
½ lb	orange peel, chopped	225 g
1 tbsp.	salt	15 ml
1 tsp.	cinnamon	5 ml
1 tsp.	allspice	5 ml
1 tsp.	mace	5 ml
1 quart	boiled cider	950 ml
	brandy	
	pastry for a double crust pie	

DIRECTIONS

Mix beef, suet, sugar, fruit, salt, spices, and cider in a large kettle. Cover and let simmer for 2 hours, stirring frequently. Stir in brandy to taste. Put into sterilized 1-quart preserve jars and seal securely. Store in a cool place to mature for at least 1 month before using. Yields 5 jars.

To make the pie: Line a 9-inch pie pan with pastry. Fill the pie with mincemeat mixture and cover with remaining pastry, rolled thin. Seal edges securely and slash top in several places so steam can escape. Bake in pre-heated 450° F (230° C) oven for 30 minutes. Serve warm.

Mince Pie (Meatless)

INGREDIENTS

1 lb	sultanas	450 g
1 lb	raisins	450 g
½ lb	currants	225 g
2	rind and juice of lemons	2
2	apples, grated or chopped	2
1 lb	Demerara sugar	450 g
12	dried figs, finely chopped	12
1 tbsp.	ground cinnamon	15 ml
½ tsp.	ground ginger	2½ ml
½ tsp.	ground nutmeg	2½ ml
½ tsp.	ground mace	2½ ml
1 cup	brandy	250 ml

DIRECTIONS

Mix together all of the ingredients and place in a large stone crock with a cork stopper, or in securely sealed preserve jars, and allow maturing for about three months before use. Yields approximately 5 lbs of mincemeat.

Make short pastry using 2 to 1 ratio of flour to shortening. Roll out pastry and cut out 2½ inch circles. Place half the pastry circles in greased tart tins and fill each with mincemeat. Place the other half of the pastry circles on top of tarts, pinch the edges together and cut two small slits into the top of each. Brush each tart with mixture of egg and milk. Bake in pre-heated oven at 450° F (230° C) until lightly golden.

Jack Horner and the Christmas Pie
Little Jack Horner sat in the corner
Eating his Christmas pie,
He put in his thumb and pulled out a plum
And said "What a good boy am I!"

(The Little Jack Horner rhyme was first published in 1725.)

Little Jack Horner was reputed to have been Richard Whiting, Steward to the Bishop of Glastonbury (1461 to 1539). Glastonbury was the largest and wealthiest abbey in England at the time. Between 1536 and 1540, after breaking away from the Catholic Church, King Henry VIII and his chief minister Thomas Cromwell undertook the systematic dissolution of all the monasteries in England with the purpose of seizing the monastic riches and land. In an apparent attempt to bribe the King and maintain his Abbey, the Bishop of Glastonbury sent his steward to deliver a gift of 12 title deeds to various English manorial estates. The deeds were said to have been hidden in a pie (valuables were often disguised in rather bizarre ways to fool thieves). Whiting (Little Jack Horner) realized that the bribe would do no good and was believed to have stolen the deed to the Manor of Mells which was the real "plum" of the 12 properties. The remaining 11 manors were given to the crown but, as Horner suspected, the Bishop's plan failed. The old Bishop was tried for treason for remaining loyal to Rome. The jury, which included his treacherous Steward Horner, found the Bishop guilty and sent the old man to a terrible death of being hung, drawn, and quartered on Glastonbury Tor. The Abbey was destroyed and Horner moved into the Manor of Mells. It is not known whether Horner actually stole the deed to the Manor or was rewarded with it for helping to convict the Bishop of Glastonbury; nevertheless, the Manor of Mells became the property of the Horner family, remaining so until the 20th century.

Humble Pie

Humble (or 'umble) pie was made from the "humbles" of a deer, which consist of the heart, liver, brains, and other organs. While the lords and ladies feasted on the more choice cuts, the servants baked these humbles into a pie to make them go further as a food source. This appears to be the origin of the phrase, "to eat humble pie." By the 17th century, humble pie had become a traditional Christmas food. Oliver

Cromwell and the Puritan government outlawed it along with other Christmas foods, rituals, and customs.

Eggnog

Today, eggnog is a firmly entrenched Christmas season drink that no festive party would be complete without. To the North American settlers facing cold winters in the new world, eggnog was not only a festive drink reminiscent of jolly old England, but it was also nutritious and revitalizing. Non-alcoholic versions of eggnog were often served to children and invalids as a tonic.

But where did this strange brew originate? There are a few different theories as to the origin of this popular festive drink. One theory states that eggnog originated in colonial America. It was originally called "eggs and grog" (grog being a colloquialism for rum). The name was gradually shortened to egg-n-grog, and finally eggnog. Another theory dates back to 17th century England, where an egg drink, mixed with sherry and milk, was served up in taverns in a small wooden cup known as a "noggin." "Nog" is an Old English dialect word also used to describe a kind of strong beer. But most believe the truth lies in a combination of the two: a drink, originally called "eggs and grog in a noggin" was likely shortened to "eggnog."

Some say it all began in Renaissance England, where eggnog was the trademark holiday drink of the upper class. The average Londoner rarely saw a glass of milk since there was no refrigeration, and even the farms belonged to the big estates. Those who could get milk and eggs to make eggnog mixed it with brandy, Madeira, or sherry. This English creation most likely descended from a hot drink called "dry sack posset," which consisted of eggs, milk, and ale or wine. The recipe for eggnog (eggs beaten with sugar, milk or cream, and the addition of some form of liquor) has travelled well, adapting to local tastes, wherever it has landed. But it became most popular in North America, where farms and dairy products were plentiful, and rum came from trade with the Caribbean.

The Germans make an eggnog, or rather egg soup, with beer (*Biersuppe*). Icelanders make a hot soup-like dessert that resembles eggnog somewhat, but contains no alcohol.

Christmas Eggnog

INGREDIENTS

6	egg yolks	6
6	egg whites	6
¾ cup	sugar	190 ml
1½ cups	brandy	375 ml
½ cup	rum	125 ml
4 cups	milk	1 litre
4 cups	whipping cream	1 litre
½ cup	confectioners' sugar	125 ml
	nutmeg	

DIRECTIONS

Beat the egg yolks, gradually adding the sugar, until the mixture is light golden. Slowly beat in the brandy and rum. Next beat in the milk and half the cream. Just before serving, whisk the egg whites until stiff and fold them into the eggnog mixture. Whip the remaining cream and confectioners' sugar until thick. Pour eggnog into serving glasses and top each with whipped cream and sprinkle with nutmeg. Yields 8 servings.

Syllabub

Syllabub is a less potent mixture than eggnog but just as rich. It was a popular dessert beverage from the 17th to 19th centuries in England and was served during celebrations, special occasions, and holidays due to its festive appearance. Syllabub was generally made with a mixture of whipped cream, whipped egg whites, white wine, sugar, lemon juice, and zest of lemon. The amount of white wine added would establish the thickness qualifying whether the mixture would be a creamy dessert or a beverage. Variations of the recipe include substituting the white wine with apple cider or other alcoholic beverages. A telltale sign of a syllabub drinker was often the thick white moustache left behind by the drink. Originally, and still on occasion today, syllabub is made by squirting fresh, warm milk directly from the cow into the bowl of spiced cider or ale.

Wassail

In the Middle Ages, the word "wassail" referred to a special drink made of hot spiced wine for toasting to each other's health on Christmas Eve, New Year's Eve, and Twelfth Night celebrations. Its origins can be found in the fifth century legend of the beautiful Saxon Princess Rowena, who toasted the health of her future husband, the English King Vortigern, with the words "*wass-hael,*" which literally meant "be of health" or "be whole" (from Old Norse *ves heill,* be well). Vortigern replied with the words "*drinc hail*" and from that day on the tradition has endured in Britain that the one who drinks first at a banquet says "was hail" to his partner, and he who drinks next says "drinc hail." Originally, the term "wassail" referred to the toast itself and not the name of the drink. Today it can mean the beverage, the toast to one's health, to go carolling house to house, or riotous drinking. The Old Saxon god, Thor, was often depicted holding a wooden wassail bowl.

Rowena's famous libation was a form of the ancient Roman *hippocras* (spiced wine), and survived to hold a prominent place in the cuisine of the wealthiest nobility up to the early Middle Ages. Incidentally, Rowena was also reputed to have killed her stepson, Vortimer, by tricking him into drinking poison. Since England's climate was not conducive to the production of wine or the exotic spices, both were imported and exorbitantly expensive. In later centuries the wine was replaced with fine local ales, giving it a different flavour, but also making it more available to the common folk. As the British developed spice plantations in their tropical Asian and Indian colonies, the cost of spices gradually decreased and they too became more accessible.

Another form of wassail was known as "Lamb's Wool" due to the appearance of a "woolly froth" on the surface of the liquid when crab apples were simmered in ale. Sometimes slabs of toasted bread were floated in the bowl giving rise to the term "toast" as in drinking to one's health.

Most families had their own unique variations of this festive drink. Some recipes call for the addition of wines and sugar, and others thickened the brew with eggs or cream, often pouring the mixture back and forth between pan and bowl to create the foam. The most popular seasonings were nutmeg, cinnamon, cloves, and grated ginger. Shakespeare makes reference to wassail in *Twelfth Night*:

> *Next crown the bowl full*
> *With gentle lamb's wool*
> *Add sugar, nutmeg, and ginger,*
> *With store of ale. too,*
> *And thus ye must do*
> *To make the wassail a swinger.*

Wassailing at one time also included the rural custom of drinking a toast to the livestock and crops during the Winter Solstice as a fertility ritual in hope that this salute would increase yield in the coming year. Toasts were addressed to corn, cows, and fruit trees. The custom was later integrated into Christmas celebrations generally occurring on the Twelfth Night, or sometimes on January 17, known as the Old Twelfth Night. Farmers and their families would feast on hot cakes and cider, then head into the orchard with more "liquid supplies." Celebratory fires were lit in fields and cider sipped in barns and orchards while gunfire was shot into the air, or amid plenty of shouting and bell ringing, to scare off evil spirits. The custom of wassailing the orchard continued into the 18th century. Robert Herrick, in *Hesperides* (1648) described it in verse:

> *Wassaile the trees, that they might beare*
> *Many a plum and many a peare:*
> *For more or lesse fruits they will bring,*
> *As you do give them wassailing.*

With the introduction of Christianity, the custom of wassailing was not abolished, but it assumed a religious aspect. Early monks called the wassail bowl the *poculum caritatis*, meaning "Loving Cup." People drank directly from the bowl and passed it around from one to another.

The term "Pig and Whistle" was often used in reference to the bowl and wassail, or the wassail cup and wassail. A "pig-gen" is an old English term for a pail, especially a milk-pail; and a "pig" was a small bowl, cup, or mug. A crockery-dealer was called a "pig-wife." The "whistle" is the wassail. A song, first referenced in 1550, goes:

Wassail, wassail, out of the milk pail,
Wassail, wassail as white as my nail,
Wassail, wassail, in snow, frost and hail,
Wassail, wassail, that much doth avail,
Wassail, wassail, that never will fail.

Traditional Wassail I

INGREDIENTS

1 gallon	apple cider or juice	4 litres
1	orange, chopped	1
1	lime, chopped	1
1	lemon, chopped	1
4	cinnamon sticks *or*	4
1 tsp.	ground cinnamon	5 ml
1 inch-square	piece of fresh ginger *or*	2.5 cm-square
¼ tsp.	ground ginger	1 ml
1 tsp.	cloves, allspice and/or star anise	5 ml

DIRECTIONS

Heat all the above ingredients together in an enamel pot and simmer over low heat for one hour; add brandy or rum (optional) and serve hot.

~ Traditional Christmas Wassail

INGREDIENTS

4 cups	brown ale	1 litre
1 cup	dry sherry or dry white wine	250 ml
3 oz.	brown sugar	90 g
4	apples	4
½	peel of lemon	½
¼ tsp.	ground nutmeg	1 ml
¼ tsp.	ground cinnamon	1 ml
¼ tsp.	ground ginger	1 ml

DIRECTIONS

Wash the apples and peel the mid-section only. Place the apples, brown sugar and 4 tbsp. of the brown ale into an oven-proof dish and bake at 350° F (175° C) for approximately 30 minutes or until the apples are tender. Remove the apples and add the remaining ale, sherry or wine, lemon peel, nutmeg, cinnamon, and ginger. Simmer gently for a few minutes. Return the apples to the brew and serve hot.

Cookies, Candies, Cakes, and Breads

Cakes and cookies of all shapes and sizes have been part of festive holiday rituals long before Christmas: they were given as presents, used as decorations and effigies, and were considered to possess magic protective powers against evil spells. Ancient Egyptians festivities included the ritual of eating wafers symbolizing their sun god. Other pagan celebrations included the tying of fruit to trees during the Winter Solstice in anticipation of the arrival of spring. One predecessor to the Christmas tree, the Paradise tree, was adorned with apples to represent the Garden of Eden. Stemming from these ancient traditions, the early Christmas trees in Europe were small tabletop trees decorated with cookies and other sweet treats that were meant to be eaten.

Many of the traditional ingredients, such as cinnamon, ginger, black pepper, almonds, and dried fruits were introduced to Europe in the Middle Ages. They were highly coveted and quickly incorporated into European baking. Most Christmas cookies, as we know them today, trace their roots to these medieval European recipes. German *Lebkuchen* (gingerbread) is believed to be the first cake or cookie traditionally associated with Christmas.

"By the 1500s, Christmas cookies had caught on all over Europe. German families baked up pans of *Lebkuchen* and buttery *Spritz* cookies. *Papparkakor* (spicy ginger and black pepper delights) were favourites in Sweden; the Norwegians made *krumkake* (thin lemon and cardamom-scented wafers). The earliest Christmas cookies in America came ashore with the Dutch in the early 1600s … but it wasn't until the 1930s that whimsically shaped cutters made of tin became less expensive and more abundant — and the Christmas-cookie boom began."[7]

Christmas cakes were usually eaten on Christmas Eve in the 19th century. Although they were often prepared well in advance, it was believed that cutting into one before December 24 would surely bring bad luck. Likewise, to ensure good luck, a portion of the Christmas cake also had to be preserved until Christmas Day itself.

In a game that mimics the social inversion rituals of the Roman Saturnalia, the Elizabethans would sometimes bake a Christmas cake that contained one bean and one pea. The cake would be divided amongst the servants and children on Twelfth Night, or sometimes on New Year's Eve. The lucky one who got the bean in his piece of cake was pronounced King of the Bean ("Lord of Misrule") and reigned for the rest of the day and night directing the carousing; whoever got the pea became, or selected, the Queen of the Pea.

In Canada, doughnuts and the Acadian *croquinoles* (fried sweet dough), sprinkled with powdered or icing sugar, were one example of a delicious traditional Christmas dessert brought over by the early French settlers. Doughnuts were often served with wild fruit preserves (jam or jelly) or with cream. Adding to the sweets selection of the early Canadian Christmas was a whole range of seasonal cookies and candies including creamy fudge. Needless to say, doughnuts have since become a popular icon of Canadian culture and an institution on their own thanks primarily to Tim Horton's.

Gingerbread Houses and Gingerbread People

Baking gingerbread in shapes dates back to at least the 15th century. *Lebkuchen,* a traditional German gingerbread, was first made many hundreds of years ago by monks in Germany. In those days the ingredients of honey and nuts and spices came from very far away and were a luxury, and therefore it was only made for special occasions. Today, *Lebkuchen* is still a specialty, one that Germans indulge in mainly at Christmas. For children, one of the best things about *Lebkuchen* is the *Lebkuchenhaus*, a house made almost entirely out of gingerbread and covered in sweets. Many families make one — gingerbread is a fantastic building material and lasts for a long time without going stale.

The tradition of decorated gingerbread houses began in Germany after the Brothers Grimm published their collection of German fairy tales in the early 1800s. Among the tales was the story of Hansel and Gretel, children left to starve in the forest, who came upon a house made of bread and sugar decorations. After the fairy tale was published, German bakers began baking houses of *Lebkuchen* and employed artists and craftsmen to decorate them. Nuremberg, Germany, became known as the "Gingerbread Capital of the World" in the 1600s when the guild employed master bakers and artisans to create intricate works of art from gingerbread, sometimes using gold leaf to decorate the houses. The houses became particularly popular during Christmas, a tradition that crossed the ocean with German immigrants. Pennsylvania, where many settled, remains a stronghold for the tradition.[8]

The first gingerbread man, however, is credited to the court of Queen Elizabeth I, who favoured important visitors with charming gingerbread likenesses of themselves. At that time, tinsmiths fashioned cookie cutters into all imaginable forms, and every woman wanted a shape that was different from anybody else's. Most of the cookies adorning 19th century Christmas trees were at least half an inch thick and cut into animal shapes or gingerbread men.[9]

"For Christmas over a hundred years ago, Pennsylvania German children in Lancaster County helped cut out and decorate foot-high cookies to stand in the front of windows of their stone or brick houses. These cookie people—often gingerbread men and women iced with rows of buttons and big smiles — were a cheerful sight to snow-cold passers-by. Figural cookie-making was practiced in Europe at least as far back as the 16th century — most of them were made using intaglio molds rather than with cutters."[10]

Recipe for Gingerbread Houses and Gingerbread People

INGREDIENTS

1¼ cup	butter at room temperature	315 ml
1¼ cup	sugar	315 ml
2	eggs	2
2 tsp.	vanilla	10 ml
1 tsp.	lemon extract	5 ml
4 cups	sifted flour	1 litre
1¼ tsp.	salt	6 ml
4 tsp.	cinnamon	20 ml
1 tsp.	ginger	5 ml

1 tsp.	cloves	5 ml
3 tsp.	nutmeg	15 ml

DIRECTIONS

Cream together butter, sugar, eggs, vanilla and lemon extract until smooth. Sift together flour, salt, cinnamon, ginger, cloves, and nutmeg. Add to butter mixture and stir until smooth, adding more flour if necessary to form firm and slightly sticky dough. Wrap dough in plastic; chill until cold and thickened. Roll and cut to shape (note: dough will need to be thicker for houses than for cookies; dough scraps can be used for decorative details; left-over dough freezes well). Bake at 350° F (175° C) until brown underneath and slightly pale on top.

German *Lebkuchen*

INGREDIENTS

¾ cup	honey	190 ml
¾ cup	packed brown sugar	190 ml
1	egg	1
3 tbsp.	freshly squeezed lemon juice	45 ml
2 tsp.	grated lemon zest	30 ml
3½ cups	flour	875 ml
½ tsp.	baking soda	3 ml
1 tsp.	ground cinnamon	5 ml
1 tsp.	ground nutmeg	5 ml
1 tsp.	allspice	5 ml
½ tsp.	ground ginger	3 ml

½ tsp.	ground cloves	3 ml
1 tsp.	salt	5 ml
½ cup	chopped candied citron	125 ml
½ cup	chopped candied lemon and/or orange peel	125 ml
½ cup	chopped candied cherries	125 ml
1 cup	chopped almonds (optional)	250 ml

FOR DECORATING

3 cups	powdered sugar	750 ml
1 tsp.	orange extract	5 ml
1 tsp.	lemon extract	5 ml
1 tsp.	rum extract	5 ml
	milk	
	candied cherries, halved	
	sliced almonds (optional)	

DIRECTIONS

In a large saucepan bring the honey to a boil. Remove from the heat and stir in the brown sugar. In a small bowl beat the egg. Add a tsp. of the honey mixture to the egg and beat rapidly. Add the egg mixture to the saucepan and beat. Add the lemon juice and zest. In a small bowl whisk together the flour, baking soda, cinnamon, nutmeg, allspice, ginger, clove and salt. Blend into the honey mixture until well mixed. Fold in the candied fruit and almonds. Place the dough in a bowl and cover tightly with plastic wrap. Chill for 48 hours.

Preheat the oven to 350° F (175° C). On a lightly floured surface roll out the dough to a ¼ inch thick. Cut the cookies with a 2-inch circular cutter and place on non-greased cookie sheets. Bake for 8 to 10 minutes or until the edges just start to turn pale golden brown. Cool the cookies on the sheets for 5 minutes before transferring to wire cooling racks.

After the cookies have cooled, mix the powder sugar with the extracts in a small bowl. Add enough milk to form a thin glaze. Place a tsp.ful of glaze on each cookie and spread evenly on top. Before the glaze dries place a candied cherry half in the centre of each cookie and fan out the almond slices around the cherry to create a flower shape.

Let cookies set overnight, then store in an airtight container allowing the cookies to mature for a minimum of 2 weeks or up to 3 months before serving.

If the cookies get slightly hard, add a thin slice of apple to each container. Cover tightly and store until cookies are re-moistened, about 1 day, then discard the apple slice.

Yields approximately four dozen cookies.

Traditional German Spritz

INGREDIENTS

1 cup	soft butter	250 ml
½ cup	sugar	125 ml
1 tsp.	vanilla or almond extract	5 ml
2 tsp.	ground cinnamon	10 ml

1	egg	1
¼ tsp.	salt	1 ml
2¼ cups	sifted all purpose flour	565 ml

DIRECTIONS

Cream together the sugar, adding a little at a time, with the butter until light and fluffy and the sugar is dissolved. Add vanilla, cinnamon, and egg. Blend thoroughly. Mix together the flour and salt. Add the flour mixture, a little at a time, to the butter mixture until the dough is soft and workable. Pack dough into a cookie press or a pastry bag and press out cookies onto lightly buttered baking sheets. Bake in a preheated 375° F (190° C) oven for 10 minutes, or until cookie edges are a light golden brown.

Yields approximately two dozen cookies.

Pfeffernuesse Cookies

(a.k.a., Peppernuts; Ginger nuts; *Peppernoten*; Gingerbread biscuits) Although *Pfeffer* is the German word for pepper, and some people do add a dash of black pepper to their recipes, the term used to refer to spices in general and not just to pepper. Likewise, although the word *Nuesse* means nuts it is not because these cookies contain nuts, but rather because of their small size and crunchy texture. Traditionally, hard cookies such as *Pfeffernuesse* were meant to be dunked into mulled wine (*Gluehwein*) during a long visiting and cookie-eating season.

German *Pfeffernuesse* I

INGREDIENTS

4 cups	all-purpose pre-sifted flour	1 litre
2 tbsp.	baking powder	30 ml
1 tbsp.	ground cinnamon	15 ml
1 tsp.	ground nutmeg	5 ml
½ tsp.	ground cloves	3 ml
4	eggs	4
2 cups	granulated sugar	500 ml
¼ cup	chopped candied citron	60 ml
1 tbsp.	grated lemon peel	15 ml
	confectioners' sugar	

DIRECTIONS

Sift flour with baking powder, cinnamon, nutmeg and cloves. Set aside. In a large bowl, beat eggs and granulated sugar until light and fluffy. Add citron and lemon peel; beat with wooden spoon until well blended. Add flour mixture, beating with wooden spoon until smooth. Refrigerate several hours or overnight.

Form the dough into 1-inch balls and place 2 inches apart on greased cookie sheets. Bake in 350° F (175° C) oven for 12 to 15 minutes or until done. Remove from oven. Cool. Sprinkle cookies with confectioners' sugar.

Yields four dozen cookies.

German *Pfeffernuesse* II

INGREDIENTS

4 cups	all-purpose flour	1 litre
½ cup	sugar	125 ml
1¼ tsp.	baking soda	6 ml
1½ tsp.	ground cinnamon	8 ml
½ tsp.	ground cloves	3 ml
½ tsp.	ground nutmeg	3 ml
¾ cup	light molasses	190 ml
½ cup	butter or margarine	250 ml
	confectioners' sugar	

DIRECTIONS

Stir together flour, sugar, baking soda and spices. In large saucepan, combine molasses and butter; heat and stir until butter melts. Cool to room temperature. Stir in eggs. Add dry ingredients to molasses mixture; mix well. Cover. Chill several hours or overnight. Shape into 1-inch balls. Place on greased cookie sheet. Bake in 350° F (175° C) oven for 12 to 14 minutes or until cookies are done. Remove. Cool. Roll in confectioners' sugar.

Yields five dozen.

🐟 Austrian *Pfeffernuesse*

INGREDIENTS

2 cups	corn syrup	500 ml
2 cups	dark molasses	500 ml
1 cup	shortening	250 ml
½ lb	brown sugar	225 g
10 cups	flour	2.5 litres
1 tsp.	baking soda	5 ml
2 tsp.	cinnamon	10 ml
¼ lb	candied citron, finely chopped	115 g
¼ lb	almonds, finely chopped	115 g
1 lemon	zest and juice of lemon	1 lemon
1	egg white	1
	confectioners' sugar	

DIRECTIONS

In a medium saucepan over medium heat combine the corn syrup and molasses; stir in shortening and lemon juice. Add brown sugar, cinnamon, citron and almonds. Cool to room temperature. In a large bowl combine baking soda and flour. Add syrup mixture to dry mixture and mix well. Roll dough into 1-inch balls and brush with egg white. Place on greased cookie sheet. Bake in 350° F (175° C) oven for 12 to 14 minutes or until cookies are done. Remove. Cool. Roll in confectioners' sugar. Yields 10 dozen cookies.

Swedish *Pepparkakor*

INGREDIENTS

½ cup	molasses	125 ml
½ cup	butter	125 ml
2 ½ cup	sifted all-purpose flour	625 ml
¼ tsp.	baking soda	1 ml
½ tsp.	cinnamon	3 ml
½ cup	sugar	3 ml
1	egg, well beaten	1
¼ tsp.	salt	1 ml
½ tsp.	ginger	3 ml

DIRECTIONS

Heat molasses in small saucepan to the boiling point and boil for one minute. Add sugar and butter and stir until butter is melted. Cool. Add beaten egg. Sift together flour, salt, soda, and spices. Add to molasses mixture and mix thoroughly. Cover bowl tightly and chill overnight. Place a workable portion of the dough at a time on lightly floured pastry board and roll thin. Cut rolled dough into desired shapes. Bake in 350° F (175° C) oven for 6 to 8 minutes. Yields approximately 10 dozen cookies.

Stollen

Stollen is another Christmas favourite in Germany. This special Christmas bread goes by many different names in German: *Stollen, Strutzel, Striezel, Stutenbrot,* or *Christstollen.* The name is derived from an Old High German word, *stollo,* meaning a support or post. The traditional German Christmas cake is a rich, sweet, colourful, and tasty concoction of nuts, raisins, currants, marzipan, candied orange and lemon peel, cinnamon, nutmeg, cardamom, mace or cloves, brandy or rum, and lots of butter.

The long, oval-shaped cake is traditionally covered in a thick layer of icing sugar, which supposedly represents the baby Jesus in his crib, swathed in white cloth. It originated in the German town of Dresden around 1300. At that time the Catholic Church, however, as part of the fasting rules in preparation for Christmas, forbade the use of butter during Advent. Thus, the *Stollen* of the middle ages was a somewhat tasteless pastry. In 1650, at the request of bakers in Dresden, Prince Ernst von Sachsen successfully petitioned Pope Urban VIII to lift the restrictions on the use of butter during Advent. The restrictions were lifted only in Dresden and thus began a baking tradition that continues to this day.

Around 1500, *Christbrote uff Weihnachten* (Christmas breads), were being sold at the Dresden *Striezelmarkt,* the oldest existing German Christmas market. Bakeries in those days were making *Stollen* cakes which weighed almost

20 kilos and were more than one and a half metres long. For many people, *Stollen* is just another Christmas treat but for the people of Dresden, *Stollen* is a huge part of their Christmas heritage.

Dresden Stollen

INGREDIENTS

¾ cup	dark raisins	190 ml
⅓ cup	chopped citron	85 ml
⅓ cup	candied orange peel or cherries	85 ml
¼ cup	rum	75 ml
1 package	active dry yeast	1 package
½ cup	warm water	125 ml
1 cup	milk	250 ml
⅔ cup	butter	170 ml
½ cup	sugar	125 ml
1 tsp.	salt	5 ml
1 tsp.	grated lemon peel	5 ml
½ tsp.	almond extract *or*	2½ ml
4 tsp.	amaretto	20 ml
2	eggs	2
4 – 4½	cups flour	950 ml–1 litre
½ cup	chopped blanched almonds	125 ml
	melted butter	
	granulated and powdered sugar	

DIRECTIONS

Place raisins, citron, orange peel and rum in a bowl and soak for one hour. Drain and reserve rum.

Sprinkle yeast into warm water and let stand until dissolved.

Heat milk and butter together over medium heat until butter melts. Pour milk and butter mixture into a mixing bowl. Add sugar, salt, lemon peel, drained rum and almond extract. Cool to lukewarm. Beat in eggs and dissolved yeast. Gradually add enough flour to make soft dough.

Dredge fruits in flour. Add fruit and almonds to dough and mix well. Knead dough on a lightly floured surface until smooth. Place in a greased bowl and butter surface of dough lightly. Cover with plastic wrap and let rise in a warm place until doubled in size, about 1½ to 2 hours.

Punch down the dough and then lightly knead on a floured surface. Divide in half. Roll each half into an oval about ¾ inch thick. Brush with melted butter and sprinkle with granulated sugar. Fold lengthwise nearly in half, so the edges are within ½ inch of meeting and the bottom edge extends beyond the top. Place the loaves on a greased baking sheet, leaving several inches between them. Brush with melted butter. Cover lightly and let rise for 45 minutes.

Bake in a preheated 350° F (175° C) oven for about 40 to 45 minutes, until nicely browned and sounds hollow when tapped. Remove from the oven, brush with melted butter and dust with the confectioner's sugar sprinkled through a sieve, then transfer to wire racks to cool. Yields 2 loaves.

Traditional Christmas Loaf

INGREDIENTS

2 cups	raisins	500 ml
2 cups	dried currants	500 ml
3 cups	warm water	750 ml
3 packages	dry yeast	3 packages
1 cup	warm water	250 ml
1 scant cup	white sugar	250 ml
½ cup	melted butter	125 ml
¼ cup	molasses	65 ml
2	eggs	2
1 tsp.	baking soda	5 ml
2½ tsp.	salt	12 ml
1 tsp.	cinnamon	5 ml
1 tsp.	nutmeg	5 ml
12 cups	white flour	3 litres

DIRECTIONS

Soak the raisins and currants in 3 cups of very warm water until soft and plump and the water has cooled to lukewarm. Dissolve the yeast in 1 cup of warm water according to the package directions. Mix all the remaining ingredients, except for the flour, in a large mixing bowl then stir in the dissolved yeast.

Next add the raisins and currants plus the liquid. Add the flour slowly and mix thoroughly. Keep adding the flour and mixing until the dough is firm enough to knead. Once the mixture is well kneaded form it into a large ball and place in a bowl and cover with wax paper or a damp tea towel. Leave the dough in a warm area until doubled in bulk. Gently punch the air out of the batter and then form the dough into loaves and place in greased or non-stick loaf pans. Cover with waxed paper and towels and let rise to double in size. Preheat oven to 400° F (200° C) and bake loaves for 10 to 15 minutes then reduce heat to 350° F (175° C) and continue baking for 20 to 30 minutes more. The baking is done when the bread has pulled away from the sides of the pan. Turn loaves out onto a wire cooling rack. Yields approximately 4 to 5 loaves.

Fruitcake

The Ancient Romans made the first fruitcake by mixing pomegranate seeds, pine nuts, and raisins into a barley mash. Later, during the medieval period, honey, dried fruits, and spices were added, and bread dough was sometimes substituted for the barley mash. Crusaders and hunters were reported to have carried a type of fruitcake to sustain themselves over long periods of time when travelling.

Though sinfully rich, fruitcake was considered sacred, and actually had laws in effect until the 18th century that restricted it to special celebrations such as Christmas, Easter, and weddings. This is most likely how it came to be associated with the holiday season. Europeans baked a type of ceremonial fruitcake at the end of the nut harvest reserving it to be consumed at the beginning of the next year's growing season to encourage another bountiful harvest.

Between 1837 and 1901, fruitcake was popular in England and served at Victorian Teas. Queen Victoria was rumoured to have waited an entire year to eat a fruitcake she received for her birthday as a show of restraint, moderation, and good taste.

Christmas Fruitcake

INGREDIENTS

1 lb	citron, chopped	450 g
¼ lb	candied orange and lemon peel, chopped	115 g
½ lb	dates, chopped	225 g
½ lb	glace cherries, chopped (reserve a few halves for decoration)	225 g
3¾ cups	raisins	875 ml
2¾ cups	currants	650 ml
½ lb	each coarsely chopped almonds and pecans (reserve a few halves for decoration)	225 g
¾ cup	brandy	175 ml
1 lb	brown sugar	450 g

1 lb	softened butter	450 g
15	egg yolks, beaten until thickened	15
15	egg whites, beaten until stiff peaks form	15
4 cups	all-purpose flour, sifted	1 litre
1 tbsp.	cloves	15 ml
1 tbsp.	nutmeg	15 ml
1 tbsp.	allspice	15 ml
1 tbsp.	cinnamon	15 ml
1½ tsp.	mace	7 ml

DIRECTIONS

Mix together the fruit, nuts, and brandy and let marinate. Meanwhile, cream together the sugar and butter. Gradually add the beaten egg yolks while constantly beating the mixture. Reserve 1 cup of the flour and sift the remaining 3 cups with the spices. Gradually add the sifted ingredients to the butter-sugar mixture, beating well after each addition. Next, gently fold in the egg whites. Sprinkle the fruit-nut-brandy mixture with the reserved 1 cup of flour, mix well, and then fold into the batter.

Preheat oven to 300° F (150° C) and place additional pans of hot water in the bottom of the oven. Grease and line a 12-inch springform pan with waxed paper. Pour the batter into the pan and bake for approximately 2½ hours. Cool the cake and wrap in brandy-soaked cheesecloth. Place in airtight container and store until ready to decorate and use. Every three weeks, re-soak the cheesecloth in brandy.

DECORATING

Before decorating the top and sides of the cake with marzipan, apply a glaze of either red currant jelly or apricot jam thinned with a little water, in order for the marzipan to adhere. Marzipan is a type of paste made of almonds, sugar and water that pastry chefs worldwide have been using for centuries in baking and for coating and filling cakes. With the addition of food colouring marzipan is also popularly used to sculpt edible, decorative forms and figurines. Marzipan must contain at least 25 percent almonds, otherwise it is considered almond paste. The finer the almonds are ground, the better the results will be.

Marzipan

INGREDIENTS

3 cups	sugar	750 ml
1 cup	water	250 ml
4 cups	ground blanched almonds	1 litre

DIRECTIONS

Add the sugar to the water in a saucepan and cook until the sugar is dissolved. Add the almonds and cook until the batter no longer sticks to the pan. Remove from heat and place onto a flat surface such as a marble slab or wooden board.

Knead the warm marzipan first with a wooden spatula and then by hand until smooth. Store in an airtight container or plastic bag.

Sugarplums

Sugarplums are exotic treats made from a combination of seeds, fruits or nuts, and sugar. Sugarplums were not actually made from plums, but were roughly the size and shape of plums, and often had little wire stalks for suspending them from Christmas trees and for other decorations. They came in an assortment of colours and flavours, and frequently had an aniseed or caraway seed at their centre. The term was in vogue from the 17th to the 19th centuries, but is now remembered primarily thanks to the Sugarplum Fairy, a character in Tchaikovsky's *Nutcracker* ballet (1892).[11]

Sugarplums belong to the comfit family, the earliest mention of which dates back to 1668. Comfit is an archaic English word for a confectionery consisting of a seed or nut coated in several layers of sugar. "In England these small, hard sugar sweets were often made with caraway seeds, known for sweetening the breath (hence kissing comfits). Up to a dozen coats of syrup were needed before the seeds were satisfactorily encrusted. Comfits were eaten as sweets, and also used in other sweet dishes; for example seed cake was made with caraway comfits rather than loose caraway seeds as in the 19th century. Confectioners as early as the 17th century recognized by varying the proportions of sugar in the syrup they could change the final texture, making pearled comfits or crisp and ragged comfits. The word comfit remained in use in English up until the 20th century: Alice, of Alice in Wonderland, has a box of comfits in her pocket."[12]

Candy Canes

Candy canes are one the most familiar and traditional sweet symbols of Christmas. But the origin of this seemingly innocuous confection is fraught with controversy.

The major claim brought forward by various religious ministries states that the candy cane's shape represents the letter "J" for Jesus. The red and white stripes represent purity (white) and the blood of Christ (red). Their version of the history tells of an anonymous candy maker from Indiana in the 1870s who began with a stick of pure white hard candy. The white symbolized the Virgin Birth and the hard candy, the rock solid foundation of the Church. He made a version in the shape of a cane, or "J," that has also been interpreted as a shepherd's hook. The three stripes are said to symbolize the Holy Trinity.

There is no historical evidence to support the claim; in fact there is much evidence to the contrary. It is highly unlikely that candy canes were created by an Indiana candy maker since plain white candy canes (circa 1670) were around long before the existence of the state of Indiana (1816). Striped canes did not appear until the early 1900s. There appears to be no mention anywhere of the candy maker's name making the plausibility of the story even more suspect. "About 1847, August Imgard of Ohio managed to decorate his Christmas tree with candy canes to entertain his nephews and nieces. Many who saw his canes went home to boil sugar and experiment with canes of their own. It took nearly another half century before someone added stripes to the canes. Christmas cards produced before 1900 show plain white canes, while striped ones appear on many cards printed early in the 20th century."[13]

Another popular legend claims that candy canes were initially created to be used as a form of covert identification among fearful European Christians during a time of persecution. This idea is also unlikely, however, considering that candy canes first appeared in the latter part of the 17th century, and by then Europe was almost entirely Christian; it was more likely to be non-Christians who were in need of a secret form of mutual identification at that time.

A more plausible connection between the origins of the candy cane and intentional Christian symbolism is a story that, sometime in the 1670s, the choirmaster of the Cologne Cathedral in Germany took an existing form of Christmas candy, straight white sticks of sugar candy, and produced bent versions which represented a shepherd's crook. The choirmaster gave these "shepherd's canes" to children during Christmas church services to ensure their good behaviour especially around the live Christmas crèche. Prior to the creation of the modern pacifier, it was not uncommon for mothers to calm their babies by letting them suck on unflavoured white sugar sticks. And so it was probably during the 17th century that hooked white sticks of sugar candy first came into use at Christmas as a sweet form of juvenile bribery.

As the early European custom of trimming the Christmas tree grew, special decorations were made for the occasion. Predominant amongst these decorations were food items such as cookies and candies. This holiday custom of giving children sugar canes spread throughout Europe and developed into fancier canes adorned with roses being used in many homes as Christmas decorations. Peppermint candy sticks with red stripes first appeared in the mid-19th century in the Swedish town of Gränna.

In 1919, Bob McCormack of McCormack's Famous Candy Company began commercial production of candy in Albany, Georgia. A few years later he changed the name to Bobs Candies, Inc. and started producing candy canes. It was a laborious process of pulling, twisting, cutting, and bending the candy by hand that could only be done on a local scale. In the 1950s, Bob's brother-in-law, Gregory Keller, a Catholic priest, invented a machine which twisted the soft candy into the spiral striping, then cut the sticks in precise measurements. The Keller Machine revolutionized the stick candy market. The final hurdle to making candy canes was surmounted in 1958 when two Bobs Candies employees, Dick Driskell and Jimmy Spratling, perfected Father Keller's machine so that it created the crook in candy canes. Packaging innovations by Bob

McCormack, Jr., made it possible to transport the delicate canes on a scale that transformed Bobs Candies, Inc. into the world's largest producer of candy canes.

Scottish Christmas Recipes

Until recent times, the celebration of Christmas was suppressed in Scotland. In 1538, the Presbyterian Church and John Knox banned Christmas for its papist origins and because there are no biblical references to Christmas celebrations nor any biblical commandments to celebrate the birthday of Christ. The Church of Scotland continued to discourage the celebration of Christmas, which remained a regular working day in Scotland as late as 1958.

New Years Eve, or *Hogmanay*, with its ancient pagan roots, was and still is the central celebration for Scots. Before the Reformation of the 16th and 17th centuries, Christmas and New Year were equally welcomed by Scots. The custom was to celebrate the birth of Christ with all solemnity; the festivities began a few days later, and spilled into New Year and Twelfth Night (also known as *Nollaig Beag* or *Latha na Bliadhn' Ur*, "Little Christmas"). The Reformation hit Scotland as hard as everywhere else. By 1583, bakers who made yule breads or cakes were fined; however, their punishment could be lessened if they divulged the names of their customers.

In the Celtic calendar, New Year fell on November 1 and

was called *Samhain.* It was a time of plenty as the stocks were returned from the hills and slaughtered before the severe winter ahead. It was also a great time for kinship, as the people who lived high up in the hills came to the gathering of the clans. In pre-Christian times, Samhain was considered a mystical, in-between time, when one year turned into another and spirits of the dead and those not yet born could walk freely among the living. Samhain celebrated the time where darkness of night prevailed over the lightness of day — winter solstice. According to Scottish mythology, Lun the Sun God was defeated by his darker side and became the Lord of Misrule. Much of the sacred symbolism of Samhain can be found in the traditions of Halloween and Hogmanay. It was customary during this season to receive a visit from a stranger (First Footer) who would bring gifts of cake (Black Bun), drink (Wassail), and a piece of coal for the fire. The Celts held alcohol in very high esteem and it was an important part of ritual.

Traditional Scottish Shortbread

Shortbread can be made into cookies or a biscuit-type cake. Shortbread is a modern version of a very ancient hard textured cake or bannock, which was baked in a large flat round shape in honour of the sun. Nowadays, cooks make marks which divide the biscuit into slices or wedges, but these marks originally were symbolic of the rays of the sun.

INGREDIENTS

½ cup	butter	125 ml
⅓ cup	very fine sugar	85 ml
1 cup	flour	250 ml
1 pinch	salt	1 pinch

DIRECTIONS

Cream together all of the ingredients to form workable dough. A few drops of cold water may be added if the dough is too crumbly. Roll out dough to ⅛ inch thick onto baking parchment paper then lift it onto a baking tray complete with the parchment. Using a large plate as a guide, cut a circle out of the dough, removing the excess edges. Make the imprint of a small circle in the centre of the large dough circle. Using a knife, draw eight evenly spaced wedges around the cake to look like rays of the sun stemming from the centre circle. Pierce each wedge three to four times with a fork. Bake in a pre-heated oven at 350° F (175° C) for about 20 minutes.

Scottish Hogmanay Black Bun

Black Bun is a very rich fruit cake, made with raisins, currants, finely-chopped peel, chopped almonds, and brown sugar, spiced with cinnamon, cloves, nutmeg, and ginger. It takes its name from the very dark colour. Some variations have the bread mixture baked inside a pastry crust. This bread is traditionally served at Hogmanay and brought by First Footers.

INGREDIENTS

¼ cup	chopped candied orange peel	63 ml
¼ cup	chopped candied lemon peel	63 ml
3 tbsp.	chopped almonds	45 ml
3 tbsp.	dark raisins	45 ml
3 tbsp.	currants	45 ml
¼ tsp.	grated nutmeg	1¼ ml
½ tsp.	ground ginger	2½ ml
¼ tsp.	ground cloves	1¼ ml
½ tsp.	ground cinnamon	2½ ml
2 tbsp.	rum or brandy	30 ml
2½–3 cups	flour	600–750 ml
½ tbsp.	active dry yeast	7 ml
½ tsp.	salt	2½ ml
4 tbsp.	unsalted butter, softened	60 ml
⅔ cup	hot water (120–130°F)	170 ml

DIRECTIONS

Soak raisins and currants in hot water for 10 minutes, then drain. Soak orange and lemon peels, almonds, raisins, currants, and spices in rum or brandy for a minimum of two hours or overnight. Combine two cups flour, yeast, salt, butter, and hot water. Mix well. Add enough remaining flour to form soft dough. Knead dough on lightly floured surface for about 10 minutes or until smooth. Place dough in greased bowl and grease the surface of the dough. Cover with a warm, slightly damp clean cloth; let rise in warm place for about one hour or until dough has doubled in size. Punch down the dough and remove two-thirds of the dough. Cover and set aside the remaining third. Knead the fruit into the two-third portion. Make a 6-inch ball. Using the one-third dough reserved, roll out a 12-inch circle. Place the smaller fruit ball in centre of the 12-inch circle and fold dough over the ball sealing the ends of the circle. Grease an 8-inch cake pan. Flatten and pierce the dough all over and completely through with a skewer in order to allow the steam to escape during baking. Place the dough in the greased pan. Bake in a preheated oven at 350° F (175° C) for 1½ hours. To brown the sides, remove bread from the pan for the last 20 minutes of baking. Place loaf on a wire rack to cool.

French Christmas Réveillon

The French word *réveillon* means "wake up" and is the name given to the nocturnal Christmas meal, eaten after the midnight mass in France and Canada. Originally it was less of a meal and more a light snack consisting simply of biscuits or a piece of *tourtière* (meat pie), along with a hot beverage. Over the years this snack has slowly evolved into a more lavish and elaborate meal. The same foods that are prepared for Christmas dinner are also served at réveillon, which is generally a family affair.

In Canada, the partaking of Christmas réveillon varies depending on the family, the period, and the cultural context. For rural francophones, Christmas réveillon was not a common practice until the 1930s. For anglophones and urban dwellers, on the other hand, Christmas réveillon was incorporated into family celebrations around 1875. The tendency to feast on Christmas Eve became increasingly more predominant as the customs of trimming the Christmas tree and exchanging presents grew.

Devout Catholics believed that reciting one thousand "Hail Marys" on December 24 would ensure the receipt of a special request; therefore, while preparing the réveillon for Christmas Eve, mothers would recite their one thousand "Hail Marys" without fail in the hopes that the Virgin Mary would grant them a small favour on behalf of one of their children or their husband.

French Canadian Tourtière

INGREDIENTS

1 lb	ground pork or veal *or*	450 g
½ lb	of both poork and veal	225 g
⅓ cup	onion, finely chopped	85 ml
1 clove	garlic, minced	1 clove
¼ cup	raisins	65 ml
⅓ cup	water	85 ml
¼ tsp.	white pepper	1 ml
1 tsp.	salt	5 ml
¼ tsp.	ground cloves	1 ml
¼ tsp.	cinnamon	1 ml

¼ tsp.	celery salt	1 ml
¼ tsp.	savoury	1 ml
1 – 2	potatoes, boiled and mashed	1 – 2
	pastry for one 8-inch	
	double-crust pie	

DIRECTIONS

Place pork, veal, onion, garlic, raisins and water in a saucepan. Simmer until meat is no longer pink. Adding seasonings; simmer for 15 minutes. Thoroughly drain meat. Mix in mashed potatoes. Fit bottom pastry into 8-inch pie plate. Fill with meat mixture. Cover with top crust. Crimp and seal edges and vent top to allow steam to escape. Bake in 425° F (215° C) oven for 10 minutes; lower oven temperature to 400° F (200° C) and bake for 20 to 25 minutes or until crust is golden brown and filling is hot. Serve hot. Serves 6.

Acadian Doughnuts

INGREDIENTS

3	eggs	3
2 cups	milk	500 ml
1½ tsp.	lemon flavouring	7 ml
3½ cups	flour	825 ml
1½ cup	granulated sugar	350 ml
3 tbsp.	melted butter	45 ml
3 tsp.	baking powder	15 ml
1 tsp.	vanilla extract	5 ml

1 tsp.	salt	5 ml
½ tsp.	nutmeg	2½ ml
2 lbs	lard for frying	900 g

DIRECTIONS

Beat eggs. Add sugar, melted butter, vanilla, and lemon flavouring. Sift together salt, nutmeg, baking powder, and flour. Combine the liquid and dry mixtures slowly and alternately to make soft dough. Turn onto a lightly floured working surface and knead until smooth. Do not overwork the dough. Roll the dough to ½-inch thickness. Cut out doughnuts (round with a hole in the middle — note the dough from the "holes" can also be cooked). Cook in deep lard at medium-high, turning once, until both sides are golden brown. Remove from lard and drain on paper towels or baking paper. Serve with jam and cream. Yields three dozen.

Rising Doughnuts

INGREDIENTS

1 package	yeast	1 package
¼ cup	lukewarm water	60 ml
¼ cup	hot milk	60 ml
2 tbsp.	sugar	30 ml
2 tbsp.	butter	30 ml
3 cups	flour	750 ml
1	egg, beaten	1
1 tsp.	salt	5 ml

DIRECTIONS

Dissolve yeast in water. Place hot milk in a bowl along with sugar, salt, and butter. When this mixture is lukewarm, add the dissolved yeast. Add half of the flour and mix with a spoon. Add the egg and mix. Add the remainder of the flour to make soft dough. Knead the dough on a lightly floured surface. Do not overwork the dough. Place the dough in a greased bowl and grease the surface of the dough. Cover with a kitchen cloth, place in a warm area, and let rise until doubled in volume. Punch down the dough lightly. Cover and let rise again — about 30 minutes. Roll the dough to about ½-inch thickness. Cut into doughnuts and deep fry until golden brown. Remove from oil and drain on paper towels.

Old Fashioned Taffy

INGREDIENTS

2 cups	brown sugar	500 ml
1 cup	molasses	250 ml
½ cup	water	120 ml
2 tbsp.	white vinegar	30 ml
1 tsp.	cream of tartar	5 ml
2 tbsp.	butter	50 ml
½ tsp.	baking soda	2½ ml

DIRECTIONS

Combine the first five ingredients in a saucepan and bring to a boil. Continue boiling and test by dropping a spoonful of the mixture into cold water — a firm ball should form when ready. Remove from heat and add butter and baking soda. Stir well and pour onto a buttered baking sheet. Let cool; then pull and cut into small pieces.

Maple Fudge

INGREDIENTS

2 cups	maple syrup	500 ml
1 tbsp.	light corn syrup	15 ml
¾ cup	chopped pecans or walnuts	190 ml
1 tbsp.	butter	15 ml
¾ cup	rich milk or cream	190 ml

DIRECTIONS

Combine the maple syrup, corn syrup, and cream in a saucepan and heat over low heat stirring constantly until it starts to boil. Continue cooking without stirring until small amounts of syrup will form a soft ball when placed in cold water. Remove from heat. Add butter. Do not stir. Cool until lukewarm. Beat until mixture thickens. Add nuts and stir. Pour into buttered pan and let cool. Cut into squares for serving.

Hot Cranberry Punch

INGREDIENTS

6 cups	cranberry juice	1.5 litres
4 cups	orange juice	1 litre
1 cup	water	250 ml

1 x 6 oz.	can frozen lemonade	170 ml
	concentrate, thawed	
½ cup	firmly packed brown sugar	120 ml
3 tsp.	whole cloves	15 ml
3 tsp.	ground allspice	15 ml
1	whole nutmeg, crushed	1
4 x 3-inch	cinnamon sticks,	4 x 7.5-cm
	broken into pieces	

DIRECTIONS

Combine first five ingredients in a large saucepan. Place spices in a piece of cheesecloth, tie with string, and add to punch. Bring to a boil, stirring occasionally. Reduce to low heat, cover, and simmer for about 30 minutes. Serve hot. Yields approximately 3 quarts of punch.

Hanukkah Recipes
Potato Latkes

INGREDIENTS

5 medium	potatoes, peeled and	5 medium
	coarsely grated	
3 tbsp.	flour or matzo meal	45 ml
1 tsp.	salt	5 ml
¼ tsp.	ground black pepper	1 ml
2	eggs, beaten	2
1	onion, chopped very fine	1
2 tbsp.	shortening for frying	30 ml

DIRECTIONS

Combine eggs and onion in a mixing bowl. Add the flour, salt, and pepper and beat until smooth. Fold in potatoes. Add shortening to a hot griddle or frying pan. Add large spoonfuls of the batter into the hot oil and fry at medium heat until crisp and golden brown (approximately 3 to 5 minutes per side). Drain fried latkes on paper towels. Serve hot with sour cream and applesauce. Yields approximately 12 pancakes.

~ Applesauce

INGREDIENTS

5 lbs	granny smith apples, peeled, cored, and cut in quarters	2.25 kg
1	juice of lemon	1
2	cinnamon sticks	2
½ cup	apple cider or apple juice	120 ml
	Brown sugar, corn syrup, or maple syrup for sweetening to taste	

DIRECTIONS

Place the apples, lemon juice, cinnamon sticks, and cider or juice in a heavy cooking pot and bring to a boil. Simmer over low heat for about 20 minutes stirring every few minutes. When apples are soft remove the cinnamon sticks, and allow to cool. Blend until smooth with hand mixer or in a food processor. Add sugar or syrup to adjust sweetness; serve cold.

🌀 Sweet Potato Latkes

INGREDIENTS

5	sweet potatoes or yams, peeled and grated	5
3	medium Yukon Gold potatoes, peeled, grated	3
1	onion, chopped fine	1
1	red bell pepper, chopped fine	1
½ cup	chives, chopped	120 ml
1 tbsp.	parsley, chopped	15 ml
3	eggs, beaten	3
	salt and freshly ground pepper to taste	
1 tbsp.	lemon juice	15 ml
3 tbsp.	flour	45 ml
approx. ½ cup	peanut or vegetable oil for frying	approx. 125 ml

DIRECTIONS

Combine grated sweet potatoes and Yukon Gold potatoes in a large cheesecloth and wring out excess liquid into a bowl — reserve this liquid and let starch settle to bottom of bowl. Transfer potatoes to a clean bowl and sprinkle with lemon juice to prevent discoloration. Add remaining ingredients, except for the oil, and stir thoroughly. Pour off the water from the reserved potato liquid retaining the starch from the bottom of the bowl. Add the starch to the potato mixture. Heat oil in a skillet or frying pan over medium-high heat. Drop large spoonfuls of the batter into the oil flattening the pancakes with the back of the spoon. Cook for 3 to 5 minutes on each side or until crisp and golden brown. Remove latkes from oil and drain on paper towels. Serve hot with sour cream. Serves 6.

Canadian Christmas Traditional Recipes

Special section by Jeff O'Neill

DRINKS

Frosted Cranberry

A non-alcoholic cocktail, with the colour of holly berries, which will delight younger and older guests alike. It is the perfect one-for-the-road drink to serve at the end of the gathering.

INGREDIENTS

½ cup	castor sugar	125 ml
2 oranges	juice of orange	2 oranges
	enough water to dissolve	
	the sugar	
4 cups	sparkling mineral water	1 litre
½ cup	cranberry juice	125 ml
	fresh cranberries, to decorate	
	fresh mint, to decorate	

DIRECTIONS

Place the sugar, orange juice, and water (enough to dissolve the sugar) into a small pan and stir over low heat until sugar has dissolved, then bring to a boil for 3 minutes. Set aside to cool. The syrup can be made in advance and stored in a covered container in the refrigerator. Pour the syrup into a chilled bowl, add the cranberry juice, and mix well. To serve, pour in the mineral water and decorate with cranberries and mint leaves.

Mulled Claret

The aroma is a blend of cinnamon, cider, and orange juice
— everything Christmas.

INGREDIENTS

1	orange	1
5 tbsp.	clear honey	75 ml
2 tbsp.	seedless raisins	30 ml
2	clementines	2
6	cloves (3 per clementine)	6
1	whole nutmeg	1
4 tbsp.	sugar	60 ml
2	cinnamon sticks	2
7 cups	inexpensive claret	1.75 litres
2 ½ cups	cider	625 ml
¼ cup	orange juice	63 ml
1 cup	brandy (optional)	250 ml

DIRECTIONS

With a sharp knife, pare off a long strip of orange peel. Place the orange peel, honey, and raisins in a large saucepan. Stud the clementines with the cloves and add them to the saucepan.

Grate a little nutmeg into the sugar and then add it to the saucepan with the cinnamon sticks.

Pour in the wine and heat over a low heat, stirring until the sugar has completely dissolved and the honey melted.

Pour the cider and the orange juice into the saucepan and continue to heat the mull over gentle heat. Do not allow it to boil or all the alcohol will evaporate.

Warm a punch bowl or other large serving bowl. Remove the cinnamon sticks from the saucepan and strain mull into the bowl to remove the raisins. Add the clementines studded with clove, and serve the mull in warm glasses.

CHRISTMAS EVE

Red Cinnamon Apples with Tiny Pork Sausages

Beautifully coloured apples with little sausages sticking out at perky angles. Great Christmas Eve supper item.

INGREDIENTS

1 cup	sugar	250 ml
½ cup	water	125 ml
¹/₃ cup	red hot cinnamon candies	85 ml
6	apples, peeled and cored	6
18	small pork link sausages	18

DIRECTIONS

Preheat oven to 350 °F (175° C).

In a pot, bring to a boil the sugar, water, and red hot cinnamon candies for 5 minutes or until sugar has dissolved and candies are melted. Place apples in the syrup, and continue cooking for 5 minutes.

Place the sausage links in a skillet over medium heat, and cook until evenly browned.

Arrange apples on a baking sheet. Place 3 sausages in the centre of each apple. Drizzle apples with remaining syrup. Bake for 25 minutes, or until apples are tender.

Yields 6 portions.

Cranberry Eggnog Salad

Cranberries are plentiful in eastern Canada.

INGREDIENTS

1 package	vanilla pudding mix	90 g
1 package	lemon Jell-O	85 g
2 tbsp.	lemon juice	30 ml
1 package	raspberry Jell-O	85 g
1 can	whole-berry cranberry sauce	1 can
½ cup	chopped celery	125 ml
¼ cup	chopped pecans	63 ml

| 1 envelope | Dream Whip | 85 g |
| ½ tsp. | nutmeg | 2½ ml |

DIRECTIONS

In a saucepan, combine the pudding mix, lemon Jell-O and 2 cups of water and bring to a boil, stirring constantly. Add lemon juice and chill until partially set. Dissolve raspberry Jell-O in 1 cup of boiling water and then stir in cranberry sauce. Fold in celery and pecans. Chill until partially set. Prepare Dream Whip, add nutmeg; fold into pudding mixture. Pour half the pudding mixture in a cake pan; carefully pour cranberry mixture over, and top with remaining pudding mixture. Chill 6 hours or overnight.

Traditional Jiggs Dinner

Newfoundland's main course and probably the most cooked dish on Christmas Eve.

INGREDIENTS

3 – 3½ lbs	salt beef (with fat trimmed)	6½ – 7½ kg
1 head	cabbage (a large bag of turnipgreens can replace the cabbage)	1 head
5 – 6	carrots	5 – 6

6 – 8	potatoes	6 – 8
1 large or 2 medium	turnip	1 large or 2 medium

Peas Pudding Ingredients

1½ cups	dried yellow split peas	375ml
1	pudding bag	1

DIRECTIONS

Soak the salt beef in cold water overnight (6 to 8 hours). Discard the water in the morning. Remove the salt meat and cut about half cup into small cubes and place to one side. Place the remaining salt meat in a large pot and add enough cold water to cover. Place the pot with the salt meat on the stove.

Place the dried yellow split peas in the pudding bag. Tightly tie the pudding bag (leaving enough space for the peas to expand) and place it in the water with the salt meat.

Cover and let boil for a total of about 2½ hours, adding more water to the pot if necessary.

Next prepare the vegetables. Peel and clean the turnip, carrot, and potato. Cut the turnip into ½ inch thick slices. If the carrots and potatoes are large, cut them in half or quarters. Clean and cut the cabbage into quarters or sixths,

depending on the size. (If you are using turnip greens, sepa-rate and clean the turnip greens.)

Cabbage is the first vegetable to go in the pot, carrot next, then turnip, and potatoes, adding more water if neces-sary. Jiggs Dinner is sometimes referred to as corned beef and cabbage (salt meat and cabbage)

How long you cook the vegetables is a matter of per-sonal taste, so you have to judge when to add them by how long you want them to cook. Some people like them cooked until they are soft and mushy and some like them crunchy. (Although the longer they are boiled, the less nutrition they have.)

Serve with pickled beets and sweet mustard pickles, fresh bread and butter.

Tourtière

A tasty miniature pie, delicious served with a spicy ketchup for a warm dish at parties

INGREDIENTS

1 tbsp.	canola oil	15 ml
1 cup	finely chopped onion	250 ml
4 cloves	garlic, minced	4
1	teaspoon ground allspice	5 ml

¾ lb	ground pork	375 g
¾ lb	ground beef	375 g
½ tsp.	salt	2 ml
1 tsp.	coarsely ground pepper	5 ml
½ cup	beef or chicken broth	125 ml
⅔ cup	fine dry breadcrumbs	85 ml
17 oz.	package flaky pie crust mix	540 g
10 tbsp.	water	150 ml
1	egg, lightly beaten	1
1 tbsp.	milk	5 ml

DIRECTIONS

Grease a 12-portion muffin pan. In a large frying pan, heat oil over medium heat. Add onions and cook for 5 minutes or until softened. Add garlic and allspice and cook for another minute or until onions become fragrant. Stir in the pork, beef, salt, and pepper and cook, breaking up ground pieces of meat, until they have become browned. Add broth and cook, uncovered, for 5 to 10 minutes or until almost all broth has evaporated. Remove from heat and stir in breadcrumbs; cool.

Preheat oven to 400° F (200° C). Combine both enve-lopes of pastry mix and water in a large bowl and stir until soft dough forms. Press dough together. Roll out two-thirds of the dough on a lightly floured surface until ⅛ inch thick.

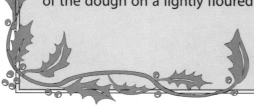

Cut 12 4½ inch circles from the pastry. You will have to re-roll pastry scraps in order to get 12 circles. Press each pastry circle into the prepared muffin pan, leaving a slight overhang of pastry at the top. Press ⅓ cup of the ground meat mixture into each pastry case.

Roll remaining pastry onto lightly floured surface until pastry is ⅛ inch thick. Cut 12 3½ inch circles from pastry. Place one circle over each of the ground meat mixtures. Using a lightly floured fork, press edges of the pastry together to seal. Whisk egg and milk together in a small bowl and brush over pastry tops. Cut 3 slits into each pastry top.

Bake, on the bottom shelf of the oven for about 35 minutes or until pastry is golden and crisp. Let stand in pan for 5 minutes before serving.

DO-AHEAD TIPS

These can be prepared one month ahead and frozen in sealed containers in freezer. Thaw in refrigerator before baking.

CHRISTMAS MORNING

Apple Pancakes from the Townships Crepes aux Pommes des Cantons

Great for Christmas morning.

INGREDIENTS

2 cups	all-purpose flour	500 ml
1 tbsp.	baking powder	15 ml
1 tsp.	baking soda	5 ml
2 tsp.	salt	10 ml
3 tbsp.	sugar	15 ml
1 tsp.	cinnamon	5 ml
2¼ cups	buttermilk	565 ml
2	egg	2
1 cup	apples, unpeeled, cut into small pieces	250 ml
6 tbsp.	melted butter	90 ml

DIRECTIONS

Sift together flour, baking powder, baking soda, salt, sugar, and cinnamon. Beat buttermilk and eggs in a small bowl. Add chopped apple and melted butter. Add the sour milk mixture to the dry ingredients. Stir well. Cook as you would ordinary pancakes in greased cast-iron frying pan. Brown on both sides. Serve plain or with butter and maple syrup.

Yields 4 servings.

Baked Peameal Bacon — the Original Canadian Bacon

Peameal bacon is a unique Canadian meat, pickled, but not

smoked, loin of pork rolled in cornmeal. Usually it is sliced and fried for breakfast but it is excellent baked whole. The cornmeal makes a crisp exterior and the meat, although quite lean, is particularly juicy, because of the pickling process. For baking it is important to select a piece from the centre cut, with a wide band of lean visible on both ends.

DIRECTIONS

Place in an open roasting pan, fat side up. Bake at 350° F (175° C) for 1½ hours. Serve hot in generous slices with baked beans, if desired.

CHRISTMAS DINNER

Brined Turkey—the Pioneer Way

Historically, brining was done as a method of preserving. Today, however, it is used primarily as a vehicle to impart flavour and moisture into a lean cut of meat.

Here are the steps to brining a turkey.

This is a general recipe. You may need to double the recipe to get enough to cover your bird. Spices may be added to this mixture to create your own unique flavour.

In a non-reactive container, mix until dissolved the following ingredients:

1 gallon	cool water	4 litres
1 cup	kosher salt	250 ml
½ cup	white sugar	125 ml

Pour the mixture over the turkey and refrigerate.

Additional spice and seasoning suggestions
Add any or all of the following to your brine mixture: bay leaves, juniper berries, black peppercorns, dried thyme, or garlic cloves.

Roast your turkey breast side down, for the appropriate time according to the weight.

Sausage, Pecan, and Cranberry Stuffing

INGREDIENTS

1 lb	pork sausage, crumbled	500 g
2 tbsp.	butter	30 ml
2 cups	chopped onions	500 ml
2 cups	sliced celery	500 ml
1	apple, peeled and chopped	1
1 tbsp.	sage, crumbled	15 ml
½ tsp.	rosemary, crumbled	2 ml
½ tsp.	marjoram	2 ml
½ tsp.	salt and pepper, each	2 ml
¼ tsp.	thyme, crumbled	1 ml

¼ cup	fresh parsley, chopped	50 ml
12 cups	breadcrumbs, lightly toasted	3 l
1½ cups	toasted pecans, chopped	375 ml
1 cup	dried cranberries	250 ml
3	eggs, lightly beaten	3
10 oz.	chicken broth*	284 ml

DIRECTIONS

Cook sausage in frying pan over medium heat until browned, about 6 minutes. Remove sausage with a slotted spoon to a paper-towel lined plate and set aside.

Drain off excess fat from frying pan. Add butter and melt over medium heat. Stir in onions and celery and sauté until softened. Add apple. Cook and stir for 2 minutes. Stir in sage, rosemary, marjoram, salt, pepper, thyme, and parsley.

Transfer mixture to a large bowl. Stir in sausage, bread-crumbs, pecans, and cranberries. Whisk together eggs and broth until blended. Add to bread mixture and stir until combined.

Spoon mixture into a greased, shallow, 4-quart (4-litre) baking dish. Cover with foil and bake at 350° F (175° C) for 40 to 50 minutes or until heated through.

Yield: serves 10-12.

* For a more moist stuffing, the broth in this recipe may be increased by ¼ to ½ cup (50 to 125 ml).

New Brunswick Maple Roasted Turkey and Gravy

Try stuffing with the Sausage, Pecan, and Cranberry Stuffing. If you have fresh marjoram on hand, use 2 tbsp. rather than the ½ tsp. dried. If you don't have fresh thyme, substitute ½ tsp. dried thyme. For an added zing of taste, 2 tbsp. of apple brandy can be added.

INGREDIENTS

2 cups	apple cider	500 ml
¹/₃ cup	real maple syrup	85 ml
2 tbsp.	chopped fresh thyme	30 ml
2 tsp.	dried marjoram	10 ml
2 ½ tsp.	grated lemon zest	12 ml
¾ cup	butter	170 ml
14 lb	whole turkey,	6.5 kilos
	neck and giblets reserved	
2 cups	hopped onion	500 ml
1 cup	chopped celery	250 ml
1 cup	coarsely chopped carrots	250 ml
2 cups	chicken stock	500 ml

GRAVY INGREDIENTS

3 cups liquid	additional chicken stock	750 ml
3 tbsp.	all-purpose flour	45 ml
1 tsp.	chopped fresh thyme	5 ml
1	bay leaf	1

DIRECTIONS

Boil apple cider and maple syrup in a heavy saucepan over medium-high heat until reduced to a ½ cup (about 20 minutes). Remove from heat and mix in half of the thyme and marjoram and all of the lemon zest. Add the butter or margarine and whisk until melted. Add salt and ground pepper to taste. Cover and refrigerate until cold (syrup can be made up to two days ahead).

Preheat oven to 375° F (190° C). Place oven rack in the lowest third of oven.

Wash and dry turkey. Place turkey in a large roasting pan. Slide hand under skin of the breast to loosen breast skin. Rub ½ cup of the maple butter mix under the skin of the breast. If planning on stuffing turkey do so now. Rub ¼ cup of the maple butter mixture over the outside of the turkey. With kitchen string, tie legs of turkey together loosely.

Arrange the chopped onion, chopped celery, and chopped carrot around the turkey in the roasting pan. If desired the neck and giblets may be added to the vegetables. Sprinkle the remaining thyme and marjoram over the vegetables and pour the chicken stock into the pan.

Roast turkey for 30 minutes. Reduce oven temperature to 350° F (175° C), and cover turkey loosely with foil (shiny side towards turkey). Continue to roast until very tender, basting occasionally with pan juices: about 3 to 4 hours not stuffed,

4 to 5 hours stuffed. Pierce the leg joint with a fork: if the juices run clear or faintly pink then the turkey is done. Transfer turkey to a platter and cove with foil. Reserve pan mixture for gravy.

DIRECTIONS FOR THE GRAVY

Strain pan juices into a measuring cup and spoon off the fat from juices. Add enough chicken stock to make 3 cups. Transfer liquid to a heavy saucepan and bring to a boil. Mix 3 tbsp. of the reserved maple butter mixture with the flour in a small bowl to form a paste. Whisk paste into broth mixture. Add the chopped fresh thyme and bay leaf. Boil until reduced and thickened slightly, whisking occasionally. Add apple brandy if desired and season with salt and ground pepper to taste.

Yields 12 servings.

Quebec-Style Roast Goose

INGREDIENTS

10 slices	white bread	10 slices
1 cup	dried currants	250 ml
4	apples, peeled and sliced	4
1 tbsp.	dried thyme	15 ml
4 tbsp.	melted butter	60 ml
	salt and pepper	

1 tbsp.	vegetable oil	15 ml
8 - 10 lbs	1 goose	3.5 – 4.5 kg
1	onion, chopped	1
1	carrot, chopped	1
1	celery stalk, chopped	1
1	garlic clove, minced	1
1	bay leaf	1
3	whole cloves	3
1 sprig	fresh thyme	1
1 sprig	fresh marjoram	1
¼ cup	white wine	63 ml
1 tsp.	tomato paste	5 ml
10 oz.	chicken stock	284 ml

DIRECTIONS

Make stuffing by combining bread, currants, apples, thyme, salt, pepper, and melted butter. Stuff and tie goose. Prick bird all over with fork. Heat oil in roasting pan, on top of stove, brown goose lightly on all sides, then drain off pan drippings. Set goose breast side up in a roasting pan, add a little water, cover and roast at 375° F (190° C) for 1 hour. Combine chopped onion, carrot, celery, garlic, bay leaf, cloves, thyme, and marjoram. Discard fat from roasting pan, add vegetable mixture and continue roasting uncovered 20 to 30 minutes per pound (3 to 4 hours in all) draining off fat at intervals and adding more water as required. Transfer cooked goose to platter and keep warm.

Skim off remaining fat in pan and heat drippings and vegetables on top of stove until mixture is reduced. Stir in white wine, tomato paste, and chicken bouillon. Simmer for 10 to 15 minutes, then strain gravy. A little cornstarch mixed with water may be blended in to thicken gravy, if desired. Serve goose with gravy, applesauce, mashed potatoes, and braised cabbage.

Yields 6 to 8 servings.

Roasted Beet Salad with Maple Vinaigrette
The earthy flavour of the beets and the sweetness of the pears make this a delicious combination.

INGREDIENTS

8	medium beets, trimmed of stalks, not peeled	8
2	ripe medium pears, peeled and thinly sliced	2
3 oz.	goat cheese, coarsely crumbled	90g

Maple Vinaigrette

¼ cup	maple syrup	60 ml
3 tbsp.	white vinegar	45 ml
2 tbsp.	olive oil	30 ml
½ tsp.	salt	2 ml
¼ tsp.	coarsely ground pepper	1 ml

DIRECTIONS

Preheat oven to 350°F (175°C). Wrap beets individually in foil. Place beets on baking sheet. Roast in preheated oven for about 1 hour, or until tender when pierced with skewer. Let stand for 10 to 15 minutes or until cool enough to handle. Peel beets. The skin should peel away easily by hand. You might want to wear clean rubber gloves to prevent your hands from being stained. Cut beets into wedges.

Arrange beets, pears and goat cheese in a medium serving bowl. Drizzle with maple vinaigrette.

DIRECTIONS FOR THE MAPLE VINAIGRETTE

Shake all ingredients together in jar until well combined.

DO-AHEAD TIPS

The beets can be roasted and peeled a day or two before serving and stored in a sealed container in the refrigerator.

The maple vinaigrette can be prepared a day or two before serving and stored in a sealed jar in refrigerator. Arrange salad just before serving.

COOKIES AND CAKES

Winter Birch Tree Cookies

INGREDIENTS

¾ cup	sugar	190 ml
½ cup	butter, softened	125 ml
1 tbsp.	milk	15 ml
2 tsp.	vanilla	10 ml
1	egg	1
2 cups	all-purpose flour	500 ml
1 tsp.	baking powder	5 ml
1 tsp.	cinnamon	5 ml
12 oz.	1 package vanilla-flavoured candy coating or almond bark, melted	354 ml
2 oz.	bittersweet chocolate, melted	60 g

DIRECTIONS

Heat oven to 400° F (200° C). Grease cookie sheet. In large bowl, combine sugar and butter; beat until well blended.

Add milk, vanilla, and egg; beat well. Lightly spoon flour into measuring cup; level off. Add flour, baking powder, and cinnamon; mix well. Shape dough into 1-inch balls. On lightly floured surface, roll balls into logs, 6 inches long. Place on greased cookie sheet.

Bake at 400° F (200° C) for 5 to 8 minutes or until light golden brown. Immediately remove from cookie sheets. Cool completely. Place melted candy coating in pie pan. Dip logs into candy coating; place on waxed paper to cool. Drizzle melted bittersweet chocolate over logs to resemble birch trees.

Yields about 40.

Apple Coffeecake with Brown Sugar Sauce

This is a scrumptious moist apple cake with a really rich caramel sauce. The recipe comes from Newfoundland.

INGREDIENTS

2	apples, peeled, cored, and chopped	2
2½ cups	all-purpose flour	625 ml
1½ cups	packed brown sugar	375 ml
¾ cup	butter, softened	190 ml
1 cup	chopped walnuts, toasted	250 ml
1 tsp.	baking soda	5 ml

1 tsp.	ground cinnamon	5 ml
½ tsp.	salt	2 ml
1	egg	1
¾ cup	sour cream	190 ml
1 tsp.	vanilla extract	5 ml

DIRECTIONS

Preheat oven to 375° F (190° C). Butter a 9-inch round cake pan or a 9½ inch spring form pan.

Using a fork, work flour with brown sugar and butter in a large bowl until crumbly. Stir in nuts. Divide mixture in half. Evenly press half into pan bottom to form a crust.

Stir baking soda, cinnamon, and salt into remaining crumb mixture until blended, and make a well in the centre.

In a small bowl, lightly beat egg with sour cream and vanilla until smooth. Add to flour mixture, stirring just until combined. Fold in apples. Evenly spread batter over crumb mixture. Bake until a cake tester inserted into centre comes out fairly clean, about 1 hour and 20 minutes. If top gets too brown before cake is baked, lightly lay a piece of foil over top for last 10 to 20 minutes of baking. Cool in pan on a rack.

Serve with Brown Sugar Sauce.

Cake keeps well at room temperature for a day. Covered, it freezes well and is easily cut while still frozen.

Yields one 9-inch round cake (12 servings).

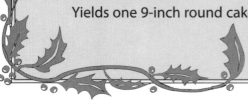

Brown Sugar Sauce

A rich topping for coffeecake! Cream may be substituted for the milk.

INGREDIENTS

¼ cup	butter	63 ml
3 tbsp.	all-purpose flour	45 ml
²/₃ cup	packed brown sugar	165 ml
1 cup	cold milk	250 ml
¼ cup	brandy	63 ml
¼ tsp.	vanilla extract	1 ml

DIRECTIONS

Melt the butter in a small saucepan set over a medium heat. In a medium-size bowl, stir flour and sugar together. Then whisk into melted butter until mixture is moistened. Stir in milk until smooth. Cook, whisking frequently until thickened and smooth, about 5 minutes. Stir in brandy and vanilla. Remove from heat. Serve right away over Apple Coffeecake with Brown Sugar Sauce. Or cover and refrigerate for a week or more. Reheat just before serving.

Yields 10 servings.

Gram's Cranberry Loaf

I can't remember a Christmas without this. One of our oldest traditions. Freezes perfectly, so make a few extra loaves.

INGREDIENTS

2 cups	all-purpose flour	500 ml
1 cup	sugar	250 ml
1½ tsp.	baking powder	7 ml
½tsp.	salt	2 ml
½ tsp.	soda	2 ml
1	egg, beaten	1
½ cup	orange juice	125 ml
2 tsp.	butter, softened,	10 ml
2 tbsp.	in hot water	30 ml
½ cup	chopped walnuts	125 ml
1	grated rind of orange	1
2 cups	raw cranberries,	500 ml
	cut in half with scissors	

DIRECTIONS

Mix dry ingredients, then mix liquid ingredients and add to dry mixture. Add the walnuts, rind, and cranberries and mix well. Bake in loaf pan for 1 hour and 10 minutes at 350º F (175° C). Chill overnight before serving.

Yields one loaf.

Quebec Maple Date Cookies

INGREDIENTS

3 cups	whole wheat flour	750 ml
1 tsp.	baking powder	5 ml
1 tsp.	baking soda	5 ml
1 cup	chopped pecans	250 ml
1 cup	chopped dates	250 ml
1 cup	butter, softened	250 ml
1½ cups	maple syrup	375 ml
3	eggs	3

DIRECTIONS

Preheat the oven to 350° F (175° C). Stir together the flour, baking powder, and baking soda. Add nuts and dates and mix well. Cream the butter and gradually add maple syrup and eggs. Gradually add the flour mixture until well incorporated. Drop by tsp. on a cookie sheet and bake 10 minutes.

Yields about 60.

Christmas Bonbons

INGREDIENTS

⅓ cup	sugar	75 ml
¼ cup	margarine; softened	60 ml
¼ cup+2 tbsp.	frozen orange juice concentrate, thawed and undiluted	90 ml
¼ cup	honey	60ml
1½ tsp.	grated orange rind	7 ml
1 tsp.	vanilla extract	5 ml
1	egg	1
½ cup+2 tbsp.	all-purpose flour	155 ml
¾ tsp.	ground cinnamon	3 ml
⅛ tsp.	baking soda	1 ml
⅛ tsp.	ground cloves	1 ml
⅛ tsp.	ground allspice	1 ml
½ cup	dried cranberries	120 ml
⅓ cup	golden raisins	165 ml
⅓ cup	finely chopped dried apricots	165 ml
3 tbsp.	chopped almonds	45 ml

DIRECTIONS

Cream sugar and margarine, using an electric mixer set at medium speed, until mixture is light and fluffy (about 5 minutes). Add juice concentrate, honey, orange rind, vanilla, and egg; beat at medium speed until blended.

Combine flour, cinnamon, baking soda, cloves and allspice. With mixer running at low speed, gradually add to orange mixture. Fold in cranberries, raisins, apricots, and almonds. Spoon batter evenly into 33 paper-lined miniature muffin pans. Bake at 350° F (175° C) for 20 minutes or until lightly browned. Cool in pans 3 minutes, remove from pans, and cool on wire rack.

Yields 33 bonbons.

Origin of
Christmas Crackers

he Christmas cracker was invented in 1847
by an enterprising young baker and con-
fectioner by the name of Tom Smith in
London, England. It was a unique creation that became an
integral part of British celebration and tradition and has even
crossed the Atlantic Ocean to Canada, becoming a popular
Christmas tradition here as well.

In its simplest form, a cracker is a small cardboard tube
covered with a brightly coloured twist of paper. When the two
ends of the cracker are pulled simultaneously in opposite
directions by two people, the friction creates a small explosive
"pop" produced by a narrow strip of chemically treated paper.
As the cracker "explodes," the cardboard tube releases its contents consisting usually of a bright paper hat, a small gift, a
balloon, confetti, and a piece of paper with a saying or joke.

At the turn to the 20th century, Tom Smith produced crackers not only for the Christmas season but also customized them in commemoration of every major event from the Paris Exhibition in 1900 to war heroes in 1918 and Edward's, the Prince of Wales, World Tour in 1926. Contents were handmade and tailored to each occasion and contained such items as grotesque or artistic masks, puzzles, conundrums, tiny treasures, jewels, games, and mottoes, plus elaborate party hats from fezzes to sheiks' headdresses. Sets of crackers came in beautiful handcrafted matching boxes that were works of art themselves. The fully illustrated cracker catalogues that date back to 1877 are considered to depict an exceptional visual history of British social and political evolvement over an entire century. Tom Smith's company has also had the honour of holding several Royal Warrants to produce Christmas crackers for Buckingham Palace.

Early History of Tom Smith

As a young lad in early 1830, Tom Smith apprenticed in a bakery and ornamental confectionery shop in London, selling sweets such as fondants, pralines, and gum pastilles. He worked hard and demonstrated an aptitude for designing and creating wedding cake ornaments and decorations. Before long he was devising new types of confections and opened up his own business in East London.

On a trip to Paris in 1840, Smith discovered the predecessor to his crackers in the form of sugared almond bonbons wrapped in a twist of tissue paper. He brought the bonbons back to London and during Christmas that year they sold extremely well, but in January demand virtually ceased. Anxious to develop the idea further and stimulate sales, Tom began marketing these bonbons as sweetheart treats with a love motto added inside the wrapping (inspired by the Chinese fortune cookie). The concept caught on and became so popular that within a short while orders were pouring in, requiring Tom to increase his staff.

Tom knew that he had a unique and potentially highly commercial idea so he decided to develop the product further. The majority of bonbons were still sold at Christmas and he began to think up ways to capitalize on this short but very profitable season and make his bonbons even more appealing. One evening as Tom was tending to the fire in his hearth while contemplating his dilemma, he kicked a log that crackled, suddenly giving him the spark of inspiration to improve his bonbons.

Creating the Snap, Crackle, and Pop
Tom thought that some sort of bang or crackle would add the necessary excitement to his novelty bonbon and now his challenge was to find a compound which would safely create a satisfactory explosion without going too far. He soon realized that something bigger than a bonbon was needed to accommodate a cracking mechanism so he first created a larger tube in which to house a compound that would make

a bang when disturbed. After much experimenting, and frequently burned hands, Smith finally perfected his chemical explosion. His solution was to use saltpetre to create a popping sound caused by friction when the wrapping was broken. This eventually became the snap, and the cracker was born.

Once again Tom Smith's business savvy proved correct and his creation was a raging success. But he was still not completely satisfied so he continued to refine his product, and included a surprise gift with the candies and small message inside. He called his new crackers *Cosaques*, after the cracking of the Cossack's whips as they rode through Paris during the Franco-Prussian wars. The name stuck for about another decade before simply being known as Christmas crackers. In early Victorian times, Twelfth Night celebrations were officially banned as being too rowdy because of the excessive use of crackers.

Around the same time, a German company, Schauer, introduce their "Sylvesters." These were apparently very similar to the cracker with a longer, slimmer shape. They were a safer, indoor version of the traditional fireworks that were lit for New Year's Eve, known as St. Sylvester's Eve in Germany.

By the turn to the 20th century, the demand for crackers was high, and Smith's factory was producing around 13 million units annually. In 1909 Tom Smith was granted his first Royal Warrant by the Prince of Wales to produce custom Christmas crackers for the Royal Family thus granting him membership in the prestigious Royal Warrant Holders Association. The company became known for filling custom orders, and for years employees would relate the story about a particular order received in 1927. Apparently, a gentleman wrote a letter to the Tom Smith Company enclosing a diamond engagement ring and a ten-shilling note as payment for the ring to be put in a special cracker for his fiancée. Unfortunately, the gentleman did not enclose an address and never contacted the company again. The ring, letter, and the ten-shilling note are said to still remain in the Company archives to this day.

Tom Smith lived to see the new branch of his firm outgrow the original premises on Goswell Road. The company moved to Finsbury Square in the City of London where it remained until 1953. When he died he left the business to his three sons, Tom, Henry, and Walter who continued to develop the cracker designs, contents, and mottoes always reflecting current affairs as well as the political and leisure activities of each period. Through a series of mergers, the Tom Smith Group is now a subsidiary of Napier Industries, considered to be the largest manufacturer of crackers in the world. Crackers are exported worldwide to 34 countries including the USA, Canada, Australia, South Africa, Hong Kong, and Japan.

New Year's Noisemakers
The custom of making as much noise as possible at midnight on New Year's Eve — such as blowing horns, setting

off pyrotechnics, discharging guns into the air — originated in ancient times with the ringing of bells, banging of metal, and shouting. The purpose was to scare off the evil spirits at this so-called "soft spot" in time so that they did not seize the opportunity of the changing of the year to slip into the world of the living and wreak havoc. In the old-style Julian calendar, the new year began on March 21, not on January 1. When the Gregorian calendar reform of 1582 dropped 10 days, some people resolutely kept their New Year's noise making on the old date, which had now become April 1, for which they were derisively called "April Fools."

First Christmas Carols

Borne on the frosty air
The Christmas song of praise
Now bids all discord cease
And joy reign everywhere.
Anonymous

rom their raucous pagan beginnings to the Puritan Reformation prohibition of carol singing, the origins of carols are not as innocent or innocuous as they may seem at first glance.

The word "carol" can be traced to the Greek *choros* (*khoraulês* or *khoros*), which means a secular circle dance performed without music. In Middle English the word became *carole*, which was again a circular dance but included singing; and the same word appears in Old French *carole*, probably stemming from late Latin *choraula*, meaning choral song; or from Latin *choraulês*, meaning accompanist.

First Christmas Carols

For most of the early history of the Church all forms of carols, whether spoken, danced, or sung, were prohibited. As the Church struggled to pull out the deep roots of pagan weeds that threatened to spoil the immaculately manicured lawn of Christianity, the singing of secular carols was shunned from its sacred services. Church hymns did exist, however these first chants, litanies, and supplications were in Latin and too theological for popular use. But outside the Church, Nativity carols were conceived, born, and raised by the voices of the people. Most of these carols were derived from raucous pagan drinking, feasting, or folk songs, often deviating from the strictly religious themes found in Church music.

In AD 1223, St. Francis of Assisi was the first to bring the peasant tradition into the Church when he introduced carols during a Christmas midnight mass service in a cave in Greccio. The 13th century fostered the rise of the carol written in the vernacular under this early influence of Francis of Assisi. During the Middle Ages people began performing special holiday plays, many notably about the Nativity. Carols would be sung at these plays and it was common for people to leave the service echoing the songs all the way home. Pageants and plays had been performed as part of the winter solstice celebrations to re-enact the creation and chaos myths so it was natural that people should want to transfer these traditions to their Christian practices.

Carols spread quickly throughout Italy, Spain, France,

England, and Germany through the 14th century with the help of travelling troubadours and wandering minstrels. The earliest extant English Christmas carol, "A child is boren amonges man," is found in a set of sermon notes written by a Franciscan friar before 1350.

The oldest existing printed Christmas carol is "The Boar's Head Carol," which was first published in 1521 by Wynken de Worde in *Christmasse Carolles*. This carol was sung in England at Christmas dinner while a boar's head was carried on a platter. The custom is still observed every Christmas at Queen's College, Oxford.

The Boar's Head Carol

1. The boar's head in hand bear I
Bedecked with bay and rosemary
I pray you, my masters, be merry
Quot estis in convivio (As you all feast so heartily).
Chorus: *Caput apri defero,*
Reddens laudes domino
(Lo, behold the head I bring
Giving praise to God we sing
or (The boar's head I bring,
 Giving praises to the Lord).

2. The boar's head, as I understand,
Is the rarest dish in all this land,

Which thus bedecked with a gay garland
Let us *servire cantico* (let us serve with a song).
Chorus

3. Our steward hath provided this
In honour of the King of bliss
Which, on this day to be served is
In Reginensi atrio (in the Queen's hall)
Chorus

4. The boar's head in hand bear I
Bedecked with bay and rosemary
I pray you, my masters, be merry
Quot estis in convivio (As you all feast so heartily).
Chorus

Some of the old carols that have survived into the present times, such as "The Boar's Head Carol," emerged from the Middle Ages and it was during this period that the practice of singing carols in the streets seems to have been firmly established. The origins of Christmas carolling in the streets, known as "wassailing," developed separately from church Christmas carols.

The ancient Celtic tradition of wassailing originated as a mid-winter fertility ritual of toasting to health, and blessing orchards, crops, and livestock. The earliest known practice of the wassail was to pour spiced ale or mulled wine onto dormant crops and orchards after the harvest to bless the ground for the spring and ward off evil.

Like many such customs originally devoted to defence against wickedness, wassailing has always been something of a festive activity associated with partying and making merry. Songs accompanied the ritual and it developed into a form of door-to-door carolling popular in the Middle Ages. Although this custom began in the pre-Christian era, the Church passively adopted it as a means of spreading Christmas good will. By not objecting to the pagan winter custom, the Church effectively gave its blessing and wassailing became a Christmas tradition. By about 1600 it had become a custom for commoners to take a wassail bowl about the streets and from house to house, offering drink from it and often expecting money in return.

The actual ingredients in traditional wassail are widely disputed. This could be attributable to the fact that festive bands who travelled from home to home often replenished the bowl with whatever liquid refreshment was available. While one home might have apple cider, another might have spirits of a stronger sort. There can be little doubt that alcohol has played a storied part of wassail's history.

As a form of recipient-initiated charitable giving, to be distinguished from begging, wassailing gave the poor the once-a-year opportunity to partake of the best food and drink from the bounteous tables of their wealthy benefactors. In turn, it allowed property owners a chance to spread good will and win the loyalty of the workers, thus preserving the status quo. Later in urban centres the custom degenerated into gangs of rowdy wassailers entering the houses of the well-to-do during the Christmas season, singing anthems to alcohol, and often demanding and receiving gifts of food, drink, and money ("Give us some figgy pudding!"). "The rich had to let them in," writes Stephen Nissenbaum in *The Battle for Christmas*, "essentially, to hold 'open house.'" The ritual walked a fine line, he notes, between merrymaking and mugging.

But not all wassailers were potential assailants. The carols they sang were often composed by the singers and conveyed musical wishes for good health; although ultimately the purpose was the solicitation of food or money:

> *"Here we come a-wassailing among the leaves*
> *   so green,*
> *Here we come a-wandering, so fair to be seen.*
> *We are not daily beggars that go from door*
> *   to door,*
> *But we are friendly neighbours that you have seen*
> *   before.*
> *Love and joy come to you, and to you your*
> *   wassail too,*
> *And God bless you and send you a happy*
> *   New Year,*
> *And God send you a happy New Year!"*
> *Our wassail cup is made of rosemary-tree,*

So is your beer of the best barley.
English Northern and Midlands traditional song

Wassail! Wassail! all over the town,
Our toast it is white and our ale it is brown,
Our bowl is made of maplin [maple] tree:
We be good fellows all—I drink to thee.
Traditional Gloucestershire song

Originally, carol singing was not limited to Christmas. Most festivals, such as New Year, Easter, and saints' days, generated their own carols. Some carols were general enough to be applicable year-round. It wasn't until the late 19th century that carol-singing become almost exclusively associated with Christmas.

The Protestant reformer, Martin Luther, in 1539 composed the song "From Heaven Above to Earth I Come" ("*Vom Himmel hoch, da komm' ich her*"). Luther wrote this hymn for the Christmas Eve festival held annually at his house. A man dressed as an angel customarily sang the opening verses. Music, written by Handel and Mendelssohn, was adapted and it became a popular Christmas carol.

One of the most famous of all Christmas carols, "Silent Night, Holy Night" (*Stille Nacht, heilige Nacht*), was written by the Austrian parish priest Joseph Mohr and composed by Franz Gruber in 1818. Another popular carol, "Oh Little Town of Bethlehem," was written as a poem in 1865 by Phillip Brooks, a Philadelphia pastor who ministered to

First Christmas Carols

Union soldiers during the Civil War. The poem was set to music three years later and was sung by a children's choir in Brooks' church, but was otherwise unknown outside his parish for a decade.

Classical composers wrote most of the Christmas carols of the 19th century. As more and more carols were written, the themes began to surpass religion, and the totality of Christmas with all that it encompasses found its way into carol music. Music became one of the greatest tributes to Christmas, and carols included some of the noblest compositions of the great musicians.

Despite the growing popularity of all things Christmas in many parts of the world, the same was not true amongst English Puritans of the British Commonwealth in the mid-17th century. Staunch Protestant Oliver Cromwell campaigned against the heathen practices of feasting, decorating, singing, and other such idolatry, which he felt desecrated the spirit of Christ. Under his leadership, the government abolished English Christmas celebrations by an act of Parliament in 1647. Puritans at that time continued to work through December 25. During this brief interlude in English history, at which time there was no monarch, Christmas-related activities remained illegal. But these activities were prohibited only as long as that Commonwealth survived, and in 1660, when Charles II restored the Stuarts to the throne, the public was once again able to partake in the singing of Christmas carols and other such Christmas celebrations. Nevertheless, the tradition of carolling at Christmastime did not resume again in England until the 1800s.

In 1659, New England Puritans of Massachusetts passed a similar law forbidding celebrations relating to Christmas due to their secular nature. This law was later repealed in 1681; however, it led to the Christmas carol almost being totally eradicated from early American society. The ban existed as law for only 22 years, but disapproval of celebrating Christmas took many more years to change. In fact, as in England, it took almost 200 years for Christmas celebrations to become fashionable in the Boston region.

After Charles Dickens' *A Christmas Carol* was published in 1843, the appeal of Christmas once again began to rise. Most of the carols that are popular today were written after 1843, although a few date back to the 13th century. The actual Christmas carol that Dickens' title refers to is "God Rest Ye Merry, Gentlemen." Christmas carol expert William Studwell observed that it was most appropriate that Dickens chose this particular song, "for no other carol has had a stronger cultural effect on London and on England as a whole than the spiritual piece which infringed on Scrooge's grouch privacy."

This popular Christmas carol is also one of the most commonly misquoted — or rather mis-punctuated — of all Christmas carols. Most people assume the line reads: "God rest ye, merry gentlemen." Note the position of the comma, which makes the line read as though the gentlemen have been celebrating rather vigorously, and are in need of a rest. On the contrary: the phrase "rest you merry" was common in the 15th century and it meant to wish merriment on someone. The original intent was to wish those gentlemen merry, or as Studwell observed, "God keep you in good spirits, gentlemen."

The First Canadian Christmas Carol

Catholic Jesuit missionary, Jean De Brébeuf wrote the first Canadian Christmas carol in Quebec, long before Canada became a nation.

In the early 1600s, Jean de Brébeuf lived among the Hurons, one of the native tribes of Quebec. Father Jean de Brébeuf was the first of 30 Jesuit missionaries to hazard the Atlantic crossing from the continent to New France with Samuel de Champlain. He spent a turbulent 24 years dedicated to the Jesuit cause of bringing Christianity to Canada's native peoples and specifically the Huron.

During his time in Canada, while recuperating from a broken clavicle, Brébeuf wrote *Jesus Ahatonnia* ("Jesus is Born"). In retelling the story of the Nativity, Father Brébeuf used symbols and figures that could be understood by the Huron, and the hymn became part of the tribe's oral tradition. He wrote this song in the native language of the Wyandot, to the music of a 16th century carol called *Une Jeune Pucelle* ("A Young Maid"). The song continued to be sung by the Huron every Christmas until 1649, when the Iroquois brutally murdered Father Brébeuf, massacred the Jesuit mission, and drove the Huron from their home. One of the last Jesuit missionaries to the Huron, Fr. De Villeneuve, wrote the old Huron words to the carol and later translated it into simple French.

Brébeuf's carol has been translated into both French and English but the most sung version is an interpretation by Jesse Edgar Middleton (1872–1960). In 1971, the Anglican Church of Canada and the United Church of Canada included Brébeuf's carol in their hymnbook. The carol is known as both "The Huron Carol," and "'Twas in the Moon of Winter Time." This version is still sung today throughout Canada and is considered a national treasure; it has also been celebrated on a set of Canadian postage stamps.

Jesuous Ahatonia (Huron Christmas Carol)
(Words: Jean de Brébeuf, ca. 1643 / Trans. by Jesse Edgar Middleton, 1926 / Music: French Canadian melody; tune name: Jesous Ahatonhia)

> *'Twas in the moon of winter time when all the birds*
>   *had fled*
> *That mighty Gitchi Manitou sent angel choirs*
>   *instead;*
> *Before their light the stars grew dim and wondering*
>   *hunters heard the hymn,*
> *Jesus your King is born, Jesus is born, in excelsis*
>   *gloria.*

First Christmas Carols

*Within a lodge of broken bark the tender babe
was found;*
*A ragged robe of rabbit skin enwrapped his
beauty 'round*
*But as the hunter braves drew nigh the angel song
rang loud and high*
*Jesus your King is born, Jesus is born, in excelsis
gloria.*

*The earliest moon of wintertime is not so round
and fair*
*As was the ring of glory on the helpless infant
there.*
*The chiefs from far before him knelt with gifts of fox
and beaver pelt.*
*Jesus your King is born, Jesus is born, in excelsis
gloria.*

O children of the forest free, O sons of Manitou
*The holy Child of earth and heaven is born today
for you.*
*Come kneel before the radiant boy who brings you
beauty, peace, and joy.*
*Jesus your King is born, Jesus is born, in excelsis
gloria.*

The Twelve Days of Christmas

There is probably no other Christmas carol that has had its origins disputed more that "The Twelve Days of Christmas." No one seems to know exactly when or by whom it was written. Various claims have been put forth regarding the true meaning of this famous Christmas carol. One such claim was suggested by Father Hal Stockert, a Byzantine Catholic parish priest from Granville, New York, in 1997. Stockert theorized that the song was written in England sometime between 1558 and 1829 as a "catechism song" during a time when the practice of Catholicism was prohibited and was intended to teach young Catholics to learn the tenets of their faith.

He claims the gifts listed in the song have hidden meanings and the "true love" mentioned in the song doesn't refer to an earthly suitor but rather it refers to God. The person receiving the presents refers to baptized Catholics. The partridge in a pear tree is Jesus Christ. Stockert claims the other symbols mean the following:

2 Turtle Doves = the Old and New Testaments

3 French Hens = faith, hope, and charity, the theological virtues

4 Calling Birds = the four Gospels and/or the four Evangelists

5 Golden Rings = the first five books of the Old Testament, the "Pentateuch," which gives the history of man's fall from grace.

6   Geese A-laying = the six days of creation
7   Swans A-swimming = the seven gifts of the Holy Spirit, the seven sacraments
8   Maids A-milking = the eight beatitudes
9   Ladies Dancing = the nine fruits of the Holy Spirit
10 Lords A-leaping = the ten commandments
11 Pipers Piping = the eleven faithful apostles
12 Drummers Drumming = the twelve points of doctrine in the Apostle's Creed

In response to Father Stockert's proclamation, the Catholic Information Network posted the following statement: "It has come to our attention that this tale is made up of both fact and fiction. Hopefully, it will be accepted in the spirit it was written. As an encouragement to people to keep their faith alive, when it is easy, and when any outward expressions of their faith could mean their life. Today there are still people living under similar conditions, may this tale give them courage and determination to use any creative means at their disposal to keep their faith alive."

Another theory asserts that the song was intended as a musical version of the popular "memory and forfeits" games that were played by the children of the time. The game was played by a leader reciting the first verse, and continued around, each player reciting the next verse. The person who missed a verse usually had to pay a penalty of some kind, decided before the game began.

According to William Henry Husk in his book, *Songs of the Nativity*, 1868, the lady who was the favoured recipient of the true love's gifts must have required extensive space for their accommodation, as at the end of the Christmas festivities she would possess 12 partridges in pear trees, 22 turtle-doves, 30 French hens, 36 colley (i.e., black) birds, 40 gold rings, 42 laying geese, 42 swimming swans, 40 milk-maids, 36 drummers, 30 pipers, 22 dancing ladies, and 12 leaping lords; in all 364 articles, one for each day of the year save one.

More likely, it is simply a secular song that celebrates the 12 days from Christmas Day to the Epiphany (January 6) of either English or French 17th or 18th century origin. Although the lyrics are obviously English, apparently the song somewhat resembles a similar French folk song.

The song's simplistic structure and versatility have spawned a vast array of parodies including the McKenzie Brothers' version with their "identifiable Canadian content" gifts such as six packs of two-four, five golden toques, four lbs of back bacon, three French toast, two turtlenecks, and a beer (eh?). The creators of Bob and Doug McKenzie are actors Dave Thomas and Rick Moranis. They recorded their version of this popular Christmas carol in 1981 (Anthem Records/ Polygram Records) on their album "The Great White North." The album went gold in the U.S. and triple platinum in

Canada as well as winning a Juno Award for the Best Comedy Album and a Grammy nomination.

Poking fun at his Ukrainian heritage, singer/song writer Metro recorded *Metro's Eleven Days from Christmas* (and other versions of traditional Christmas carols with a Ukrainian twist — Singwell Studios, Vancouver, BC) with gifts that his "Mrs. gave for me," such as 11 pails of *borshch* [beet soup], 10 lbs of *chisnek* [garlic], nine months pregnant, "eight" all my supper, seven four-by-two slabs, six overalls, five golden rings of *kolbasa* [sausage], four *holubtsi* [cabbage rolls], three rubber boots, two *perogies* [dumplings] and a bowl of sour cream.

Mummering

> *I open the door, I enter in,*
> *I beg your pardon to begin,*
> *Whether we rise, stand, sit or fall,*
> *We'll do our duty to please you all...*

Aboriginal people have been acting out creation stories with the use of masks, costumes and dances as part of their winter solstice celebrations for as long as 40,000 years. Although no written documentation exists from that time, archaeological evidence combined with the aboriginal dedication to preserving their culture through oral history speaks volumes. From Inuit mythology to Scandinavian folklore to Norse to Teutonic to Goth to Egyptian to ancient Greek mythology to Romans parading in the streets wearing masks during Saturnalia, the dots all connect to a tradition which continues today in the form of "mummers." Mummering (or mumming) means "making diversion in disguise," or "one who goes merrymaking in disguise during festivals." The term Mummers is only one of the collective names used. Others are: Guisers, Christmas Rhymers, Belsnickers, Janneys, Plough Jags, Plough Bullocks, Tipteerers, and even Morris Dancers, although the actors may never have performed a dance.

Mummers' plays have been performed in England, Scotland, Wales, and Ireland for many centuries. They are folk dramas that in post-Christian times became based on the legend of St. George and the Seven Champions of Christendom. The story of St. George and the dragon developed out of a typical Egyptian solar myth of the sun god, Marduk, doing battle with the five-headed dragon, Tiamat. The dramas were originally mime or silent shows (mummers refers to the Middle English word *mum*, meaning silent, although the origin may also be connected with *mommo* the Greek word for mask.) All the characters were played by men, who tended to perform the same role for many years running. Dialogue was eventually added, but was passed on by oral tradition. Consequently, over the centuries the original story's significance has been lost, making present day performances very entertaining but virtually meaningless to most audiences.

The principle characters of most mummers' plays are St. George, Captain Slasher, the Turkish Knight, the King of Egypt, Doctor, and several soldiers who challenge St. George to a duel and are subsequently slain. The Doctor enters and demonstrates his skill by resuscitating the dead knights. Essentially this drama is an allegory for the death of the year, and celebration of its rebirth in the spring.

The province of Newfoundland has a 200-year long tradition of mummering between Christmas and Twelfth Night (January 6). The early settlers from the u.k. brought the custom of mummering to Canada, where it is also known as janneying. Sadly, it has been banned in most places because of some of the practices involved, namely begging door to door. Mummering was also discouraged after the tragic and violent death of Isaac Mercer in 1861. Mercer sustained a brutal beating at the hands of a group of inebriated, disguised mummers.

Mummering's ancient pagan origins included "very rough and violent activity in which the costumes consisted of dried skins, horns, and tails from caribou, seals, and other animals and these traditions carried on to the present although most people do not relate the reason. The event usually took the form of a parade in the street and became very loud and rowdy, with the participants carrying sticks. People were injured and property was damaged by those whose identity was hidden. People were quite frightened by the mummers, and as a result the activity was banned."[14]

Here is how J.B. Jukes described mummering in Newfoundland in 1842:

> "This was the season of general holiday. The lower orders ceased work; and, during Christmas, they amused themselves by what seemed the relics of an old English custom, which, I believe, was imported from the West of England, where it still lingers. Men dressed in all kinds of fantastic disguises, and some in women's clothes, with gaudy colours and painted faces, and generally armed with a bladder full of pebbles tied to a kind of whip, paraded the streets, playing practical jokes on each other and on the passers by, performing rude dances, and soliciting money or grog. They called themselves Fools and Mummers."

The use of the "bladder full of pebbles" in the Newfoundland mummering tradition may present a clue to a connection with Inuit folklore whereby animal bladders are considered sacred holders of the soul and according to their creation stories the sun was created from a bladder tied to a string. "The Inuit believe that souls are continually recycled, and that, if properly honoured, the *inua* of a dead animal will be reincarnated as future prey. Thus in the winter Bladder Festival, the inflated bladders of seals and other mammals are pushed back into the sea through holes made in the ice."

First Christmas Carols

When mummering was brought to Canada by English immigrants the tradition developed in a unique way once removed from the "mother land" and in so doing incorporated some local flavour as the different cultures "rubbed shoulders" sharing and blending their celebrations.

Prairie Carolling — *Koljada*
In many of western Canada's early Ukrainian communities, carolling, or *koljada/koliadky,* was one of the most important social events to take place during the Christmas season. From New Year's to Epiphany (Ukrainian Christmas, January 6), groups of carollers would travel from homestead to homestead singing to raise funds or collect donations for the church or some other community charity. In the earliest years of Canada's Ukrainian settlements, only men went carolling. Although Ukrainian carolling bears striking resemblance to mummering, stemming from the same roots, prairie carolling seems to have maintained civility perhaps because of its relationship to the community church. This type of carolling, however, was not completely immune to the rowdiness, intoxication, and lewdness from whence it originated.

Although carolling was an enjoyable part of the festive season, it was not always an easy task for the men, who had to leave their farm chores behind, and travel considerable distance between all the farms in a parish. Carolling required extensive preparation. First, a leader had to be selected. Another member of the carolling group was elected to play the part of the goat, and costumed accordingly. The custom of the goat accompanying the carollers has its origin in the pagan times when the goat represented the god of fertility. Another member was chosen to be the bag carrier, or the collector of all the gifts people would give them. And yet another member would be given the task of carrying a six-pointed star attached to a long stick with a light in its centre, symbolizing the Star of Bethlehem. In pre-Christian times, this light would have signified the sun and the anticipation of winter giving way to spring.

Carolling in the Canadian-Ukrainian community was not a simple singing of Christmas songs; it was more of a folk opera originating from the old country. The carollers first had to ask for permission to sing — hearkening back to a time when this form of "guising" was banned. Then, if allowed, they entered the house and sang carols glorifying each and every member of the family. These songs would extol praise upon their work as well as their personal traits. Sometimes the carollers even performed slow ritualistic dances. They also enacted a short, humorous skit involving the goat. The skit portrayed the goat dying and then being brought back to life symbolizing the death of winter and the birth of spring. The carols themselves often focused on the cycles of nature, with incantations for prosperity, good health, and a successful harvest. One such popular pagan carol told the tale of a landowner who was awakened one Christmas Eve by a swallow and told to make preparations to receive three very

First Christmas Carols

important deities: the sun, the moon, and the rain spirits. In the Christianized version, the three guests become Jesus Christ, Saint Nicholas, and St. George.

Another Ukrainian Christmas Carol from Galica explains the creation of the world:

When there was in the beginning no world,
Then there was neither heaven nor earth.
Everywhere was a blue sea,
And on the midst of the sea, a green plane-tree
On the plane tree three doves,
Three doves take counsel,
Take counsel as how to create the world.
Let us plunge to the bottom of the sea.
Let us gather fine sand;
Let us scatter fine sand,
That it may become for us black earth.
Let us get golden rocks;
Let us scatter golden rocks.
Let there be for us a bright sky,
A bright sky, a shining sun,
A shining sun and bright moon,
A bright moon, a bright morning star,
A bright morning star and little starlets.

Much later versions have God, St. Peter, and St. Paul riding the doves as the actual creators.

The carolling always ended with short well-wishing poems, appropriately selected for each home and sometimes before departing performers would demand treats with threats for refusal. The treats, also called *koljada,* usually took the form of little pastries, or *korovki,* in the shape of cows or goats.

> *If you don't give us a tart — We'll take your cow by the horns.*
> *If you don't give us a sausage — We'll grab your pig by the head.*
> *If you don't give us a bliny — We'll give the host a kick.*

The tricks played by those who were refused rewards could be quite destructive. Garbage might be gathered from all over the village and piled in front of the offending host's gate, their gate might be torn off, or their livestock let loose.

Sometimes, carollers would carry a bundle of hazel twigs and after receiving *koljada,* would gently hit his host with a small stick while wishing him happiness and health in the coming New Year. A small twig was left with the farmer who would then nail it above his door for wealth and protection.

Some people believe Christmas carollers should never be sent away empty-handed, no matter how badly they sing or perform, for fear of inviting bad luck, or these destructive tricks. One of those carollers could be a king in disguise so best to be safe and always offer food, a drink, or a bit of money just in case. There is also a superstition that says singing Christmas carols at any time other than during the festive season could bring bad luck.

The Origin and Evolution of Santa Claus

"After you stop believing in Santa Claus,
The whole world just goes downhill."
Tom Clancy, *The Sum of All Fears*

S anta Claus (a.k.a. *Noel Baba*, Father Christmas, Father Frost, *Joulupukki, Kris Kringle, Père Noël, Sabdiklos,* Saint Nicholas, *Sinter Klaas, Weihnachtsmann, Ruhklas, Pelznickel, Klasbur, Belsnickle, Aschen Klaus*) is known throughout the world and is an inseparable part of Christmas. In fact, in some form or another he has been an inseparable part of midwinter celebrations for many millennia. Santa Claus is a folk figure with multicultural roots so deep that the origins of this legend have become legends themselves. He embodies characteristics of Norse, Celtic, Teutonic, Inuit, Russian, Greek, and Roman mythological characters as well as a third century Catholic bishop, by the name of Nicholas, whose life stories and miracles have achieved mythical proportions.

Saint Nicholas

Legends of mysterious gift-givers, who judge right from wrong, good from bad, are as old almost as time itself. Around the same time that the Church was struggling to get a foothold in Europe, there lived a pious young man named Nicholas in what is now the country of Turkey. He was born about AD 280 in Patara of Lycia, 350 miles northwest of Bethlehem, of devout and wealthy parents who provided him with a Christian upbringing and education. He was orphaned at an early age inheriting a considerable amount of money, which he reputedly gave away to the needy. He was ordained the Bishop of Myra whilst still a very young man. Soon after his appointment to bishop, the government of the Eastern Roman Empire, under Emperors Diocletian and Maximian, jailed all Christian bishops who did not publicly sacrifice to the pagan gods of Rome. Nicholas remained in prison for nearly 10 years until Emperor Constantine conquered the East and put an end to the persecution of Christians. It has been claimed that Nicholas took part in the Council of Nicaea in AD 325 — the Council that attempted to resolve the existing differences in Christian beliefs and set the date of December 25 as the birthday of Christ.

There is much speculation about the life of Saint Nicholas and many stories relate his good deeds and habit of coming to the aid of the underprivileged, particularly children. There are legends of him performing at least 21 miracles including saving his city from starvation during a harsh famine, rescuing three sailors from drowning, and resurrecting three boys who had been murdered by an evil innkeeper. Even the story of how he came to be elected bishop was considered nothing short of a miracle. When his predecessor died and the other bishops met to elect a new bishop, they gave themselves up to fasting and prayer for inspiration and guidance in making their decision. One very influential bishop claimed he heard a voice telling him to watch at the doors of the church at daybreak, and to consecrate as bishop the first man he saw coming to church, whose name would be Nicholas. Guess who came to the church at sunrise to pray?

The most famous story of all about Saint Nicholas tells of his gracious deed of giving three bags of gold to a poor man with three daughters. In those days a young maiden's father was required by custom to offer prospective husbands something of value, called a "dowry." The larger the dowry was, the better the chance that a young woman would find a good husband. Without a dowry, a maiden was unlikely to marry and unable to support herself. Therefore, this poor man's daughters were destined to a wretched life of slavery or prostitution. When Nicholas heard of the poor family's plight he wanted to help, but as a shy man he did not like to receive credit for his gifts. So he devised a plan that would enable him to help the family yet remain anonymous. On three different occasions he went to the family's home and tossed a bag of gold down the chimney, or through an open window, where they landed in the girls' stockings or shoes left before the fire to dry. This is believed to have led to the custom of children hanging stockings or putting out shoes, eagerly awaiting gifts from Saint Nicholas. To the poor father, the miraculous appearance of the bags of gold provided the needed dowries. On the last occasion, the father had spied to see who this generous benefactor was. Nicholas begged the poor man to keep the secret, but of course the news got out. From then on, whenever anyone received an unexpected gift, they attributed it to Nicholas.

The three bags of gold Nicholas gave to the poor family made him the focus of merchants in northern Italy. Statues and pictures had depicted him holding the three bags and when taken as the patron saint of the merchants, the bags became three gold balls, representing moneylenders and today, pawnbrokers. This is why pawnbrokers' shops usually have three gold balls hanging over the entranceway. Also, the frequent association of the number three with Saint Nicholas is no coincidence. This was no doubt an attempt on the part of the Catholic Church to emphasize the Holy Trinity, which according to legend again, Nicholas played a part in establishing at the Council of Nicaea.

Legend also tells that Nicholas loved children and often

went out at night disguised in a hooded cloak, to leave necessary gifts of money, clothing, or food at the windows of
unfortunate families. In modern Europe, many people decorate the outside of their homes with figures of Saint Nicholas
climbing a ladder or a rope to a window. In that part of the
world he is not said to enter through rooftop chimneys nor
does he fly in a sleigh pulled by eight reindeer as does his
North American counterpart, Santa Claus.

Bishop Nicholas died on the sixth of December circa
AD 343. The exact day of his death may be an adaptation of
Poseidon's feast day to connect Nicholas with the sea and
mariners. An elaborate basilica was built over his tomb in
AD 540 and dedicated to the saint by the Roman emperor
Justinian I at Constantinople, now Istanbul.

By AD 800, the Eastern Catholic Church officially recognized Nicholas as a saint. And in 850, the clergy of Cologne
cathedral were commemorating the death of the saint by
giving special treats of fruit and cookies to the students of
the cathedral school, on December 6. By the ninth century, the first hymns to Saint Nicholas were composed.
Nicholas became patron saint of Russia in 987 by decree of
Duke Vladimir, where he was henceforth known as *Nikolai
Choodovoritz* (Nicholas, Miracle Maker). Around this time,
the Russians began to transpose their pagan winter folk spirit
of Father Frost with *Nikolai Choodovoritz* who they believed
lived in an arctic environment, dressed in furs with a long
white beard and rode in a sleigh drawn by reindeer.

The Origin and Evolution of Santa Claus

In the year 1087, 47 Italian soldiers stole the bones of Saint Nicholas from his tomb in Demre, Turkey and on May 9 brought his body to Bari, Italy where it remains to this day enshrined in the 11th century *Basilica di San Nicola.* This removal greatly increased his popularity, and Bari became a much visited pilgrimage centre. For this reason Saint Nicholas is often referred to as the Bishop of Bari. The theft was unofficially approved by the Church, who feared the shrine of the saint could be desecrated in the many wars and attacks in the Demre region. Also, by that time the split had occurred in the Universal Church, creating Roman Catholic and Eastern Orthodox, and the Roman Catholics felt that they should be the safeguards of the relics of this most popular of saints. In this same year, by sacred decree of the Holy Roman Catholic Church, Nicholas achieved sainthood and was granted power over the air and ordained Supreme Controller of the Winds and henceforth Saint Nicholas had the "power to fly like the wind."

Some time in the early part of the 12th century, nuns in Belgium and France began the practice of giving gifts to the children of the poor on December 6. This is among the first instance where gift giving is performed in the name of Saint Nicholas. Still, it took another century before December 6 began to be celebrated as Saint Nicholas Day, a religious holiday in France, Germany, and Holland when people give gifts to their children and the poor in the name of Saint Nicholas.

The earliest writings about the life of Saint Nicholas date back to AD 842 in an account written in Greek by Saint Methodius, Bishop of Constantinople. By AD 1400, over 500 songs and hymns had been written in honour of the popular saint. And on December 6, 1492, Christopher Columbus arrived in Haiti naming the port Saint Nicholas in honour of the safe journey. By end of the 1400s, Saint Nicholas was the third most popular religious figure, after Jesus and Mary. There were more than 2000 chapels and monasteries named after him, exceeded only by the Virgin Mary. More than 700 churches in Britain alone were dedicated to Saint Nicholas.

Over time, the date of his death, December 6, was commemorated with an annual feast throughout Europe, which gradually came to mark the beginning of the medieval Christmas season. The anniversary of Nicholas's death is so close to Christmas that, in many countries, the two merged. But in Germany and the Netherlands, the two remain separate.

Devotion to Saint Nicholas grew worldwide; his name has been given to places in many countries and numerous surnames of persons are derived from Nicholas. Because of his wisdom and sensitivity, many groups claimed Saint Nicholas as their patron saint, including:

- Russia and Greece, Moscow, Paris, and Fribourg (Switzerland);
- Pilgrims, preachers, infants, children, orphans, scholars, students, and spinsters;

- sailors and seamen, fishermen, boatmen, ferrymen, longshoremen, bargemen, plankmen, dockers, shipwrights and gaugers, navigators, sea voyagers, and those in shipwreck;
- As patron saint of sailors, his effigy was the figurehead of many ships, and thus his cult spread from Asia Minor to Italy, Spain, Holland, Britain as well as the New World;
- thieves, prisoners, registrars, notaries, clerks of court, lawyers, and judges;
- bakers, pawnbrokers, merchants and shopkeepers;
- those involved in the cloth trade: button makers, tatters, weavers, drapers, haberdashers, and cloth merchants;
- tallow merchants and candle makers, chandlers and oil merchants, perfumers, bottlers, florists, and embalmers, pharmacists and apothecaries;
- commission grain dealers and merchants, seed merchants, grain carriers, weighers, millers, grocers, and brewers;
- wine porters, wine merchants and wine vendors, coopers and brewers;
- tanners and butchers;
- and, Saint Nicholas was even made the patron saint of wolves. Wolves are featured often in European folklore in association with many of the pagan forerunners of his legendary character.

Pagan Origins

Originally the idea of a Santa Claus-like folk figure emerged thousands of years ago, before Christ and Saint Nicholas, in ancient Norse, Inuit, Saxon, Celtic, Greek, Roman, and Babylonian mythology to name a few. Albeit his earliest incarnations were considerably more wild and rugged than the "right jolly old elf" of 20th century mythology, but the character has had millennia to evolve.

The Norse peoples believed that the cold, the dark, and the howling winds of winter were the work of ice giants who battled the gods and the humans. Odin, also known as Woden to the Germanic peoples, was their leader in the battle against this icy chaos that threatened them each winter. Odin would ride out the storms in the sky on his fast eight-footed white horse, Sleipnir. At first a belligerent and loud god, Odin evolved over time to embody wisdom and justice, often meting out rewards or punishments. One of the characteristics of Odin was his ability to foresee the future. He travelled with his two black ravens Hugin and Munin ("thought" and "memory").

The raven is a significant character in ancient folklore including Norse, Teutonic, Inuit, and Japanese. All seem to agree that the raven (or crow) has always been the thinker, the trouble-maker, the cunning and clever one, the shape-shifter and trickster, and sometimes even the saviour. According to the Inuit, ravens are one of those rare creatures that possess *isuma* (human-like awareness), which make them good companions. Inuit mythology tells the story of how the raven is responsible for bringing daylight into the world. He also created man, and thus has the power to take it all away as well. But these cultures seem to have mixed reactions to ravens. Throughout various locations in Europe as well as from east to west across the Arctic, the raven fades from a lighter, more admirable character, to a darker, diabolical cast. These dual characteristics are significant to the later development of Saint Nicholas and specifically to his helpers.

Odin's ravens were his trusty companions who kept him informed about people. Odin's name means "the inspired one" and he was depicted as a tall, white-bearded, cloaked old man carrying his never missing spear, Gungnir. Odin was represented by 12 characters, one for each month of the year. His December character was called Jule and the month was called Jultid, which is where the term Yuletide originates ("turning the wheel of the seasons"). The Vikings believed that Odin walked among men on Earth during Jultid, disguised as a traveller in a long blue-hooded cloak, carrying a staff and a satchel of bread. He would sometimes leave the bread as a gift at poor homesteads while checking to see that humans were kind in offering hospitality to weary travellers and those in need of protection. At that time of year, the Vikings were unable to go to sea so they congregated in great halls to drink and talk of their exploits, and to honour their gods in thanks for a good year.

Odin's son Thor, god of agriculture, thunder, and war,

made his home in the far north. His weapon was lightning and he was associated with the colour red. Sometimes, while his father travelled amongst humans, it would be Thor who fought the giants of ice and snow, conquering the cold thereby allowing spring to come. Thor travelled the skies in a chariot drawn by two goats named Gnasher and Cracker and he was often depicted carrying a wassail bowl. Thor, as the god of agriculture and fertility, was revered during the mid-winter celebration known as Mothernite.

Eventually as Christianity became more and more widespread, worship of Odin and his pantheon slowly died out and a familiar mythology grew around Saint Nicholas; although it sometimes became hard to tell where the legend of Saint Nicholas began and that of Odin (or Woden) ended. Nevertheless, Odin and his son, Thor, are still honoured weekly to this day: Odin's sacred day, Woden's Day, became Wednesday in English and Thor's Day became Thursday.

Until about the 14th century, Nicholas was portrayed with a short dark beard, like an Eastern Bishop. Belief in Odin, flying through the skies on his white horse, with his long white beard flowing, was superimposed over the Saint's characteristics. He was further merged with the Germanic character of "Winterman" who was said to descend from the mountains with the snows, dressed in furs and skins, herald-ing winter. This character was also known in Scandinavia, where the Lapps believed that he herded the reindeer down to lower pastures, signalling the arrival of winter; hence the later American addition of reindeer as the flying bearers of Santa's sleigh. Lapps lived in dome-shaped dwellings called yurts. These homes were made of birch and reindeer hide with one opening, usually on top, that served as both a door and a smoke hole: another explanation for Santa's entry down the chimney.

The Finnish version of Saint Nicholas may have evolved from Ukko, chief god of the Finnish pantheon in pagan times. Ukko was the ancient father who reigned the heavens, supporting the world and controlling the clouds, thunder and rain. His name was similar to the Finnish word for thunder, *ukkonen.* He was often invoked by the Finns when all other gods had failed them. Ukko was also called on in many difficult situations, such as curing the sick or when luck in the hunt was vital. He eventually became the protector of the poor, the downtrodden, the outcast, and children. Some believe that Ukko was one of the original ancestors of Santa Claus. He was often described as an old man with a long, white moustache, but with no beard, which was possibly a Mongolian influence. In Finnish mythology, Lapland, the region above the Arctic Circle, was considered to be the home of magical singers, enchanters, devils, shamans, sorcerers, witches, fairies, trolls, and wildmen. Ukko was the lord of this mystical locale and made his home there, on a hill called Korvantunturi. The Sami are the indigenous, reindeer-herding people of Lapland and their Shaman, or *Noid,* was believed to have the gift of second sight, invisibility, shape-shifting, visions, and the capability to create false apparitions. Because of this power, Martin Luther called Lapland the home of the devil.

To the Inuit people of the Arctic, the *Angakut,* or Shaman, is the spiritual leader of each tribe. The Shaman's role was that of priest, healer, magician as well as the inter-preter and teacher of taboo; of what was right and what was wrong; watching for who was respectful of the laws of nature and who disobeyed them. He dressed in furs, carried a medi-cine bag or sack that contained mysterious tools of his trade. He received payment or gifts in exchange for his services. He travelled by sled pulled by dogs and lived in a land where reindeer (or caribou) were revered.

Archaeological discoveries have convinced some scien-tists that the ancestors of the Inuit, the Thule, also identified in parts of Scandinavia, may have arrived in the Canadian Arctic as far back as 12,000 BC (although some natives believe that their ancestors emerged from beneath the earth into the present world through a hole in the earth's surface). The Canadian Arctic has been described in Norse legends and there are many similarities between Scandinavian and Inuit folklore including that of shy, short-yet-robust beings, odd in their nature, possessing ancient wisdom most likely devel-oping from their contact with the now extinct Tunit people. Perhaps it is reasonable to conclude that the legend of Santa Claus really did originate from the North Pole. "The exces-sive cold, the winter, and the reputed mystical powers of the hyperborean [the far cold north] people have long attracted the imagination of writers, adventurers, and seekers of mystic powers. Surely, Santa Claus lives in the North because, like a holy magi, he holds the great supernatural power of the *noid* [shaman]."[15]

The Evil Sidekick

So out of this hodgepodge of feared-yet-loved mythological pagan deities and gift-bearing winter figures, blended with a judgmental yet benevolent Catholic bishop, emerged the various personas collectively known as Saint Nicholas. European Saint Nicholas traditions still vary widely from region to region in guise and name. He appears variously as *Ruhklas, Pelznickel, Klasbur, Sinterklaas, Ashenclos,* and others. Sometimes he travels on foot, and other times he rides a white or grey horse, a mule, or even a goat. But, more diverse than those of the saintly Nicholas, are the many legends and traditions surrounding his often wild companions. The pagan folklore origin of his various sidekicks is evident and, like Saint Nicholas himself, his companion is a conglomerate of many characters developing out of the animism and duality of the mythology.

In Norse mythology, there are giants, elves, and dwarfs. The elves and dwarfs were generally thought to side with the gods, although their role was shadowy. According to Scandinavian folklore the good elves, called the *tomte* or *nisse* were said to take care of the house or barn while the owners slept. The race of dwarfs, or *wights*, lived underground and could pose quite a menace to humans. Tricksters, who could take animal or human form, were also common elements of many ancient and pre-historic mythologies. Tricksters were irrepressible practical-jokers who flouted convention and caused mischief but who were simultaneously associated with creative and magical powers.

Sometimes a female figure appears as Saint Nicholas's helper; usually a boy dressed up as *Budelfrau* in Lower Austria, *Berchtel* in Swabia, and *Buzebergt* in Augsburg. *Buzebergt* wears black rags, has a blackened face and unkempt hair. Others include *Rumpelklas, Bellzebub, Pelznickel, Pelzebock, Hans Muff, Klaubauf, Bartel, Krampus, Drapp, Hoesacker,* or *Zwarte Piet,* and other such characters who often took the form of a rather hideous, hairy monster with horns and sometimes even covered in bells and dragging chains. His is a character found throughout Germanic folklore and most of his various names are appreciably synonymous with "devil."

"The devil is also known as Nikolas, or Old Nick for short, while *nickel* is a term for a demon. In various regions, the wildman is known as *Chläus, Div, Djadek, Jass, Kinderfresser* (child eater), *Klapperbok,* Old Scratch, *Thomasniklo,* and *Schrat.* Over the ages, the brutal wildman figure evolved into a character more like a clown or holiday fool. *How the Grinch Stole Christmas* by Dr. Seuss follows a classic wildman scenario: The Grinch is a hairy, Bigfoot-like creature that lives in an alpine cave in a mountain similar to the Matterhorn."[16]

Saint Nick's best known companion in Germany is *Knecht Ruprecht, Knecht* meaning servant. Historically, *Ruprecht* (Robert) was a dark and sinister figure, clad in a tattered robe carrying a sack on his back, which, according to legend, he uses to carry away all naughty children. The English counterpart of Knecht Ruprecht is thought to be Robin Goodfellow who, documented as early as 1489, had a loud "Ho Ho Ho" laugh. Numerous supernatural "little people" were associated with Saint Nicholas in German folklore, contributing to his eventual elfin status and collaboration with elf helpers in the American creation of Santa Claus.

All the children love Saint Nicholas, but they're quite afraid of his helper. For it is the helper who keeps track of who is good and who is bad. Naughty children may get only switches, or worse — they may even be carried away in the helper's bag until they learn to be good. Parents, seizing the opportunity to coerce good behaviour from their children, played up this helper of Saint Nick's. Previously in some regions, the parents would have enlisted the aid of the local priest whom they would inform about their children's behaviour. The priest would then personally visit the homes dressed in the traditional Christian garment and threaten the children with rod-beatings. Saint Nicholas and Knecht Ruprecht conveniently took on this role, letting parents and priests off the hook.

So when a child had the "the devil" in him, instead of calling on the priest to perform the exorcism parents would threaten the child with an even worse devil to scare him straight. As attitudes towards raising children and their place in the world changed, so did the role of Saint Nicholas and his wildman devilish characters.

"Reformed" Santa

Saint Nicholas's development took a detour in the Middle Ages due mostly to the changes that were taking place within the Roman Catholic Church. One of the most pivotal changes occurred on October 31, 1517, when German monk Martin Luther posted his 95 theses on the Wittenberg Castle Church door, marking the beginning of the Protestant Reformation. The rise of Protestantism throughout Europe and the development of the Puritan movement had a profound effect upon the veneration of all Catholic saints including Saint Nicholas.

Laws were passed in England and colonial America to abolish the celebration of Christmas and as a result Protestants throughout Europe ceased to worship Saint Nicholas. But the fact that the Puritans had to pass laws to that effect demonstrates that their religious zeal was not shared by all and try as they might, the Puritan government could not legislate Christmas and Saint Nicholas entirely out of existence.

Although the feasting and veneration of Catholic saints were prohibited, people had become accustomed to the annual visit from their gift-giving saint and many refused to forget the purpose of the holiday. Therefore, in some countries, the festivities of Saint Nicholas's Day were amalgamated with Christmas celebrations, and although the gift-bearer was outfitted with new, secular associations, he still reflected the saint's generous spirit.

In England, they favoured Father Christmas, who was not related to the Church. He evolved out of the Roman god of agriculture and fertility, Saturn, as well as the legends of later conquerors. Saturn was worshipped in England after the Romans invaded in AD 43, and was thought to bring food, wine and good fortune to the Roman Empire each year. When the Saxons invaded and settled Britain, circa AD 600, they brought the tradition of welcoming King Frost and Lord Snow into their homes in the hopes that the elements would be less harsh on them. They enacted this gesture by dressing an actor in a pointed cap, or fur hat, and a cloak or cape draped with ivy, and inviting him join in their feast. As a representative of the season, he was treated with full respect and many glasses were raised in toast to him. The arrival of the Vikings in England during the ninth and tenth centuries further influenced the winter tradition of gift giving by a god-like or elemental figure. The Vikings brought with them their beliefs in the northern deities, and their chief god Odin, who in the guise of his December character came to earth dressed in a hooded cloak, to sit and listen to his people and see if they were contented. He was portrayed as a sage with a long white beard and hair, carrying a satchel full of bounty, which he distributed to the needy or worthy. This character later became known as Father

Christmas portrayed as a large man who wore a scarlet robe lined with fur and a crown of holly, ivy, or mistletoe.

Beginning in 1645, after Oliver Cromwell's parliament banned Christmas, the traditional British mummers' plays changed to include a visit by Father Christmas, rather than Saint Nicholas, who issued a defiant challenge to the Puritan government: "In comes I, Old Father Christmas, Be I welcome or be I not, I hope that Christmas will ne'er be forgot." England began the transformation of Saint Nicholas into Father Christmas and from there he migrated into countries where the Reformed Churches were in the majority.

In Germany, Martin Luther objected to the practice of gifts being given to children in the name of a Catholic saint and instead sought to re-emphasize the position of Christ by promoting the *Christkindlein* (Christ Child) as the Christmas gift giver. The *Christkindlein* was typically portrayed by a fair-haired young girl. In this tradition, Saint Nicholas was relegated to the status of the assistant to the *Christkindlein*. In his new position he was called *Weihnachtsmann* (Christmas Man), *Schimmelreiter* (Rider of the White Horse), or under a number of other guises, including:

- *Ru Klaus*: meaning Rough Nicholas so named because of his rugged appearance.
- *Aschen Klaus* or *Ashenclos*: meaning Ash Nicholas, because he carried a sack of ashes as well as a bundle of switches.

- *Pelze Nicol* or *Pelznickle*: meaning Furry Nicholas, referring to his fur-clad appearance.
- *Belsnickle* or *Buller Clos*: Nicholas with bells.

In some regions of Germany, Saint Nicholas in any of a number of guises remained the gift giver, accompanied still by his faithful, fearsome servant *Knecht Ruprecht* who kept track of who was naughty and who was good. And again it was not only his duty to reward good children, but also to punish naughty children who could not recite their prayers. Good children were rewarded with a gift. Naughty children got only a lump of coal, or switches with which their parents could administer appropriate punishment (or, in some cases, the assistant was reputed to administer the punishment).

Saint Nicholas, as the patron saint of sailors and navigators, was admired at the Dutch maritime centre of Amsterdam, who made him a hero. The Dutch also celebrated the god Woden who wore a full white beard, had a magic cloak, rode a horse, and dispensed gifts to children. As in other regions of Europe, eventually Woden merged into Saint Nicholas. During the Reformation, a ban was placed on the celebration of Saint Nicholas Eve in the Netherlands, forbidding the long-entrenched custom of distributing sweets to children. Notwithstanding the Reformation, some Dutch kept the Saint Nicholas tradition alive.

In the Low Countries of Belgium, the Netherlands, and Luxembourg, Saint Nicholas is known in the Dutch language as *Sint Nikolaas, Sanct Herr Nicholaas, Sinterklaas,* or *Sinter Claes,* who sails on a steamship from his castle in Madrid, Spain, with his white horse, *Schimmel,* to the Netherlands. In 1556, Holland was united with Spain and it became the custom for Holland's bishops to take summer vacations in Spain, including the fictitious Saint Nicholas. According to legend, he was inundated with updating his ledgers on children's behaviour and rewards, so he hired a Moorish youth named *Zwarte Piet* to keep his records. His name means Black Peter in English, and was later attributed to his blackened and dirty appearance from climbing down chimneys, although originally he may have represented the feared dark-skinned Moors of old Spain, which was enough to frighten any medieval Dutch child into being good. The legend may also stem from the story that the real Bishop Nicholas had purchased the freedom of an Ethiopian slave named Piter who remained in his service. *Zwarte Piet* accompanied *Sinterklaas* to Holland and carried a sack full of birch rods and lumps of coal for bad children. An old tradition has the bad children stuffed into *Zwarte Piet's* sack, and dropped into the sea as *Sinterklaas* and Piet make their way back home to Spain. A less drastic treatment says that the bad children were taken back to Spain where the kindly saint and his assistants attempted to rehabilitate them. This was probably a reflection of the Dutch sentiments towards the Spanish with their history of oppressive occupation leading to the Dutch war of independence from 1568 to 1648, combined with the ancient belief that the devil carried souls to hell on his back.

On the eve of his Feast Day, December 6, *Sinterklaas* rides his white horse through the sky, landing on roof-tops and descending through chimneys. In anticipation of *Sinterklaas*'s arrival, Dutch children fill their wooden shoes with hay, bread, or a carrot for *Schimmel*. If the children were good, they find presents, fruit, and money in their clogs when they awake on the Saint's feast day. The tradition of leaving food out for Saint Nicholas may stem from the ancient Winter Solstice custom of leaving food for the spirits of the dead who were believed to visit on the longest night.

Santa Immigrates to America

It is commonly, albeit erroneously, believed in America today, that when the Dutch immigrated to America they brought their patron Saint Nicholas with them. In AD 1626, a fleet of Dutch ships left Holland for the New World and legend has it that at the prow of the ship *Goede Vrouw* (Good Wife) was a figurehead of Saint Nicholas, the patron saint of merchants, sailors, seafarers, and travellers. He report-edly wore a broad-brimmed hat and held a long-stemmed Dutch pipe. Although the legend also states that a statue and church were erected in his honour, there is, however, no evi-dence that Saint Nicholas was favoured in New Amsterdam. Contrarily, the Dutch colonists, being Reformists, would not have had any interest in venerating a Catholic saint. Some suggest this myth was fabricated by one of the original creators of the American Santa Claus, Washington Irving in 1809. The American version of Santa Claus was a deliberate creation by an elite group of New Yorkers who drew upon the legends and folklore of Dutch, German, and Scandinavian settlers.

Upon arrival in the New World, the Dutch purchased some land from the Iroquois, in exchange for goods with a value of 60 guilders (about $24) and named the village *Nieuw Amsterdam* (New Amsterdam). Just a few years later in 1651, the state legislature of Massachusetts, settled by English Puritans, passed an act forbidding all observation of Christmas. Thirty years after that, the law was repealed, but the ghost of no Christmas past continued to have a profound chilling effect on the celebration of Christmas in New England until the start of the 20th century.

Under Charles II, who ousted the Puritans in England, the English took New Amsterdam in 1664, gifting it to the Duke of York who renamed it New York. But the Dutch origins could not be entirely erased. Whether or not there existed an active cult of Saint Nicholas amongst the Dutch who settled in New Amsterdam, his influence ultimately prevailed many years later when the Dutch name for Saint Nicholas, *Sinter Klaas* was anglicized to Santa Claus by English Americans. The first documented reference to Santa Claus occurred on December 23, 1773 when a New York newspaper, *Rivington's Gazetteer*, reported "Last Monday, the anniversary of Saint

Nicholas, otherwise called Santa Claus, was celebrated at Protestant Hall, at Mr. Waldron's; where a great number of sons of the ancient saint celebrated the day with great joy and festivity." Santa Claus, a.k.a. Saint Nicholas, was mentioned in the New York newspaper again the following Christmas, but no further reference was evident for the next 20 years.

One group of early settlers to America, who did bring their love of Christmas with them, was the Germans. They brought their custom of setting out a basket of hay in the barnyard for *Christkind's* donkey on Christmas Eve. On Christmas Day, they'd find the basket filled with *snits* (dried apple slices), *choosets* (candy), walnuts, and gingerbread. As the Germans intermarried with the English, the dialect for *Christkind* (also called *Christkindlein* or *Christkindle* in parts of Germany) became *Kristkingle* or *Krisskringle*. Eventually the Kris Kringle replaced the Christ child figure entirely, a substitute akin to Santa Claus.

By the latter half of the 19th century, Kris Kringle was the most common Christmas gift-giver in Pennsylvania. Thus, despite the intentions of the Reform movement to replace the Catholic Saint Nicholas with the Christ child as the gift-bearer, the original meaning of the word has faded. Once thought to be the Christ child's chief helper, the image of Kris Kringle has reverted back to an image of Saint Nicholas. Today the name Kris Kringle is virtually synonymous with Santa Claus in North America. It is interesting to note that the "Pennsylvania Dutch" were actually from Germany. The word

"Dutch" in this instance is a corruption of the German word *Deutsch*, which means German.

Sinterklaas's helper, *Zwarte Piet*, and his multitude of European guises, did not seem to have made the journey to America; or more likely he could not survive outside his native environment. It is believed this character was either omitted as being too scary in the years ahead as writers and artists transformed Saint Nicholas into Santa Claus, or he was amalgamated into the transformation. But Santa was not doomed to conduct his daunting tasks alone in the New World, and eventually Black Peter et al. were replaced by a tribe of happy elves who were more in tune with Santa's new image.

Santa's New Image

In the melting pot of America, Santa Claus eventually emerged from a combination of the Dutch Saint Nicholas/*Sinterklaas*, the English Father Christmas, and included elements from German and Scandinavian traditions, and Norse mythology. The major contributors to this amalgamation were the 19th century American writers Washington Irving and Clement Clarke Moore, and the illustrator Thomas Nast, who created the image of Santa as a white-bearded, pot-bellied, jolly man.

Most of the central features of the Americanized Santa Claus legend, such as his climb down the chimney and the switches he leaves for naughty children, are said to be of Dutch origin. His red suit trimmed with white fur resembles the red bishop's mitre and cape worn by the Dutch version of

Saint Nicholas. This Dutch emphasis in this new creation was neither accidental nor organic.

John Pintard and the New York Historical Society

After the American Revolution, many New Yorkers took pride in remembering the colony's nearly forgotten Dutch roots, even those who were not of Dutch descent. John Pintard, influential patriot and antiquarian, who founded the New York Historical Society in 1804, promoted Saint Nicholas as patron saint of both the society and city. Some claim that the very beginnings of Santa Claus — as distinct from Saint Nicholas — might be traced to John Pintard who included Saint Nicholas in his private almanac as early as 1793. Pintard and many others were gravely concerned about how the Christmas and New Year's holidays were being celebrated. Often the celebrations featured gunfire, drunkenness, sexual licentious, home intrusions (by "wassailers"), and riots.[17] After a period of Puritan repression the celebration of Christmas had reverted back to its origins of midwinter revelry and misrule to such an extent that the government was forced to intervene by criminalizing rowdy behaviour, outlawing begging, and creating the first professional police force in New York in 1828. But just as the Church was powerless to overcome the pagan Winter Solstice celebrations centuries before, the government was also failing in its attempts to quell the "Saturnalian-like" revival. So the power brokers of New York's elite society took a different approach, headed by Pintard with his desire to take the celebration of Christmas off the streets and into the home.

Pintard launched an all-out campaign using culture and invented traditions to tame the wildness of the Christmas season. He saw the need for an orderly ritualized way for the social classes to co-exist in harmony during the holidays and to neutralize the tradition of misrule which threatened the established social order. Not only did he promote Saint Nicholas as the patron saint of New York, but in 1810 he paid for a Christmas flyer promoting Saint Nicholas as a friend and benefactor, distributing gifts to good children. With the help of one of the Historical Society's members, the young American writer Washington Irving, and one of Pintard's acquaintances, Dr. Clement Moore, Saint Nicholas and Christmas were reinvented.

Pintard, and his fellow wealthy gentry, felt their authority was being threatened by newcomers. These men were so conservative that they were actually opposed to democracy. They envisioned the re-introduction of Saint Nicholas as a nondenominational, working-class character into New York society as a cultural counterbalance to the booming urban commercial development and democratic misrule they were experiencing at the time.

Washington Irving (1783–1859)

It was the popular author Washington Irving who gave America the first detailed description of what would become the present-day Santa Claus. On Saint Nicholas Day, December 6, 1809, under the pseudonym Diedrich Knickerbocker, Irving published *A History of New York from the Beginning of the World to the End of the Dutch Dynasty*, a satire that has been called the first great book of comic literature written by an American. Purporting to be a scholarly account of the Dutch occupation of the New World, the book is a parody of history books as well as a satire of politics in his own time.

Irving dedicated his lampoon of Dutch culture to the New York Historical Society, whose members were predominantly old city conservative aristocracy of British Episcopalian descent who referred to themselves as "Knickerbockers." Originally the word Knickerbocker was used to describe any New Yorker who could trace his family to the original Dutch settlers and later it came to mean anyone from New York. There is an old Winter Solstice/Christmas custom in the Netherlands whereby people are expected to mock and make fun of each other's characters and peculiarities. Thus although Irving himself was of Scottish-English descent, his satire in which a Dutchman mocks his fellow countrymen would not have been considered strange.

In this piece, Irving made dozens of references to an impish, pipe-smoking Saint Nicholas who, riding over the treetops in a wagon, brings gifts down chimneys, and in so doing Irving began a legend that would travel round the world and begin the domestication of the traditions of Christmas. Irving's new Santa Claus was quite a different depiction from the stern, bishop-like, Dutch *Sinterklaa*s, accompanied by the loathsome Black Peter. Irving also made a dramatic departure in his physical description of the saint: he changed the bishop's vestments to more traditional Flemish attire replacing the bishop's robe, mitre, and staff, with a wide brimmed hat, pants, and a long Dutch clay pipe. Irving transformed Saint Nicholas from a bishop into a Dutch gentleman.

The significance of Irving's role in the creation of Santa Claus cannot be understated. In his aptly titled book, *Saint Nicholas of Myra, Bari, and Manhattan: Biography of a Legend*, Charles W. Jones noted, "Without Irving there would be no Santa Claus. The history contains two dozen allusions to him, many of them among the most delightful flights of imagination in the volumes. Here is the source of all the legends about Saint Nicholas in New Amsterdam—of the emigrant ship *Goede Vrouw*, like a Dutch matron as broad as she was long, with a figurehead of Saint Nicholas at the prow; here are the descriptions of festivities on N[icholas] Day in the colony, and of the church dedicated to him; here is the description of Santa Claus bringing gifts, parking his horse and wagon on the roof while he slides down the chimney—all sheer fictions produced by Irving's *Salmagundi* crowd." Irving's comic fiction had such an impact that within his lifetime, the tale he spun was actually believed by the general public to be historical fact, when in reality Irving was "forging a pseudo-Dutch identity for New York, a placid 'folk' identity," as noted by Nissenbaum in *The Battle for Christmas*.

In 1819–1820 Washington Irving further contributed to the image of the ideal traditional English Christmas celebration when he published a serial collection of short stories, under another pen name, entitled *The Sketchbook of Geoffrey Crayon, Gent* which was an instant success in England as well as America. Some of the stories described an old Yorkshire country Christmas with carolling, yule log burning, mingling of masters and servants, and decorations of holly, ivy, and mistletoe. Irving apparently later admitted that some elements of the sketches were products of his imagination. Nevertheless at the time, they served as an immediate reinforcement of the motivation to bring Christmas into the home. This same collection of short stories included Irving's classics *The Legend of Sleepy Hollow,* in which the schoolmaster Ichabod Crane meets with a headless horseman, as well as *Rip Van Winkle* about a young Dutchman who falls asleep for 20 years and awakens to find himself in a totally transformed world where he doesn't fit in anymore. Both these stories were based on old German folktales.

Clement C. Moore (1779–1863)

The more recent changes in Santa were largely brought about in 1823 by the poem *A Visit from St. Nicholas,* more commonly recognized as *The Night Before Christmas* by Reverend Clement C. Moore. Moore was a learned professor, a poet, and a student of European folklore, including that of the German and Scandinavian immigrants who had settle in the northern United States. He gathered together all the elements of European lore, deities, and folk-characters, melded them with Irving's Dutch-American version, and created a poem which was to become the single most important blueprint for the modern Santa Claus. Moore's description of Saint Nick's attire recollects the pagan folklore imagery of the wild companion: "He was dressed all in fur, from his head to his foot, / And his clothes were all tarnished with ashes and soot."

The poem transformed a stern and dignified Saint Nicholas into a jolly old elf, Santa Claus, a magical figure who brought only gifts, minus the punishments or threats. Just as important, the poem provided a simple and effective ceremony that enabled its readers to restrict the holiday to their own family. *The Night before Christmas* moved the Christmas gift exchange off the streets and into the home, shifting the focus away from the rowdy, demanding wassailers and onto the deserving children.

The following poem, published in 1821 by New York printer William B. Gilley in a small hand-coloured book entitled *A Children's Friend*, is the first documented reference associating Santa Claus with Christmas on December 25, rather than Saint Nicholas's gift giving saint's day, December 6. Gilley was a friend and neighbour of Moore's and the book was written and illustrated by another acquaintance of Moore's, Presbyterian minister Arthur J. Stansbury.

The poem is also believed to be the first publication depicting Santa with a reindeer, both in the words and in one of the illustrations showing Santa with a sleigh and a single reindeer.

Old Santeclaus with much delight
His reindeer drives this frosty night.
O'er chimney tops, and tracks of snow,
To bring his yearly gifts to you ...
Each Christmas eve he joys to come
Where love and peace have made their home

It is possible that Moore was familiar with Stansbury's book prior to composing *The Night Before Christmas*. Moore's verse expanded Santa's transportation from a single reindeer to a team of eight. He also added such characteristic details as Santa Claus's laughs, winks, and nods as well as describing the method the "jolly old elf" uses to return up the chimney. Moore claimed to have composed the poem in 1822, as a Christmas Eve story for his children and that without his permission the poem went public when a friend, Miss Harriet Butler of Troy, New York, sent a copy of it to newspaper editor Orville L. Holly. It was published for the first time in the Troy *Sentinel* on December 23, 1823, without attribution. Although the poem appeared in print numerous times over the next few years, Moore's name was not associated with it until 1844 when he included it in a volume of his poetry.

Thomas Nast (1840–1902)

In 1863 Thomas Nast, a caricaturist for *Harper's Weekly*, began developing his own image of Santa. Nast was born on September 27, 1840, and immigrated to the United States from Landau, Bavaria, when he was six years old with his mother and older sister. Recalling his childhood memories of Christmas in Germany, and inspired by Moore's 1823 poem, Nast's Santa was an overly fat, jovial, white-bearded elf, dressed from head to toe in fur. His illustrations were also the first to establish Santa as a toymaker, reading letters from children, and preparing the "naughty and nice" list. In 1869, a widely distributed children's book entitled *Santa Claus and His Works* contained a collection of new Nast colour illustrations and a poem by George P. Webster that identified the North Pole as Santa's home. Webster also has the elfin Santa transported by a team of airborne deer from the mountains. Nast's images of Santa later included the telltale red and white suit and became incorporated into the Santa lore.

During the American Civil War in the 1860s, many of Nast's drawings had a pro-Union flavour, portraying Santa Claus as the patron of the Union soldier. President Lincoln is said to have made the observation that Nast, through his use of the Santa character, had become the North's "best recruiting sergeant."

From 1864 to 1886 Thomas Nast continued to draw Santa Claus every year, and became known as "the" Santa Claus artist. Nast influenced later artists, such as Norman Rockwell, who illustrated similar Santas for commercial publications such as the *Saturday Evening Post*.

In 1956, the United States Embassy marked the military barracks in Landau, Bavaria, where Thomas Nast was born, with a bas-relief bust of the artist and bronze plaque with an inscription dedicating the *gift to the German people in friendship and in memory of Thomas Nast*.

Santa Claus and Coca-Cola

In 1931, Archie Lee of the D'Arcy Advertising Agency proposed that the Coca-Cola Company use a realistic, robust-looking Santa Claus for its upcoming holiday advertising campaign. Commercial illustrator Hadden H.Sundblom painted this image in oil. The original model was Lou Prentice, a retired salesman who passed away not long after his image became the Santa Claus that is now known around the world.

For the next 35 years, the Coca-Cola Company continued to run annual Christmas advertisements that featured Sundblom paintings of a human-size Santa Claus (not elf-size) drinking Coke. In some of his paintings Sundblom used his own image. These ads did much to bolster the modern image of Santa Claus in the public consciousness (and the drinking of Coke!).

Due to Santa's long standing association with Coca-Cola, some people seem to think that he wears red and white because those are the Coca-Cola colours. Evidence indicates otherwise, however. Santa Claus is in part descended from

Saint Nicholas, Bishop of Myra, and a bishop's robes are red. An English Father Christmas was first recorded in his traditional red and white attire in a 1653 woodcut. And when Louis Prang depicted Santa Claus on Christmas cards in 1885 and 1886, he showed him wearing a red suit. Sundblom didn't create the red-coated Santa, but he did foster a consistent image for Santa every year for over 30 years.

The Coca-Cola Company was not the first to commercialize Santa Claus. Stores in the United States were advertising Christmas shopping in 1820, and by the 1840s, newspapers were creating special sections for holiday advertisements, which often featured images of the newly popular Santa Claus. As early as 1841, Santa had been used as a promotional gimmick when stores declared themselves "Santa's Headquarters" or "Kris Kringle's Headquarters."

By the 1870s, Santa Claus was making regular Christmas appearances in department stores in the United States and Canada. Before the turn to the new century, department stores across America had added a throne for Santa Claus so children could sit on his knee, see their hero face to face, and tell him their Christmas wishes. During the 1890s, Father Christmas began to appear in English stores where his habitat was referred to as a "grotto."

In the early 1890s, the Salvation Army began raising money to pay for the free Christmas meals it provided to needy families by dressing up unemployed men in red Santa Claus suits and having them solicit donations on the streets of New York. Those familiar Salvation Army Santas have been ringing bells on the street corners of American and Canadian cities ever since.

The Santa Claus Parade

A Canadian tradition, the Santa Clause parade had its inception in commercialism. Santa Claus and his elves had already been setting up a workshop in large department stores for several years when he had his first parade through the streets of Montreal in 1925. Staged at a cost of $100,000 by Eaton's department store, this first parade was a huge festival for children and adults alike.

A month prior to the event itself, Eaton's started to announce on the radio through "Santagrams" that Santa Claus was coming. These daily bulletins followed his progress from the North Pole to Montreal. When he "arrived," Santa paraded through the working class areas of Montreal, stopping in the centre of town, before ending up at Eaton's department store. Downtown, the company's directors, including President John David Eaton, greeted the distinguished visitor with great pomp and ceremony. This tradition was maintained right up to the mid-1950s.

Other 20th century additions to the image of Santa Claus include the appearance of Mrs. Claus and the practice of leaving out small food gifts for Santa on Christmas Eve (although Europeans had been doing this for their gift-givers for centuries). In 1899, Katherine Lee Bates, the author of "America the Beautiful," wrote a Christmas book entitled *Goody Santa Claus, A Sleigh Ride.* This was possibly the first recorded mention of the existence of Mrs. Santa Claus. "Goody" was a common contraction for "goodwife."

In 1925, it was discovered that there are no reindeer at the North Pole. There are, however, lots of reindeer in Lapland, Finland. In 1927, the great secret of Santa's address was revealed by Markus Rautio ("Uncle Markus") who hosted the popular Finnish public radio program "Children's Hour." He declared that Santa Claus lives on Lapland's Korvatunturi Mountain on the Finnish-Russian border. At 500 metres (1,640 feet), it actually is only a large hill, but it is off-limits to people. Korvantunturi, which means "Ear Fell," and somewhat resembles a hare's ears is said to be Santa Claus's ears, with which he listens to hear if the world's children are behaving. Santa has the assistance of a busy group of elves, who have quite their own history in Scandinavian legend.

In the early 1900s, Santa was depicted as a craftsman who personally made all the toys by hand in a small work-shop. Over time that image changed, and Santa became the "foreman" overseeing the work of elves responsible for hand-crafting the annual cache of toys. By the end of the 20th century, the reality of mechanized mass production invaded the image of the North Pole toy factory managed by Santa and Mrs. Claus. This image has been perpetuated by the many advertisements and commercials depicting a workforce of disgruntled elves playing mischievous pranks on the boss.

Santa's evolution is a unique example of the blending of countless beliefs and practices from around the world and a symbolic reflection of the popular ideology of the times. He was a fertility symbol and shaman in a time when humanity was closer to nature; a benevolent but stern bishop once Christianity became widespread; a model of propriety in a period of misrule; and, an advertising spokesman when western culture began bowing to big business and commerce. Like all good mythic figures, Santa Claus will likely live on; what form he is given in this millennium will depend on what gods society chooses to revere.

Santa's Elves

As mentioned, the North America version of the Christmas "gift giver" evolved into the roly-poly jolly Santa Claus who lives with Mrs. Claus and the elves at the North Pole. Santa has flying reindeer to pull a sleigh full of toys that are made by the elves working in his workshop.

In Clement Moore's *Night Before Christmas*, Santa himself is referred to as a "jolly old elf." In this poem, Santa Claus must be small enough to go down a chimney and he rides in a "miniature sleigh with eight tiny reindeer." But neither Moore's nor Walker's poems mentioned any help that Santa might be receiving. Thomas Nast also depicted Santa as elfin. Having emigrated from Bavaria he would have been familiar with *Pelznichol*, as well as the industrious dwarfs of Germanic mythology who were often depicted as busily making things.

The first mention of other elves helping Santa came in 1859 when *Harper's Weekly* published the anonymous poem *The Wonders of Santa Claus*:

In his house upon the top of a hill
And almost out of sight,
He keeps a great many elves at work,
All working with all their might,
To make a million of pretty things,
Cakes, sugar-plums, and toys,
To fill the stockings, hung up you know
By the little girls and boys.

The Scandinavian settlers to America may have contributed to the interjection of gift-giving elves, *nissen* and *tomten*, into the North American Santa lore. Elves are creatures of Germanic mythology that have survived in northern European folklore. Originally a race of minor gods of nature and fertility, they are often depicted as small, youth-like men and women of great beauty living in forests and other natural places, underground, or in wells and springs. They have been said to be long-lived or immortal and have magical powers attributed to them.

International Christmas Gift-bearers

In Germany, children eagerly clean and polish their shoes to put out for *Sankt Nikolaus*'s visit to their homes in the evening of December 5. After the children have gone to bed Saint Nicholas delivers candy and other sweets to be opened on December 6, *Nikolaustag* (Saint Nicholas Day) by deserving children. The lucky children in Germany get another visit from a Christmas gift-giver on Christmas Eve, December 24. In the mainly Protestant regions of Germany, it is tradition that *Christkind* (the Christ Child) sends the gifts on Christmas Eve. This was the favourite gift-giver of Martin Luther. In northern areas, Christmas Eve presents are usually brought by the *Weihnachtsmann* (Christmas Man). *Sankt Nicolaus, Christkind* and *Weihnachtsmann* all look the same and to children nowadays, they are the same person. In their infinite wisdom, or blissful innocence, children don't question why these gift bringers have different names and methods — the children are simply happy to receive gifts and candy twice in one month.

Knecht Ruprecht, with his sack of switches, is also associated with the holiday season. Sometimes misbehaving children would receive a stick instead of treats from Saint Nicholas, a warning from Nicholas that unless they improve by Christmas Eve, Nicholas's servant Ruprecht will come and beat them with the stick and they won't get any Christmas gifts from *Weihnachtsman.*

The Baby Jesus also delivers the gifts under various names in other countries: *Christkind* (Austria, Belgium); *El Nino Jesus* (Colombia, Costa Rica); *Le Petit Jésus* (France); *Menino Jesus de Natal* (Portugal); *Babbo Natal* (Italy);

Jezisek (Czech Republic); *Jouluvana* (Estonia); *Jezussek* (Slovenia). On Christmas Eve in Great Britain, Australia, New Zealand, and Switzerland, children hang up stockings for Father Christmas, the British version of Santa Claus, to fill with presents. In Switzerland, his wife Lucy (a derivative of Saint Lucia) accompanies Father Christmas. Father Christmas is depicted as a bearded old man in a fur-trimmed robe with sprigs of holly in his long white hair who rides a donkey or a white goat on his Yuletide rounds. He incorporates many traditions from different European countries plus newer American customs. Letters are sent to him by children with their Christmas gift requests and wishes. Instead of mailing these letters, they are thrown into the fireplace. If they go up the chimney, the wish will be granted; if not, then sadly the wish goes unfulfilled. Children hang their Christmas stockings on the hearth or at the foot of their bed to receive small presents, which are opened Christmas morning.

Father Christmas is also known by other names: *Bonhomme Noël* or *Père Noël* (France); *Papia Noel* (Brazil, Peru, and Spain); *Pa Norsk* (Norway); *Pia Natal* (Portugal); *Kaledu Senis* (Lithuania).

In France, *Père Noël* is a kindly old gentleman with the trademark white beard and red suit trimmed with white fur. He travels through the country on Christmas Eve and leaves gifts in shoes left out for him by the children. *Père Noël* travels with his stern disciplinarian companion *Pre* (or *Père*)

Fouettard. It is *Pre Fouettard* who reminds *Père Noël* just how each child has behaved during the past year and he is much feared. According to legend *Pre Fouettard*, also known as *Houseckler*, was an evil, murderous butcher whose penance now is to follow *Père Noël* as his servant. In some parts of France, *Père Noël* brings small gifts on Saint Nicholas Eve (December 5) and visits again on Christmas Eve (December 24). In other French homes, it is *Le Petit Jésus* who brings the gifts. In one area of France, *Père Noël* may have some competition from Aunt Airie, a fairy who wears a cape, travels with a donkey, and also gives out gifts to deserving children.

In the Netherlands, Belgium, and Luxembourg, Saint Nicholas is known as *Sinterklaas* and Santa Claus is known as *Kerstman.* The traditions became a bit convoluted after America developed one of its important Christmas icons — Santa Claus — in part from traditions imported by Dutch immigrants. While the Dutch exported *Sinterklaas* to America, America after World War II, exported Santa Claus back to the Netherlands. This has meant a real bonanza to Dutch children who now receive gifts from both *Sinterklaas* and Santa Claus, first on Saint Nicholas Day and next on Christmas Day.

A few weeks before his feast day, actors portraying *Sinterklaas* and his helpers or *pieten,* journey to the Netherlands from his home in Spain on a steamer loaded with all the presents. While in the Netherlands, he travels on his white horse called *Schimmel* with his trusty sidekick,

Zwarte Piet (Black Peter). From his arrival until his feast day, the children can put their shoes in front of the fireplace in hopes of receiving treats come morning. Sometimes the children put straw, carrots, and water by their shoes for the horse.

Sinterklaas together with his *pieten* visit children to punish the evil ones and to reward the good ones. Good children receive sweets (called *pepernoten, taai-taai,* or *schuimpjes*) and presents in their shoes. The worst punishment is to be taken to Spain in *Zwarte Piet*'s bag, and a less radical punishment is to get the *roede* (rod) or lump of coal instead of presents. On the eve of his feast day, *Sinterklaas* purportedly visits all children. After knocking on the door, he leaves a bag full of presents (if they were good children). Early in the morning of December 6, when he has visited everyone, he is said to return to Spain without any fanfare or farewell.

On Christmas Eve, *Kerstman,* having the same profile as Santa Claus, travels in a sleigh borne by flying reindeer and comes down the chimney bringing presents for good boys and girls. Unlike *Sinterklaas,* he is not accompanied by an evil sidekick.

Throughout Scandinavia, there was a widely believed superstition in the existence of tiny magical creatures called *nisse,* who lived in attics and cellars and brought good luck into a household. The growing popularity of Santa Claus and other holiday gift-bearers had an influence on the Scandinavians too, so they gave the *nisse* a red suit and a long white beard and called him *Julenisse.* In the mid-1800s some Scandinavian writers "revealed" the true purpose of the *nissen* by linking them to Father Christmas as his helpers.

In Denmark, the festive gift-bearer is known as *Julemanden* and arrives in a sleigh drawn by reindeer, carrying a sack over his back. He is assisted with his Yuletide chores by attic-dwelling elves called *Juul Nisse.*

In Norway, the popularity of Santa Claus brought about the rebirth of the ancient Norse folkloric figure, *Julesvenn.* In ancient times, he would come during the feast of *Jul* to hide lucky barley stalks around the house as talismen for the new year's crop. Nowadays he comes on Christmas Eve to bring gifts to deserving children.

In Sweden, gifts are brought by the *Jultomten,* a Christmas elf (*tomte*) who lives in the barn, if there is one. *Jultomten* is a mischievous character who likes playing practical jokes. Apart from wearing woollen clothes with a red cap, long red stockings, and wooden clogs, he is not easy to spot except by the family cat. He can, however, be distracted from his propensity for practical jokes by his favourite food, rice pudding. Originally *Jultomten* was a sort of wild man of the forest: he was short and stocky, bearded, and dressed in furs. He cared for animals and had shamanistic powers over the elements. According to legend, *Jultomten* lived deep in the forest long before he showed himself to humans. It is said that he used to roam around the Swedes' farms during the night. He would sneak into children's rooms, touching them to bestow prophetic dreams. To this day, on Christmas Eve Swedes still leave porridge, milk, or tobacco to appease the mischievous little elf, similar to Americans leaving milk and cookies for Santa.

Sweden also honours the early Christian martyr Saint Lucia, or Queen of Light. *Lucia* is derived from the Latin word for light. On her feast day, December 13, a family's eldest daughter dresses as St. Lucia in a bride-like white robe and a candle crown, and serves a special meal to the family. St. Lucia's feast day is also known as Little Yule. Like Saint Nicholas, the veneration and image of Saint Lucia came about as a blending of ancient Norse mythology and Christian legends.

In Finland, Father Christmas is known as *Joulupukki* (literally meaning "Yule Buck"). As part of their Winter Solstice festivities, Finland's pagan ancestors held big celebrations to ward of evil spirits. The embodiment of these spirits of darkness was a creature who wore goatskins and horns. Originally this creature didn't give presents, but demanded them, and in return he would not wreak havoc upon the people. Eventually this character evolved into the Christmas Goat but used to frighten the kids and was in every way very loathsome. *Joulupukki* has mellowed in his old age and today he is a much kinder, gentler, gift-bearing character.

Finland also has another gift-giver named *Ukko* who evolved from the principle pagan god of the sky to become the protector of children. Even after the Finns accepted

Christianity, the memory of *Ukko* persisted. *Ukko* travels from Lapland on a sleigh drawn by reindeer, and is believed to be one of the first gift givers depicted using this mode of transportation. Today he is also accompanied by several Christmas elves who help to distribute the presents to the children. He is possibly one of the earliest ancestors of Santa Claus.

In Greece, a large log called a *skakantzalos* is burned much like a yule log to ward off wicked elves called *kallikantzaroi*. Sometimes the Greeks will also burn old shoes, the smell of which keeps the wicked elves away. Children born on Christmas eve or Christmas day were feared to be *kallikantzaroi*. In fact, children born within the Christmas festival were sometimes bound in braids of garlic or straw and their toenails singed to expel the evil. The Greeks also honour *Aghios Vassilis*, St. Basil, on his Feast Day of January 1. The Greeks consider St. Basil the gift bringer. Born in the town of Caesarea in Asia Minor in AD 329; he was a contemporary of Saint Nicholas of Myra, although the two never met. Children receive gifts from St. Basil on his feast day and traditional *Vasilopita*, "Basil" cakes, are eaten to honour this patron saint of Greece.

In Italy the traditional Christmas gift-bearer is a woman or witch by the name of *La Befana*, which means "The Epiphany." Each year on January 6, the children of Italy awaken in hopes that *La Befana* has made a visit to their house. This is a significant day to Italians because it marks the end of the Christmas season and the day that the Magi visited the Christ child. Many children in Italy look forward to the Epiphany even more than Christmas. According to legend, *La Befana* was an old woman from Palestine who refused an offer to go with the Magi to see the baby Jesus because she had too much housework to do. A few hours after they left, she changed her mind, and set out to catch up with them. After many hours of searching she still had not found them. Thinking of the opportunity she had missed, the old woman stopped every child to give it a small treat in hopes that one was the Christ child. Each year on the eve of the Epiphany she sets out looking for the baby Jesus. She stops at each child's house to leave treats for good children, or a lump of coal for naughty children, in their stockings or shoes.

In Russia, *Babushka* was a witch-like old woman who gave the Magi wrong directions on their journey to Bethlehem. In order to atone for her prank, she was condemned to roam around Russia on Epiphany Eve, giving treats and small gifts to all good children. *Babushka* was very popular in Russia until the Communist revolution, after which she was outlawed due to her religious association.

Saint Nicholas was also particularly revered in Russia. Legend has it that the 11th century Prince Vladimir returned from a baptismal journey to Constantinople with tales of the Saint's miraculous feats and henceforth made Saint Nicholas the patron saint of Russia (Nicholas is a very common name for Russian males). The long celebrated Feast of Saint Nicholas was also put to rest with the dawn of Communism.

In response to this, the Russians developed another gift-bearer, *Ded Moroz*, or Grandfather Frost, who together with his niece or granddaughter, *Sneguochka*, the Snow Maiden, goes from house to house on New Year's Day, delivering presents and spreading holiday cheer. With the fall of the Communist regime, *Babushka* has returned in a limited role, and all three characters are now involved in holiday gift-giving.

In some areas of Russia, the remnants of the pagan legend of *Kolyada*, who was believed to be the goddess of winter and the earth, still exist. Clad all in white, she travels from house to house on a sled bringing gifts, accompanied by her maiden attendants who sing the *Kolyada*, or carols. Her journey begins when the days start to grow longer and she is thought to be joining her consort, the sun god.

In Poland, the *Gwaizor*, or Star Man, is a religious figure similar to Saint Nicholas. The parish priest in disguise often plays *Gwaizor*, accompanied by his Star Boy helpers, giving gifts to children. In Poland, Christmas is often described as the Festival of the Star, commemorating one of the most significant symbols of Christmas, the star of Bethlehem.

Although the population of Japan is less than one percent Christian, that has not deterred them from adopting many Western Christmas customs, including exchanging gifts. The Japanese people have even manifested their own

gift-bearer, *Hoteiosho*, an old Japanese god who was originally one of the seven gods of good fortune. He is an amiable
peaceful deity depicted as a Buddhist priest with large ear-
lobes and a huge stomach, which is believed to be a symbol
of his large soul. He is always depicted as joyously laughing,
whether alone or surrounded by children. He holds a fan in
one hand and carries on his back the linen bag (*hotei*) from
which he derives his name and retrieves the gifts for good
children. He does not need a helper to check on the children's
behaviour because he has eyes in the back of his head allowing him to see everything. He has become popular in Europe
under the name of *Pusa*.

While China does not officially recognize Christianity
as a religion, there are an estimated 10 million baptized
Christians living in China. For those who do celebrate
Christmas, it is *Dun Che Lao Ren* or Old Man Christmas who
fills the stockings of Chinese Christian children. Through
Western influence and exposure to modern practices in
Japan, large malls and department stores in China now have
actors dressed as Santa Claus handing out treats to children.

Although Christmas Day is not a public holiday in
China, *Ta Chiu* is a Taoist festival of peace and renewal that
takes place in Hong Kong on December 27. At the end of the
festivities Taoist priests read aloud the names of everyone
who lives in the area. When the priest has finished reading
the list, the names are attached to a paper horse and burned
in the hopes that the smoke will carry the names to heaven.

In Spain, Christmas is a highly religious festival, and the Spanish traditionally do not recognize Santa Claus. Children do however look forward to receiving gifts during the season. On January 5 (Eve of Epiphany), children leave their shoes on the window ledge full of straw, carrots, and barley to feed the horse and donkeys of the three Wise Men (*Los Reyes Magos*). The Wise Man, Balthasar, is a particularly welcome visitor and the closest equivalent in Spain to Santa Claus. By morning, the children's shoes are filled with gifts. Parents encourage children to write to the Three Kings with their gift requests.

In parts of Labrador, populated with Moravian immigrants, Inuit traditions gradually blended with Moravian Christmas feast days. A typical example of this is the masked *Nalujuks* who make an appearance in Labrador's Moravian villages on the Eve of Twelfth Night, January 5 (also the date of the Eastern Orthodox Christmas Eve).

The *Nalujuk* represented the change from nature worship to Christianity. These masked spirit figures would visit the village at the end of the Christmas gathering, just before everyone was ready to go back to their normal life. *Nalujuks* entered from the east, carrying walking sticks and small gifts, reminding children to act in a Christian way throughout the year. Children were expected to respond by singing a hymn thus showing their commitment to Christianity. Bad children might be punished while the good children would be rewarded.

This action by the *Nalujuk* relates to *Suporgoksoak*, the feared and respected spirit who was the controller of the wildlife and determined if people were worthy of receiving his bounty. Converted Inuit Christians adapted this idea, combining their beliefs with the story of the three Wise Men, in the figure of *Nalujuk*. Today, the tradition has a jovial element, as the children taunt and chase the *Nalujuk*, who try to capture them. The *Nalujuks* then make them sing songs to gain their release.

Reindeer Names

ost people can name Santa's eight reindeer, or a least some of them, from Clement C. Moore's poem, *The Night Before Christmas*. But the now-famous names of two of the reindeer had a rather tumultuous beginning. The following is how the lines naming St. Nick's reindeer appeared in the poem's print debut in Troy, New York's newspaper, the *Sentinel*, on December 23, 1823:

> *"Now Dasher! now, Dancer! now, Prancer and Vixen!*
> *On, Comet! on, Cupid! on Dunder and Blixem!*
> *To the top of the porch! to the top of the wall!*
> *Now, dash away! dash away! dash away all!"*

The Dunder Blunder

In this first printing, the last two reindeer's names read "Dunder and Blixem." The poem was submitted anonymously and was reprinted this way many times before it finally appeared in an 1844 collection of Clement C. Moore's verse (originally called *A Visit from St. Nicholas*). In Moore's collection, the names were spelled "Donder and Blitzen."

In 1994, *Washington Post* newspaper journalists set out to determine if Moore meant to name his seventh reindeer "Donder" or "Donner." The results of their investigation were published in an article on December 21, 1993 where they concluded that Moore must have meant "Donner" since that word means "thunder" in German and "Donder," insofar as they could find, doesn't mean anything. Plus, they located 25 geographical places named "Donner" and none for "Donder." Therefore, "Donder" must have been a misprint. But the case could not be closed that easily, as they wrote in a follow-up report of January 11, 1994, under the headline, *Corrections Roll in like a Clap of Donder.*

"No sooner had this heresy appeared in print than a somewhat vexed Ms. H.J. Zegers-ten Horn, of Bethesda, dashed off a letter that blitzed through the mails like a comet, pranced into the building, danced through the newsroom and landed like a fat Cupid on the editor's desk. Donder, asserted Zegers-ten Horn with the deflating assurance of someone born in the Netherlands does mean something: 'It is the Dutch, not German, writing and pronounciation [*sic*]

of the word "thunder."' ...Still reeling from these developments, the *Post* was next broadsided by Mr. John A. Dodds,
of Arlington, who maintained that his two sources identified
the seventh reindeer not as 'Donner,' not as 'Donder,' but as
'Dunder,' as in 'dunderhead.'"

Undaunted by this setback, the *Post* forged ahead with
its quest, landing at the Library of Congress where a friendly
librarian named Kresh came to their aid. "Kresh, a graybeard-
ed 53, is a published poet and career librarian who came to
the reference room 27 years ago and, he said, 'never left.'
Who can blame him? The place he works in was built in 1897,
feels like a cathedral and appears on souvenir plates at the
airport." (The obvious resemblance of the librarian's name to
"crèche" is such a coincidence that one wonders if it wasn't
fabricated by the *Post!*)

Kresh located a volume of the 1844 "Poems," by Clement
C. Moore. Once Kresh had the book, he turned to Page 125,
and there it was: "Donder." "More important," Kresh said,
"Moore wrote the introduction, an indication that 'Donder'
was the way he wanted it spelled."

According to the newspaper report, further confirma-
tion came quickly. In *The Annotated Night Before Christmas*,
which discusses the poem in an elegantly illustrated modern presentation, editor Martin Gardner notes that the *Troy
Sentinel* used "Dunder" (one for Dodds), but dismisses this as
a typo. Gardner cites the 1844 spelling as definitive, but also
found that Moore wrote "Donder" in a longhand rendering

of the poem penned the year before he died: "That pretty well sews it up," concluded Kresh. Kresh said he found the search "interesting" because no one had ever asked about Donder before. Now, he said, he could make a permanent file like the one he has for questions about "Hoosier poet" James Whitcomb Riley and an "old outhouse."

According to Christmas music historian, Douglas Anderson, the transformation of Donder to Donner was made in error by Robert L. May in his children's book, *Rudolph, the Red-Nosed Reindeer* published in 1939. May, however, was not the first to publish the name as Donner. It had appeared on at least seven different occasions in *The New York Times* as Donner between 1906 and 1949. When May's brother-in-law, Johnny Marks, wrote the lyrics for the 1949 hit song *Rudolph the Red-Nosed Reindeer* (sung and recorded by Gene Autry) he used Donner and Blitzen as well.

So that solves the great mystery of the "Dunder" blunder, but what of the "Blixem" mix-up? "Donder" is the Dutch word for "thunder" and "Blixem" is the corresponding Dutch word for "lightning." "Blitzen" is the German word for "lightning" and a better rhyming fit with Vixen. In 1837, publisher Charles Fenno Hoffman printed a version of *A Visit from Saint Nicholas* with several alterations from earlier versions, including the changing of "Blixem" to "Blixen" and "Dunder" to "Donder." This has led to the theory that Moore, also liking the change, adopted it when he published the poem in his collection of verse. Moore's original poem has been lost, however he did produce other longhand versions, one of which sold for $255,500 in 1994 at a Christie's auction.

To further confuse matters, there is also speculation as to whether Dr. Moore is the real author of the poem. Some experts believe the poem was actually penned by a New York children's literature writer of Dutch descent named Henry Livingston. If in fact, Livingston was the true author of *A Visit* then it stands to reason that the original names of reindeer would have been the Dutch thunder and lightning, "Donder" and "Blixem," later to be changed by Moore to the German thunder and lightning, "Donner" and "Blitzen." The mystery may never be resolved.

Reindeer Names in German from a Song
Eine Version des Liedes lautet so:
Die Rentiere kamen daher wie der Wind,
und der Alte, der pfiff, und er rief: "Geschwind!
Renn, Renner! Tanz, Tänzer! Flieg, fliegende Hitz'!
Hui, Sternschnupp'! Hui, Liebling! Hui, Donner
  und Blitz!
Die Veranda hinauf, und die Hauswand hinan!
Immer fort mit euch! Fort mit euch! Hui, mein
  Gespann!

Origin of Rudolph the Red-Nosed Reindeer
The much-loved character of Rudolph the Red-Nosed

Reindeer, immortalized in song and film, has been an essential part of North American Christmas folklore for as long as most people today can remember. But Rudolph is a 20th-century creation. Rudolph became the ninth reindeer of Santa's team in 1939, when he was created by Robert L. May. May was an advertising writer for the Chicago-based department store chain, Montgomery Ward Company.

May's boss wanted Montgomery Ward to produce a give-away children's Christmas book in-house as a promotional gimmick to attract customers to the stores. The task of coming up with a story was assigned to Robert May, who had a talent for writing children's stories and rhymes, and in January 1939 he started to create his story. Fashioning his protagonist in part after "The Ugly Duckling" fable, as well as from his own childhood memories of being teased for being small and shy, May created the misfit reindeer Rudolph. He wrote the story in verse form as a series of rhyming couplets, testing his progress out on his four-year-old daughter, Barbara. The story was a hit with Barbara, but it was initially rejected by May's boss because the image of the red nose was associated with overindulging in alcohol. But May persisted, and with the addition of illustrations by Denver Gillen it was accepted by the boss and completed in August. That Christmas, Montgomery Ward printed and distributed 2.5 million copies.

The give-away projects were suspended during the war years but Wards reissued the book in 1946 and distributed more than 3.5 million copies. That same year, Sewell Avery, chairman of Montgomery Ward, turned over the copyright to Robert May. May was heavily in debt from medical bills accumulated during his wife Evelyn's long struggle with cancer (she passed away when May was almost finished writing his story). With the copyright in hand, May was able to get himself out of debt, and later put his six children through college.

"Christmas of 1947 was the brightest ever for Bob May, his family, and Rudolph. Some 6,000,000 copies of the booklet had been given away or sold — making Rudolph one of the most widely distributed books in the world. The demand for Rudolph sponsored products increased so much in variety and number that educators and historians predicted Rudolph would come to occupy a permanent niche in the Christmas legend."[18]

In 1949, Johnny Marks turned the story of Rudolph into a song. Gene Autry recorded it; taking it to number one on the Hit Parade, and selling two million copies. The film version of Rudolph, narrated by Burl Ives, first aired in 1964. Both the story and song have been translated into over 25 languages making it one of the most popular Christmas tunes in history.

In 1958 May donated his original "Rudolph" manuscript to the Baker Library at Dartmouth College, which now houses the Robert L. May Collection. May resigned from Wards in 1951 to manage Rudolph's career, but returned to the company in 1958. He retired in 1970 and died in 1976.

Christmas Stockings

'Twas the night before Christmas, when all through the house
Not a creature was stirring, not even a mouse;
The stockings were hung by the chimney with care,
In hopes that St. Nicholas soon would be there.
Clement C. Moore, *'Twas the Night before Christmas*

n North America, the tradition of hanging Christmas stockings for Santa Claus to fill with treats dates back to the end of the 19th century. The first literary reference to Christmas stockings being hung by the chimney was in 1809 by Washington Irving in *A History of New York from the Beginning of the World to the End of the Dutch Dynasty*. Clement C. Moore's infamous 1823 poem cemented the image and practice in North American culture. A visual record of this now common custom can be found in the many Christmas illustrations by German-born, American artist Thomas Nash. The custom of hanging Christmas stockings started in the United

States although some believe it was Dutch settlers who introduced this Christmas Eve tradition to America. It was told that sometime during the 16th century, children in the Netherlands started the custom of leaving their clogs filled with straw by the hearth for *Sinterklaas*'s horse. A treat for *Sinterklaas* was also left in the house near the fire. In return *Sinterklaas* would leave the children treats. In America the clogs would become stockings, and the saint known to all would become Santa Claus.

On Christmas Eve in Quebec and Acadia, children traditionally put their shoes close to the fireplace in the hopes of receiving gifts from the Baby Jesus or *Père Noël* (Father Christmas), a custom brought to Canada by French settlers. This custom is still practiced in many parts of Europe on December 5, the eve of Saint Nicholas Day, rather than Christmas Eve. Today in Canada, the shoes have been replaced with the more common, and commercial, Christmas stockings, which are also becoming more popular worldwide as a result of American cultural influence.

The custom may have originated from the legend of Saint Nicholas's anonymous gift of bags filled with gold coins to a poor man for his daughters' dowries. According to the legend, the bags of gold were thrown down the chimney where they landed in the girls' stockings, which were hanging on the hearth to dry. In other versions of the story the coins were placed inside a sock and then thrown down the chimney.

The modern tradition of receiving an orange in the toe of a Christmas stocking or foil-covered chocolate coins is said to symbolize Saint Nicholas's bags of gold. Stories of deities leaving anonymous gifts of gold coins, however, can be found in many ancient folktales. One such example is the Germanic Mother Goddess, Holda, wife of Woden. Her feast day is December 13. One of her roles is a protector of children and she gives gifts of gold coins to those who do good deeds. Stories of Winter Solstice gift-bearers have a long history but the origin of the shoe-stocking tradition remains elusive.

Long before the legends of Saint Nicholas received wide circulation, it seems shoes, stockings, and even feet were targets of superstitions, some of which have retained a foothold in modern times.

- A common belief in the Middle Ages, and even as late as the 19th century, was that worn shoes retained the spirit and character of their owners. Many fairy tales were based on this premise.
- Old shoes were put on the roof of old houses to fend off evil spirits.
- Feet and shoes were associated with good luck and an old shoe was valued as a good luck charm.
- In modern Greece old shoes are burned to prevent *kallikantzaroi*, naughty goblins, from invading the home during Christmas time.

- In the Middle Ages, footwear was expensive and the common practice was to bequeath one's footwear to members of the family. The saying "following in your father's footsteps" may have arisen from this custom and implied following the good fortune associated with shoes.
- Travelling carried with it many perils and subsequently many rituals were practised to avoid an ill fate. It was customary to drop an old shoe outside the front door before setting out on a long journey.
- Throwing shoes after someone going on a journey was also thought to bring good luck.
- Tying old shoes to the wedding car would give the strength of the shoe's character and bring good luck to the couple as well as chase off evil spirits.
- Dressing has many superstitions and custom dictates the right shoe should be put on and removed before the left shoe, otherwise bad luck could ensue.
- Leaving shoes in the shape of the cross is considered to bring bad luck. To undo the bad luck another person must pick up the shoes.
- Placing the left foot on the ground first when getting out of bed will bring bad luck.
- Walking around with one shoe on and the other off will bring bad luck for a year.

- To receive shoes as a gift on Christmas Day is considered bad luck as was wearing new shoes on Christmas Day.
- Superstition dictates putting salt and pepper in the left boot for good fortune.
- Leaving stockings in the shoes overnight brings good luck.
- Wearing a stocking inside out is a sign of receiving a gift in the near future.
- An old English superstition claims: "If you do not give a new pair of shoes to a poor person at least once in your lifetime, you will go barefoot in the next world."
- Never accept a gift of old boots or you will walk in the former owners' troubles.
- The Labrador Inuit people believed a miniature pair of boots represented the spirit of the real pair. As long as the miniature was in good condition, it was believed that the real boots would not wear out.
- There is an ancient custom in many cultures of placing shoes outside a home as a sign of welcome.

Not only did shoes and stockings hold a significant place in the hearts and minds of people long ago, but who was in the first shoes that stepped over the threshold on New

Year's Eve was of the utmost importance. An ancient Celtic tradition called "First-Footing" dictates that the first person to cross a home's threshold after midnight on New Year's Eve will determine the homeowner's luck for the new year. The ideal visitor is a dark-haired stranger bearing gifts — preferably whiskey, a lump of coal for the fire, small cakes, or coins. A wide variety of items were brought, but most of them symbolized the essentials of life such as food, drink, heat, or light. The lump of coal began as a lucky omen for the household, but became a thing of dread in later transmutations of the gift-bearing stranger into Saint Nicholas and Santa Claus. The significance of the dark hair hearkens back to the fourth century or earlier, when the presumably fair-haired Vikings invaded Scotland: a blond visitor was not a good omen.

First-footing remains a strong tradition in rural areas of Scotland. In some districts added significance is attached to a high arched foot, or "the foot water runs under" in a first-footer. It is considered unlucky if the person's feet are flat. On the Isle of Man, a good first-footer is a dark man of good appearance with insteps "high enough to allow a mouse to run through." Some sources also indicate it is considered bad luck if the first-footer is a woman. Other undesirable features of a first-footer include people who are pious and sanctimonious, miserly, lame, with a blind eye, midwives, ministers, doctors, gravediggers, thieves, and people with bare feet. In other words, the first-footer must be whole, socially acceptable, and lucky, to guarantee those desirable qualities for the household in the coming year.

It seems shoes, stockings, and feet may have held much more symbolic significance for many of our ancestors than they do today. But nonetheless, why shoes, or stockings, as the vessel of choice in which to receive the blessings of a saint? The last things a person would want to be without in the dead of winter are socks and shoes. Around the time the custom began most people, children included, only owned one pair of shoes and good hygiene was severely lacking by today's standards. Charcoal is a very effective odour absorber so perhaps this has something to do with the origins of the "lump of coal" in the shoes or stockings of naughty children. Likewise, perhaps the custom originated as a way for parents to get their children to clean and polish their shoes at least once a year!

Christmas Presents

I n its purest Christian intent, to celebrate the birth of Jesus is to celebrate God's greatest gift to humanity. According to legend, the Wise Men knew the importance of the gift. They were the original Christmas gift-bearers and strange as their choice of gifts were for a child, the symbolism behind these three rare and precious presents was significant. "Incense (frankincense) was used in temple worship at Jerusalem. Gold was the precious metal of kings. Myrrh was used in Jewish burial practices. The coded message is that the Christ child is both God and King who will experience a salvific death."[19]

In honour of the Magi, many cultures exchange gifts on January 6, Feast of the Epiphany, also known as Twelfth Night and Three Kings Day. There also exists a multitude of stories and legends about the beauty and graciousness of the simple and humble gifts given to the Christ child, usually by children, reinforcing that the value of a gift lies in the intention with which it is given.

In his book, *The Battle for Christmas*, Stephen Nissenbaum points to another significance of the gesture behind the gifts: "The Gifts of the Magi, too, represented the high-in-status waiting on the low—three kings paying homage to an infant lying in squalor." This was essentially a continuation of a tradition that had been perpetuated for many millennia in the seasonal ritual of social inversion and masters serving slaves. In the Middle Ages, this gesture of giving over to the lower classes continued during the Christmas festivities but so did the accompanying carnival atmosphere with its raucous public drunkenness, begging, and general rowdiness. Many chose to celebrate Twelfth Night, as well as much of the Christmas season, in the tradition of the Master of Misrule demanding free food and drinks from the upper classes.

By the 19th century, this misrule had got so out of hand that something had to be done. So begging was banned and the "cultural media directors" of the time started a campaign of sorts to shift the focus of Christmas on the family and off the streets which resulted in the creation of a new consumerism and new forms of gift giving. This sudden interest in gift giving may be attributed to the rise of Clement Moore's poem, *A Visit from St. Nicholas*. From the growing popularity of Santa Claus, the new recipients of the gifts became the children instead of the lower classes. "An important factor here is that you could not give children what you gave beggars — they already eat your best food! And so you had to go shopping, and spend. Christmas helped create the new consumer society because people were not in the habit of buying luxury — but the essence of the Christmas present is that it cannot be a necessity, when you are giving inside the family it needs to be something special, a luxury item. This was the way that for many people the consumer economy got created. Even in times of depression you must buy something nice, some luxury for your own dear ones. The only people we still give necessities to are the poor!"[20]

In England, where Calvinistic puritans had reduced Christmas to a staid religious observation purged of merriment, a similar Christmas transformation was occurring. Just as popular writers Washington Irving and Clement C. Moore were responsible for creating a new type of Christmas in America, Charles Dickens, through his 1843 story *A Christmas Carol*, re-invented English Christmas. The Dickensian Christmas encompasses charity, goodwill, family togetherness, feasts, parties, gifts, and children's games. Dickens' Christmas story was translated into dozens of languages and became famous throughout the world as an instruction manual for the modern Christmas. Up until the Victorian era, the attitude toward children was that they "should be seen and not heard." But under the reign of Queen Victoria this changed and the emphasis on children as the centre of Christmas became more predominant. Parties were held not only for the adults, but for children as well at Christmas time. The following poem appeared in a British newspaper in the 1860s indicating the emphasis on children and presents at Christmas:

Christmas has come, with gifts and toys,
For little girls as well as boys.
Mary has got a picture-book,
And Jane has got a gilded fan,
And something nice has come for Ann,
Baby has got a neat doll, dressed
In scarlet coat and bright blue vest -
Mary and Jane, and Ann I know,
When Christmas comes with frost & snow
Will think upon the girls and boys
Who get no pretty Christmas toys
Who suffer want, and cold, and care,
And help them both with alms and prayer.

In response to this new consumerism, department stores such as Eaton's and Simpson's in Toronto, and Dupuis Frères in Montreal, seized the opportunity and started publishing and distributing Christmas catalogues thereby launching a new way of shopping by mail-order in Canada. This opened up the door to shopping in advance as well as from rural areas. Department store Christmas catalogues practically became legendary in Canada in the last century just as Internet shopping is changing consumerism in this millennium.

Origin of the Snowman

The first big snowfall of the season is typically greeted with squeals of excitement and enthusiasm by children eager to get outside and build a snowman, or even an entire snow family. The image of a snowman is commonly connected with Christmas and is embedded in western culture although the first snowman could even date back to the cavemen as a primitive sort of "scarecrow" or false figure intended to fool a foe. Other theories suggest that snowmen were first created in Russia over 2500 years ago in response to the apparent sightings of the Siberian Yeti or the Abominable Snowman.

A snowman is a human-like figure constructed from compacted snow. Although a snowman's shape can take many forms the most common variety consists of rolling a large ball of snow for the base of the body; a second smaller ball for the midsection; a third and even smaller ball for the head. Facial features, such as eyes and a mouth are tradition-ally added using coal or small stones, as are buttons. A nose may be added, using a piece of fruit or a vegetable, such as a carrot; sticks are sometimes added as arms. Snowmen are often depicted with a pipe and a hat.

One famous snowman is also an important "resident" of Zurich, Switzerland. He is the centrepiece of the spring *Sechselauten* holiday, similar to Groundhog Day in North America, celebrating the end of winter. This popular event involves a parade complete with costumed marchers, floats, horses, bands, and people throwing gifts into the crowd. The climax of the parade features the burning of the snowman. He is mounted on top of a large wood pyre that is set ablaze at 6 p.m., and using a complicated mathematical formula, the time it takes to completely melt him is used to calculate the arrival of spring. The detonation of an explosive charge placed in his head adds to the excitement and drama. The burning of the snowman symbolizes the "death" of winter and the triumph of the sun.

An old Ukrainian folktale tells of an aged couple who are lonely for a child. The old woman makes a pair of white fur slip-pers for her imaginary dream-child and magically, a little snow child dressed in sparkling white appears the next day, wearing the white fur slippers! From then on, every winter, this snow child comes and lives with the old couple, filling their lives with love and joy. She dances through the snow, paints frost leaves on the windows, and digs snow tunnels in the yard, but she cannot bear to come inside where it's warm. Every spring, the old folks are sad when their snow child melts, but consoled by the knowledge that she will return with next year's snowfall.

This myth is one of many such legends that tell of a snow person coming to live with mortals and is another example of ancient folkloric symbolism of the cycle of the seasons; of birth, death, and resurrection so indelibly associated with Winter Solstice. Snowmen, like *Frosty*, continue to symbolize this magic even today. They stand as silent sentinels guarding our homes, preserving the past, and inspiring our imaginations.

A similar, but more detailed, legend from Russia tells the story of Grandfather Frost and the Snow Maiden. "A Russian tale tells of a woodcutter and his wife who were childless. They were a good and kind couple but they were lonely. One winter day, to ease their loneliness, they began to roll large snowballs together and in a short while they made a *snequrochka*, a Snow Maiden. She looked so beautiful that they called her their daughter.

"At that same moment, hiding and crackling among the fir trees, was Grandfather Frost. He was an old winter god with a long, white beard and he carried a great staff that was filled with wonderful magic. He had overheard the couple and felt sorry for them for people who were kind and good always touched his heart. And so he raised his great staff and suddenly the Snow Maiden came to life.

"Some said the Snow Maiden was the daughter of Grandfather Frost and Mother Snow, sent to comfort the couple for a time. Others said she was really a spirit-princess come to earth. Whatever her nature, she remained with the couple as a true and dutiful daughter would be.

"Now as spring approached and people began to leave their houses, the Snow Maiden fell in love with a young man from the village. But the price of surrendering her heart in love would be to lose her human mortality. Grandfather Frost continued to watch her from a distance for he knew what would soon happen to her.

"One day she was walking with her beloved through a birch wood. The youth played his flute; the Snow Maiden walked beside him turning her face to the sun. Suddenly she gave the faintest sigh and began to melt. She was still a creature of ice and snow and could not stand the springtime sun. Soon there was nothing left but an icy mist, drifting upward into the blue sky. The frail creature could not survive the breath of spring.

"But her spirit had leapt into the waiting arms of Grandfather Frost and Mother Snow and they carried her away over the stars to the far north where she plays all through the summer on the frozen seas.

"But each year in winter, on the first day of the New Year, Grandfather Frost and the Snow Maiden return to Russia. And they continue to work their magic for those who are kind and good. And they visit, in particular, the children, bringing them gifts and helping them to make their dreams come true, as they did long ago for the woodcutter and his wife."[21]

Perhaps the most famous snowman, at least in North America, is *Frosty the Snowman.* The song, *Frosty the Snowman,* was a "Tin Pan Alley" novelty song created by Jack Nelson and Steve Rollins in 1950. It was intended as a follow-up to *Rudolph the Red-Nosed Reindeer* and sold to Gene Autry, who recorded it that year. While *Frosty the Snowman* is often thought of as a Christmas song, it's really just a winter song like *Jingle Bells, Suzy Snowflake,* and *Winter Wonderland,* and makes no reference to Christmas. It was a huge success with millions of records sold and a new legend was born. The title was taken up for a children's book, illustrated by Corinne Malvern, and published in 1950 by Golden Books. In 1968, it went on to become a popular children's television cartoon by Rankin & Bass. The cartoon, in which Jimmy Durante narrates the story and sings the title song, has become a Christmas classic about Frosty's adventures with an evil magician, echoing the ancient Winter Solstice theme of the cycle of death and rebirth.

According to the *Random House Dictionary of the English Language* the word "snowman" didn't come into existence until sometime between the years 1820 and 1830. Snow was not popularly associated with the imagery of Christmas until the 19th century, when Santa Claus was identified as coming from the North Pole. But by the 20th century, snow-men were predominant on Christmas cards and Christmas decorations. Many patents have even been granted for snowman-related items such as Snowman Accessory Kits, Snowman Moulds, Snowman Dolls, and even a Lawn Leaf Bag with Printed Snowman Image.

The Nutcracker

D uring the Victorian era, silver nutcrackers matched the table settings for serving nuts at the end of the meal, originating the expression "from soup to nuts."

Even before Russian composer Peter Tchaikovsky's famous 1891 score, *The Nutcracker*, made the toy a popular collectable object, they were a common and economical Christmas gift that could be handmade from a scrap of wood. According to German folklore, nutcrackers were given as keepsakes to bring good luck to the family and protect the home. *The Nutcracker* ballet's 1892 premiere in St. Petersburg, choreographed by Marius Petipa and Lev Ivanov, was a box office and critical failure. Tchaikovsky re-wrote the music and turned it into a suite which went on to become a huge success and *The Nutcracker* is now one of the most well known and well loved ballets. Set on Christmas Eve, it tells the story of young Clara, who is given a nutcracker that comes alive in the night and transforms into a handsome Nutcracker Prince. After Tchaikovsky's ballet, the nutcrackers were usually dressed as soldiers or government officials.

The Erzgebirge (Ore Mountain) region is located in the eastern part of Germany not far from Dresden at the Czech border. About 400 years ago, when silver mining subsided in that region, the silver miners turned to toy making in order to make a living. Over the centuries they developed extraordinary woodcarving skills that were passed down from one generation to the next. More than 150 family-owned enterprises from the village of Seiffen and the surrounding areas have formed a co-operative of woodworkers called Dregeno Seiffen e.G. The village of Seiffen was located close to the so-called "salt street," a trade route that brought salt from the Halle/Leipzig region to Prague. Using this route, the toy makers from the Erzgebirge sent their products to Leipzig, a trading place for European goods for more than a thousand years.

The nutcracker's career began in the Biedermeier period in Germany, roughly equivalent to England's Victorian era. It was during that period that Christmas began to be celebrated as a truly family event focusing on the children. In the toy making centre of Sonneberg in the Thuringian Forest there was mention in 1735 of "nut-biter" devices that operated according to the principles of leverage. These nut-biters were described as sturdy energetic forms with large heads. Two moving arms on the back of the head allowed the lower jaw to push the nut against the upper jaw. In a carnival parade in 1783, students from Freisingen presented large models of Berchtesgaden wares, including a nut-biter in the form of a little man whose mouth and stomach were one and the same. By the time the Brothers Grimm put together their first dictionary of High German (1830s), the term *Nussknacker* (nutcracker) was defined as "often in the form of a misshaped little man, in whose mouth the nut, by means of a lever or screw, is cracked open."

The original Seiffen nutcrackers were never dressed up. Collectors recognize the value of the art of painting the nutcracker or its pure woodwork in its original variety. Nutcrackers of all types from the Erz Mountains were first offered for public sale at the Christmas Market in Dresden in 1745. However, figural nutcrackers were not found in catalogues or price lists from the region until 1850.

The nutcracker's illustrious literary life began in 1816 with the publication of E.T.A. Hoffmann's fairy tale "The Nutcracker and the Mouse King" ("*Nussknacker und Mausekönig*"), on which the famous ballet is based. The original "Nutcracker," as written by E.T.A. Hoffman, was a morbid story and not particularly suitable reading for children. The story was revised by Alexander Dumas in a children's story about a little girl named Clara who received a nutcracker doll for Christmas from her beloved godfather. On Christmas Eve she had a dream in which many of her toys came to life including her nutcracker who became a handsome prince, who took Clara to an enchanted land. When she awoke from the dream, Clara was saddened that the prince was gone, but found herself under the Christmas tree surrounded by her loving family all looking forward to a wonderful Christmas.

Thirty-five years later Heinrich Hoffmann's *King Nutcracker and Poor Reinhold* (1851) was published. In Hoffmann's picture book, the Nutcracker brings the poor, ailing Reinhold into a dream world full of toys, which he then finds under the Christmas tree the next morning. All the toys in the dream such as houses, trees, horsemen, soldiers, and Noah's Ark with animals, were made in Seiffen and were very popular at the time. The book inspired toy makers to create a replica of the Hoffmann nutcracker. In 1870, Wilhelm Friedrich Fuechtner (1844–1923) created the first of a new type of the now-famous Erz Mountain nutcracker. Fuechtner became known as the "father of the nutcracker" and was the first to make commercial nutcrackers using a lathe. The production of Fuechtner nutcrackers has been carried on by the next four generations: Albert Fuechtner (1875–1953), Kurt Fuechtner (1903–1970), and Werner Fuechtner (born in 1930) and his sons.

Portrayals of nutcrackers changed over time, from good-hearted fairy tale kings to society's authority figures. The feeling of resentment for these authority figures was the basis for carving the nutcrackers in their images. Toy makers who found themselves at the mercy of soldiers, foresters, and policemen, took great pleasure in using wooden figures in these uniforms to crack nuts. The purpose was not to honour these people, but to satirize them as they cracked the symbolic "hard nut." By the end of the 19th century, the nutcracker appeared almost consistently in the catalogues of the toy wholesalers as a representative of contemporary authorities. What started out as a practical tool often ended up as an expression of light irony and a social critique by common folks. But even in this role, the colourfully painted nutcrackers were just as well loved as children's toys and a useful household gadget.

As time passed and the tradition grew, the nutcracker could be found in nearly every home in Germany. Eventually this folk craft was influenced by the industrial revolution and manufacturers began to mass produce the nutcrackers using a process called turning. Today the largest manufacturer of wooden nutcrackers is Christian Steinbach of Germany. Other designers include Lothar Junghanel, Christian Ulbricht, Helgard Peterson, Franz Karl, and Olaf Kolbe, to name a few. Although nutcrackers are made in Czechoslovskia, Poland, and Taiwan, as well as in Germany, the German nutcrackers are considered to be more colourful and better made. With the substantial population of German immigrants in Canada, and the large numbers of Canadian Armed Forces personnel stationed for some time in Germany, it is now also quite common to see original Erzgebirge nutcrackers displayed in Canadian homes during the Christmas season.

The Importance
of Frankincense

S moke and incense have long played an important role in human life and religious ritual. The ancient Romans, Persians, Babylonians, and Assyrians all burned frankincense on their pagan altars, at cremations, in their homes, and on state occasions. It was also used in purification ceremonies and was believed to expel evil spirits as well as protect from ill health. The mythical phoenix was said to build its funeral pyre out of frankincense and myrrh. According to Herodotus, frankincense in the amount of 1,000 talents weight was offered every year, during the feast honouring the god Baal, on the great altar of his temple in Babylon. According to *A Modern Herbal*, by Maud Grieve, frankincense also has medicinal applications: "it is stimulant, but seldom used now internally, though formerly was in great repute. Pliny mentions it as an antidote to hemlock. Avicenna (10th century) recommends it for tumours, ulcers, vomiting, dysentery and fevers. In China it is used for leprosy."

In the Christmas story, frankincense was one of the three gifts the Wise Men gave Jesus and it was considered a luxury. Legend says that it was presented to the Christ child by Balthasar, the black king from Ethiopia or Saba, in fulfilment of Isaiah's prophecy that gold and frankincense would be brought from the Gentiles to honour the heavenly king.

Frankincense was the purest incense. It is a sweet smelling gum resin derived from certain Boswellia trees which, at the time of Christ, grew in Arabia, India, and Ethiopia. The frankincense trade was at its height during the rule of the Roman Empire at which time this resin was considered as valuable as gems or precious metals. When burned it produced a white smoke which was believed to represent the prayers and praises of the faithful ascending to heaven.

The custom of burning incense came to Europe from the Middle East with Turkish merchants and the Crusaders. Incense was very expensive and therefore only used for the Twelve Days of Christmas from December 25 to January 6, The Epiphany.

Burning incense at Christmas had been a custom in Germany long before the creation of the smoker figurine. Smokers originated from the same region in Germany as the Nutcracker. Ferdinand Froh and his nephew, Gotthelf Friedrich Haustein designed and made the first incense burning smoker in 1856, at the village of Heidelberg in the Erzgebirge region. The first smokers are found in pattern books and price lists from circa 1850.

As a marketing tactic Ferdinand and Gotthelf designed the smoker as a smoking person with the most popular figurines being Turks, merchants, and gypsies. Other first models for smokers were the common "man of the street" or villagers, such as wood cutters, peddlers, miners, mailmen, chimney sweeps, night watchmen, toy makers, priests, and bakers. As years passed and the smoker grew in popularity more designs were added, such as the typical Christmas figures of Saint Nicholas and snowmen, all to add to the festive act of incense burning. Early producers of smokers used a special type of dough to form faces and arms. Today nearly all smokers are made entirely of wood.

Origin of the Crèche

Away in a manger, no crib for His bed,
The little Lord Jesus laid down His sweet head;
The stars in the sky looked down where He lay,
The little Lord Jesus, asleep in the hay.
(Author unknown; first published in Philadelphia in *1885*
in *Little Children's Book for Schools and Families,* by J.C. File)

One of the most beautiful family Christmas traditions is setting up a crèche during the Advent season. A crèche is a model of the Nativity scene of the birth of Christ in Bethlehem. It can be a small tabletop-size model in the home or a large life-size scene set up in a church or on a lawn. The term "crèche" is French for a manger or a crib and is derived from the Old German word *Krippe*. The first crèche is said to have been created in 1223 by Saint Francis of Assisi in Greccio, Italy. Saint

Francis held midnight mass in a cave in Greccio, where men and beasts re-enacted the Nativity by candlelight. Churches had built Nativity mangers prior to this time but they were ostentatious depictions covered with gold, silver, and jewels. St. Francis wanted to remind people that Jesus was born in humble stable. Life-size crèches are commonly seen throughout Italy to this day.

Church crèches were very widespread in Italy and Germany from the 16th century, where the large Nativity figures were usually made of wood or clay. The less costly ones had carved heads, hands, and feet with clothed bodies over wire or straw. The Italians were accustomed to displaying the pious *santi belli*, statues of household saints, in their homes already and by the 18th century smaller versions of the Nativity figures were being added at Christmas time. Sometimes, very elaborate versions of these statues became prestigious features in royal residences.

From Italy, the custom spread to the neighbouring provinces of southern France. Crèches with Italian influence could be found in the churches of Provence starting in the 18th century although the appeal of crèches was seen in France as early as the 17th century in upper and middle class homes. These forerunners of the domestic crèche began to appear in the form of decorated glass-fronted boxes called *grottoes* or rockeries.

The *santi belli* were also well received by the French who called them *santons* which means "little saints." The figures were made of wax, bread dough, or spun glass and were often set in exotic imaginary landscapes created with moss, flowers, stones, and animals. Initially the scenes included only the biblical figures, but more and more characters joined the ensemble and before long some scenes contained up to 40 different pastoral folks.

In the 18th century, a small cottage industry sprang up in the Midi of France, making all the characters for the crèche. The *santons* became especially popular during the French Revolution when the Convention of 1795 forbade midnight mass and church crèches, resulting in people displaying crèches in their homes instead.

The industry was revolutionized in 1798 by Louis Lagnel's introduction of pre-fabricated plaster moulds. In 1803, artisans began selling their *santons* at the Christmas fair in Marseille and the popularity exploded. Much like the incense smokers of Germany the classical figures of the crèche were joined every year by traditional village characters representing Provençal town or country trades people: bakers, milkmaids, basket weavers, fishmongers, pie sellers, coopers, cobblers, pilgrims, among many others.

Religious orders from France brought the tradition to Canada, where church crèches representing Nativity figures appeared from the very beginnings of the colony. Although the church Christmas crèche was part of early religious traditions in Quebec, it was not until after 1875 that crèches began to appear in homes as part of family customs. Even before decorated Christmas trees became the custom, the crèche already had a place of honour in French-Canadian homes.

The custom of setting up a crèche under the Christmas tree became very popular during the 1930s. Many families built their own small stables in which to display commercially bought figures. Before long, whole villages of little houses and shops sprang up at the foot of the tree to accommodate the vast array of village characters. Next electric toy train sets were added to the ever expanding villages and eventually there was no more room for the Nativity scene under the tree!

From Quebec the popularity of these Nativity *santons* spread south of the border to New England where the tradition continues to thrive today supplied in large part by French and Canadian *santoniers*.

The Night the
Animals Could Speak

At the hour of midnight
In the midst of winter
Bright with Heaven's starlight
Born was our Redeemer
At the hour of midnight
Roosters were all crowing
"Christ, our heav'nly sunlight comes
His peace bestowing."
From a Puerto Rican Christmas Carol

During the Roman Saturnalia celebration, people paraded the streets wearing animal masks in personification of deities, re-enacting the chaos and creation myths. The eve of winter solstice was the longest, darkest night of the year (December 24/25 by the Julian calendar) and ancient people believed it to be a magical night when portals or bridges to other realms opened for a brief time. On that night animals were said to speak like humans and give advice.

Christmas Eve with its atmosphere of wonder also offers infinite possibilities to people's imagination. It was said that on the stroke of midnight on Christmas Eve, farm animals were briefly blessed with the gift of speech, in honour of the animals present in the manger when Jesus was born. Oxen, horses, pigs, roosters, and sheep began to speak to one another revealing secrets and stories about their masters. But for humans to witness this miracle was considered extremely bad luck, and one could be struck dumb by overhearing the animals talking.

In some rural traditions, on Christmas Eve, the farm animals are either fed before the family eats, or they are given the leftovers from the special feast in respect of the animals' role in the Nativity. Another belief states that on every Christmas Eve at midnight, farm cattle kneel in the stable to worship the infant Jesus and that honey bees wake up from their winter slumber humming a song of praise to Jesus. There is an old belief that early on Christmas morning, all bees will leave their hives, swarm about for a short while, and then return. Many people tell tales of having witnessed this phenomenon. One explanation is that bees get curious about their surroundings, and if there is unexpected activity they will want to check out any potential danger. As people were often up and about on Christmas Eve observing various traditions, or just returning from the night services, the bees would sense the disturbance and venture out of their hive to investigate.

The Origin of Christmas Cards

ood engravers had been producing prints with religious themes as far back as the Middle Ages in Europe. The oldest known greeting card in existence is a Valentine made in the 1400s, now held in the British Museum. In the 15th century, Germans presented seasonal gifts called *Andachtsbilder*, a sort of greeting card with a religious picture for the home. They were often designed to look like a scroll with a depiction of the Christ child bearing a cross with the inscription "*Ein gut selig jar*," meaning "A good and blessed year." The New Year greeting card did not gain popularity until the late 1700s. Following the 1796 invention of lithography by Alois Senefelder, it became common practice for German merchants to send greeting cards to their customers for best wishes in the new year. Lithography is the technique whereby

large numbers of drawings or text are first drawn on finely textured stone and then reproduced on paper.

In the early 18th century, special printed items were given during the holidays. The first holiday greeting cards of sorts were the "Christmas Pieces" made by school children to demonstrate their calligraphy and writing skills for their parents. Another early custom was the use of decorative notepaper with matching envelopes by the British gentry to send personalized hand-written Christmas letters to their friends, family, and associates.

The first Christmas card was probably made in Germany centuries earlier, but it was a card designed in 1843 in England that truly marked the birth of the commercial Christmas card. Coincidentally, that is the same year that Charles Dickens wrote *A Christmas Carol.*

The credit for designing this infamous first commercial Christmas card is given to John Calcott Horsley (1817–1903). He was a well known painter who later became the Rector of the Royal Academy from 1875 to 1890. He designed the first Christmas card in the summer of 1843 at the request of his friend Sir Henry Cole (1808–1882), founding director of the South Kensington Museum (renamed the Victoria and Albert Museum in 1899) and one of the organizers of the Great Exhibition of 1851. Sir Henry Cole was a prominent innovator in the 1800s, responsible for the modernization of the British postal system, and in his spare time he ran an art shop that specialized in decorative objects for the home.

He was also an assistant at the Public Records Office and a writer and publisher of books and journals. He wrote books on art collections and architecture under the pseudonym Felix Summerly and founded *The Journal of Design* as well as *Summerly's Home Treasury* for publishing children's books, some of which he edited himself.

With all his ventures, Cole had little time for the cumbersome task of inscribing countless personal Christmas greetings, so he asked Horsley to produce for him a Christmas card with a single message that could be duplicated and sent to all on his list. The card Horsley created for Sir Henry was a Christmas triptych. The centre panel depicted a happy family of children, parents, and grandparents all seated at the Christmas dinner table, some raising their glasses of wine for a toast. Flanking this scene are the two side panels depicting acts of Christmas charity: to the left, feeding the poor; to the right, clothing the needy. Below the images is written the now familiar phrase "A Merry Christmas and a Happy New Year to You."

The intention of this image was to remind people that Christmas is not only a time for family but also a time to help those less fortunate. But so much for good intentions: the image drew criticism and was condemned by the British Temperance Movement for "promoting drunkenness" and for "fostering the moral corruption of children." Such criticism was ironic considering Cole's founding purpose for the *Summerly's Home Treasury* was to change the current approach to children's books which he termed "hurtful to children." The irony of the criticism goes further in light of John Horsley's public image of being "the greatest prude of all"! Horsley objected to painting from life classes and to paintings of the nude. His boisterous condemnation of this area of art earned him the nickname "Clothes Horsley" and a fair amount of ridicule.

One thousand copies of the card were printed in 1843 by Jobbins of Warwick Court, Holborn, London, with the excess being sold at Felix Summerly's (Cole's) Home Treasury Office for one shilling each. The cards were printed on stiff cardboard, 5 1/8 by 3 1/4 inches in black and white and then coloured by hand. Of the 1,000 original Christmas cards printed, only 12 are known to still exist, two of which are in the Hallmark Historical Collection. Copies of a facsimile reprint issued in 1955 can still be found today. One of the originals went to auction in 2001 and sold for a record £22,500 (around c$53,000). This particular card was inscribed to "Granny and Auntie Char" and was signed by Sir Henry himself, which makes it exceptionally rare. Ordinarily, one of these cards is expected to fetch between £3,000 and £6,000.

Due to the high cost of postage, initially only the upper classes sent Christmas cards. The "penny post," however, was created with the British Postal System's passage of the Postal Act of 1870. The practice of sending Christmas cards then became accessible to many more people and, as printing methods improved, Christmas card production increased.

Popularity of cards grew so quickly that by the 1880s, sales figures were in the millions. Indeed, Christmas cards became so successful that by 1880, the Postmaster General was already warning everyone to "post early for Christmas."

Some of the favourite holiday cards of the late 1800s and early 1900s were those designed by Kate Greenaway, a Victorian children's writer and illustrator, Frances Brundage, and Ellen H. Clapsaddle. Most cards were very elaborate, adorned with fringe, silk, and satin, and cut into a variety of shapes such as fans, bells, birds, candles, and even plum puddings. Other popular styles folded like maps or fitted together as puzzles, as well as pop-up varieties that revealed tiny mangers, ice skaters, or other festive winter scenes.

While Christmas cards were relatively popular in England by 1860, the custom had not yet caught on in North America. The first Christmas greetings in the United States are thought to be those produced by New York engraver Richard Pease in 1851. When the custom finally did catch on, Americans imported greeting cards from England until mass production came to Boston by way of a German immigrant, Louis Prang (1824–1909).

Louis Prang opened a lithographic shop in 1850 with only $250. His initial creations featured flowers and birds, and were sold only in England in 1873. Prang's first line of U.S. cards were published in 1875 (two years after the introduction of the "penny post" card in the United States). By 1881, Prang was producing more than five million Christmas cards each year. His yuletide greetings began to feature winter scenes, glowing fireplaces, and children playing with toys. Prang was an innovator in the field of mass produced lithography, and wrote many books and articles on the subject. His painstaking craftsmanship and perfection of the chromolithographic printing technique have made his cards a favourite of collectors today and earned him the title "father of the American Christmas card."

Unfortunately, Prang's high-quality cards were costly, and although Americans took to Christmas cards, they preferred the penny Christmas postcards and cheaper imports from Germany. Prang was forced to close his business in 1890. The German-made cards remained popular in America until World War I, when they were removed from the shelves, and by the end of the war America's modern greeting card industry had been born. Today, more than two billion Christmas cards are exchanged annually within North America alone making Christmas the number one card-selling holiday of the year.

Another popular form of season greeting was the calendar. Calendars and almanacs became common New Year gifts and advertising give-aways, because they would remain with the recipient long after the other greetings had left the mantle place. The greeting calendar came into general use in the 1870s and '80s, initially as an extension of the novelty almanac, and later as a popular hanging wall decoration. These almanacs and calendars played an important role in the lives of Canadians in the 19th and 20th centuries.

The almanac was often hung by a string somewhere in the kitchen. Although religious, agricultural, medical, or other similar information made up the majority of the text, it was the calendar pages that were the most useful. Interleaved with blank pages for notes, these almanacs were used as daily journals. Nineteenth century Canadians did not use the almanac to plan ahead, as the daytimer is used today, but recorded information such as family histories, planting of crops, social events, letters sent, sales made, and, of course, the weather.

Christmas Stamps

At one time, mail was sent for free and the burden of the cost was on the recipient. In 1837, an English schoolmaster named Rowland Hill noticed that although the post office was providing the service, a vast number of recipients were refusing delivery and the post office was losing money. Hill wrote a pamphlet called "The Post Office Reform" wherein he proposed the concept of prepaid stamps and on May 1, 1840, the first stamps went on sale in Britain. These first postage stamps were called "One-Penny Black" and "Two-Pence Blue" stamps and featured images of Queen Victoria. In 1870, the British Post Office introduced a halfpenny stamp for mailing postcards. At this point sheets of postage stamps were not perforated and a cutting implement was required to separate the stamps. In 1847 an Irish engineer named Henry Archer submitted a design to the British Post Office for perforating the stamp sheets. By 1854, Archer's machine was sufficiently perfected to produce the first tear-off stamps.

The First Christmas Stamp

It's not very often Canadians get to take credit for starting Christmas traditions, since so many were well established before Canada was. But the first Christmas stamp is an exception. In 1898, an "Imperial Penny Postage" stamp was issued in Canada to mark the advent of penny postage throughout the British Empire. The stamp showed a Mercator world map with the colonies and islands of the British Empire highlighted in red; it was inscribed "Christmas 1898." This was Canada's first bi-coloured stamp and the world's first Christmas stamp. Philatelists (stamp collectors) had to wait until 1964, however, before Canada began regularly issuing Christmas stamps. Other countries issued first Christmas stamps as follows: Austria in 1937, Brazil in 1939, Hungary in 1941, United States of America in 1962, and the Netherlands in 1987.

Beginnings of
Boxing Day

B oxing Day is observed in most
Commonwealth nations: Australia, Great
Britain, New Zealand, and Canada. But the
reason why December 26 is a statutory holiday is not often
common knowledge. Contrary to some claims, the name
"Boxing Day" does not originate from the desire to rid the
home of empty boxes the day after Christmas. The name also
has nothing to do with returning unsuitable gifts to the stores
they came from. In fact, most stores nowadays will not even
take merchandise returns on Boxing Day.

Boxing Day has also been known as Offering Day, Saint
Stephen's Day, or the Feast of Saint Stephen (in honour of
Saint Stephen who was one of the first seven deacons chosen
by the early church in the Acts of the Apostles). Saint Stephen
is widely regarded to be the first martyr, or the Protomartyr,

of Christianity. The Feast of Saint Stephen is celebrated on December 26 in the Western Church and on December 27 in the Eastern Church.

The Boxing Day tradition may date from the Middle Ages (AD 400s to 1500s), but the exact origin is unknown. As a holiday, it originated in England in the middle of the 19th century under Queen Victoria. Its roots are found in a long ago practice of giving cash or wares to the less fortunate. Gifts among peers were exchanged on or before Christmas Day, but presents to the lower classes were bestowed the next day.

There is considerable speculation how the name of Boxing Day came about or precisely what unequal relationships are being recognized. The following theories have been espoused.

- The earliest boxes were not boxes at all. They were earthenware containers with a slit in the top (similar to piggy banks.) These earthenware "boxes" were used by the Romans for collecting money to help pay for the festivities at the winter Saturnalia celebrations.
- Christmas celebrations of old entailed bringing everyone together from all over a large estate, thus creating one of the rare instances when everyone could be found in one place at one time. This gathering presented the lord of the manor with an opportunity to easily distribute the year's

stipend of provisions. After all the holiday partying was over and it was almost time to go back to distant homesteads, serfs were presented with their annual allotment of practical goods. The nature of the allotment was determined by the status of the worker and his relative family size. The items handed out included such things as cloth, leather goods, food staples, tools, and other such necessities. The lord of the manor was obligated to supply these goods and this was not a voluntary contribution. These provisions were put into boxes, one box for each family, to make transporting the results of this annual restocking easier.

• Hundreds of years ago, members of the merchant class gave boxes of food, gifts, and money as a token of appreciation to tradespeople and servants who had provided services throughout the year (for example, postmen, lamplighters, parish beadles, parish watchmen, chimney sweeps). These boxes were distributed the day after Christmas as a form of yuletide tip.

• There was a time in Britain when servants brought boxes with them to work on the day after Christmas into which their masters would put coins as a special year end gift or Christmas bonus.

- A 17th century Christmas custom involved apprentices collecting money from their masters' customers. They collected this money in earthenware containers, which could be opened only by being smashed. On Boxing Day, the apprentices would eagerly break open the boxes to see how much they had received.
- Around Christmas time, boxes were placed in churches to collect alms for the poor from the congregation. These donation boxes were opened on Christmas Day by the clergy who would then distribute the contents to the needy the next day.
- At one time, a donation box was kept onboard every ship that sailed on long voyages. The donations collected were presented to the priest who, in return, would offer masses for the safety of the expedition and all aboard. The mass was at that time called "Christmass," and the boxes kept to pay for it were named "Christmass-boxes." The opening of these boxes was known as "Christmass-boxing day," later shortened to Boxing Day.

The one common denominator of all these theories is the theme of the "haves" giving to the "have-nots." As mentioned, people of equal status exchanged gifts on or before Christmas Day whereas those of lower social status received their gifts on the day after. The social superiors did not receive anything back from those they endowed; a gift in return would have been construed as a presumptuous claim of equality, and the antithesis of what Boxing Day actually represented — the preservation of class lines. So the next time your boss gives you a Christmas present just remember, according to tradition, you do not have to reciprocate (but do send a thank-you).

Today in Canada, Boxing Day is not celebrated in the traditional manner. Although, throughout the Christmas season many individuals and organizations do keep the original meaning of Boxing Day alive by donating their time, energy, and money to fill Food Banks and provide gifts for the poor. December 26 is usually synonymous with Boxing Day sales, where retail stores offer extreme discounts on Christmas merchandise, making it the biggest shopping day of the year in Canada.

It is also a time for family and friends to gather with lots of food and fun. Sports such as hockey, curling, soccer, horse racing, and hunting are popular on this holiday. Saint Stephen is the patron saint of horses, so Boxing Day became associated with horseracing and hunting.

The Three
Wise Men

The Three Wise Men of the Nativity, also commonly referred to as the Magi or the Three Kings, are actually not identified by number in the Bible. Matthew 2:11 does, however, mention three gifts of frankincense, gold, and myrrh from which Christian tradition has set their number as three and called them kings. Eastern Orthodox traditions believe there were 12 Magi who visited the Christ child. There is also no biblical source that indicates they were kings. The revelation of the divinity of Christ to the Gentiles (the Wise Men) was called an "epiphany" (a word now associated with a sudden realization of a fundamental truth), and would have been equivalent to a type of "academic certification" of the authenticity of his divinity. The 12 days of Christmas ends on January 6 with the Feast of Epiphany, also called

"The Adoration of the Magi" or "Three Kings Day," commemorating their visit.

The Bible also does not say anything about the Wise Men visiting the manger but rather states that they visited a "house" and saw "the young child" (Matthew 2:11). Many believe that the wise men did not arrive until quite some time after Jesus' birth. According to Luke 2, shepherds visited the infant Jesus in the manger, not Wise Men

The Magi were a caste of Zoroastrian priests of ancient Persia, and were revered by classic authors as astrologers and practitioners of medicine renowned for their wisdom. Because they were alleged to have power over demons, they were given the name "magi" meaning "sorcerer." The Western tradition of the names and descriptions of the Magi is derived from an early sixth century Greek manuscript and subsequent translations:

- Melchoir, King of Arabia, was the oldest of the Magi. He had a long grey beard and gave gold as a gift, symbolizing the acknowledgment of Christ as King.
- Balthasar, King of Ethiopia, was middle-aged, dark in colouring, bearded, and bore the gift of frankincense, symbolizing Christ as the High Priest.
- Caspar, King of Tarsus, was in his twenties. His gift was myrrh, which was used in making

medicines, symbolized Christ as the healer and great physician.

Legends claim that after discovering and honouring the Saviour, the Magi returned home and surrendered their property and positions, giving all their riches to the poor, and set out to spread the Gospel. The apostle St. Thomas reportedly baptized them 40 years later in India, ordaining them as priests. Melchior is said to have died on January 1, AD 54 at the age of 116; Balthasar on January 6 at the age of 112; and, Caspar on January 11 at the age of 109. They were also said to have been martyred and buried in the walls of Jerusalem.

The Empress St. Helena, mother of Constantine I, supposedly discovered their bodies in Persia in AD 325 during her pilgrimage to the Holy Land and brought their remains to Constantinople. She is credited with establishing their identity within the early Church, although the Magi were not referred to as saints until the 12th century. Shortly after that, their remains were taken to Milan where they remained until 1162 when the Holy Roman Emperor Friedrich I took them after capturing the city. In 1163, he presented them to Germany as a gift where they remain to this day in Cologne Cathedral. The Cathedral Church of Saints Peter and Mary in Cologne, which took 632 years to complete (1248–1880), is the largest Gothic structure in northern Europe. It is currently the most visited building in Germany — with 15 million people a year coming to view its beauty and its treasures. The shrine of the Three Wise Men is so famous that the church itself has become popularly known as the *Dreikoenigenkirche* (the Church of the Three Kings).

The Blessing of Doorways
In earlier times, the 12 holy nights between Christmas and Epiphany were called "Smoke Nights" due to the custom of burning incense throughout the homes and barns to bless homesteads.

In the Middle Ages, it was customary to bless homes with holy Epiphany water. The patriarch would lead the family procession carrying a shovel of charcoal on which he burned incense, while the oldest son carried a bowl of holy water, sprinkling it in each room. The rest of the family followed along saying the rosary and singing hymns.

While the father and oldest son were incensing and blessing the house, the youngest child carried chalk that had been blessed in a special ceremony after morning mass. With the blessed chalk, the father wrote over every doorway that led from the house into the open: AD 18+C+M+B+67 which stands for "the three Holy Kings, Caspar, Melchior, Balthasar, in the year of our Lord 1867" or whatever the current year was. This inscription, which also included three crosses, indicated that the three kings were protecting the house against all evil spirits.

This tradition of blessing the doorways is meant to symbolize the family's commitment to welcome Christ into their homes on a daily basis throughout the year. This tradition is observed in Poland, Czechoslovakia, and Sweden by the Star Boys on their Epiphany visits. According to tradition, the homes marked with these holy symbols will receive good fortune throughout the year.

Groundhog Day and Candlemas

If Candlemas Day is bright and clear,
there'll be two winters in the year.
Scottish couplet

hat does Groundhog Day have to do with Christmas? The name "Groundhog Day" is unique to Canada and the United States but the practice, which came to North America from Europe, actually has its origins in the early Christian observance of Candlemas which in turn has its origins in pagan celebrations.

Candlemas is the last festival in the Christian year that is dated by reference to Christmas; subsequent holidays are calculated with reference to Easter, therefore Candlemas is considered to mark the end of the Christmas and Epiphany season. It is celebrated on February 2, the 40th day after

Christmas, and is more formally known as the "Purification of the Blessed Virgin Mary" or the "Presentation of Jesus in the Temple". Christians were observing this holiday in Jerusalem at least as early as the fourth century AD. By the middle of the fifth century, candles were lit on this day to symbolize the association of light with Christ. This was also the day on which all candles that would be used for the next year were blessed by the clergy, hence the name "Candlemas."

The Feast of the Purification was based on the Jewish tradition that women were considered unclean after the birth of a child and were not permitted to enter the Temple to worship. At the end of the purification period, 40 days after the birth of a son or 60 days after a daughter, the mother was brought to the Temple or synagogue and ritually purified. This feast is now celebrated as the Presentation of the Lord, when the infant Jesus was taken to the Temple by his parents according to Jewish custom.[22]

The relationship between purification rituals and the month of February also hark back to the days of nature-based worship. The etymology of the work derives from Middle English *Februarie*, from Old English *Februarius*, from Latin *Februa*, meaning "feast of purification." The pagan Roman purification ritual of *Lupercalia* took place in February. This festival was celebrated to ensure fertility for the people, fields, and flocks.

Likewise, similarities have also been drawn between Candlemas and the ancient Greek *Thesmophoria* festival, associated with the annual disappearance and reappearance of Persephone the daughter of Demeter, goddess of the harvest. Festivities were held to mark the transformation from death to life and the beginning of the agricultural year. The festival included a special meal of roast pig, a ritual tossing of bones into a cavern for a "bone fire," recovering the ashes of the bones, and sowing them with the new seeds in spring to mark the return of Persephone and the new harvest to come.

The pre-Christian Celtic *Imbolc*, or *Oimelc*, festival was a celebration marking the half-way point between the winter solstice and the spring equinox. As one of the cross-quarter festivals it was celebrated from the eve of the holiday through the following night. *Imbolc* literally means "in the womb" and *Oimelc* means "ewes milk" in reference to lambing season. *Imbolc* was dedicated to the Celtic goddess Brigit, who was associated with learning, poetry, fire, smithcrafts, healing, and birth and midwifery. Candlelight processions were held to bless fields and seeds and sacred bonfires were burned as part of the purification and cleansing rituals, much like those held at Yule. Many of Brigit's pagan characteristics were retained when she was made a saint by the Roman Catholic Church who claimed that she was actually a Christian missionary, thereby enabling the Irish to retain their beloved goddess. The date of *Imbolc* was very close to the date of the Eastern Church Candlemas giving rise to the theory that Candlemas may have been in part a Christianization of the pagan festival.

Candlemas was also widely believed to be a good day for weather forecasting. Taking place on the same date as earlier pagan festivals associated with nature the same principles of weather prediction apply. The long held belief was that if February 2 were a sunny day, there would be 40 more days of cold and snow. In the British Isles, good weather at Candlemas has always been taken as a sign foretelling severe winter weather ahead. It is also the date that bears and wolves emerge from winter hibernation to inspect the weather. If they return to their dens on this day it is interpreted to mean that severe weather will continue for a minimum of 40 more days. In western Europe, this was also the time for preparing the fields for the first planting.

One old English rhyme says:

If Candlemas Day be fair and bright,
Winter will have another flight;
But if it be dark with clouds and rain,
Winter is gone, and will not come again.
Another variation of the rhyme hails from Scotland:
If Candlemas day be dry and fair,
The half o' winter to come and mair,
If Candlemas day be wet and foul,
The half of winter's gone at Yule.

The Roman legions, during the conquest of the northern country, are thought to be responsible for bringing this tradition to the Teutons, (early Germans), who adopted it and concluded that if the sun made an appearance on Candlemas Day, the hedgehog, upon emerging from hibernation would cast a shadow, thus predicting a "second winter" consisting of six more weeks of bad weather. This belief was further carried into folklore tradition in England, Scotland, Mexico, the United States, and Canada (as Groundhog Day), and many other places.

Groundhog Day is a traditional festival celebrated in Canada as well as in the USA on February 2. The theory and custom behind this festival is that, like in Europe, one must observe a groundhog's burrow on this day to determine if winter will continue or spring will arrive early. If the groundhog surfaces and fails to see his shadow due to clouds covering the sun, winter will soon end. If the groundhog glimpses his shadow because the sun is shining, however, this will frighten him back into his hole, and six more weeks of winter can be expected. Groundhogs have proven to be very reliable in over a century of observance.

The first official Groundhog Day was held in Punxsutawney, Pennsylvania, on February 2, 1887. Pennsylvania's earliest settlers were Germans and they found groundhogs to be in abundance in many parts of the state. The groundhog somewhat resembled the European hedgehog, which they had been observing annually on February 2 as their weather predictor. The Germans would recite the following couplet on February 2:

Groundhog Day and Candelmas

For as the sun shines on Candlemas Day,
So far will the snow swirl until the May.

Br'er Groundhog was the name given to the first official weather forecasting groundhog, but it was later changed to Punxsatawney Phil in honour of King Phillip. Canada has her share of famous meteorological media hogging rodents as well, including Wiarton Willie, Balzac Billy, and Shubenacadie Sam.

Candlemas Superstitions

Candlemas, which represented the last festival of the Christmas season, was also considered the day on which all Christmas decorations must be taken down and the greenery removed from the home. Some superstitions specified that all Christmas greenery should be disposed of by ritually burning it on Candlemas Eve. Any traces of holly or other evergreens left behind were considered a harbinger of death. Likewise, anyone hearing funeral bells tolling on Candlemas was doomed to soon receive news of the death of a relative or close friend; the number of times the bell tolled represented the number of days that would pass before the devastating news was revealed. It is considered acceptable, however, and even advisable, to bring home evergreens from a church and display them in the house all year to promote good luck.

345

Many carols referred to Candlemas as the conclusion of the Christmas season. Robert Herrick (1591–1674) wrote at least four poems concerning Candlemas. The following excerpt is from "Ceremony upon Candlemas Eve":

Down with the rosemary, and so
Down with the bays and misletoe
Down with the holly, ivy, all,
Wherewith ye dress'd the Christmas Hall
That so the superstitious find
No one least branch there left behind
For look, how many leaves there be
Neglected, there (maids, trust to me)
So many goblins you shall see.

Old Slavic
Winter Solstice
and Christmas
Superstitions

edieval Slavic peasants did not embrace
Christianity on any more than a surface
level. This gave rise to what the Russians
call *dvoeverie* or "double-faith." According to historians,
Christianity's foothold was so weak that many peasants did
not even know the name of the man on the cross to whom
they prayed.

Old customs connected with Christmas have flour-
ished for years in the countryside, although the city has
retained only a few of them. On the eve of Winter Solstice
(*Koljada*), the longest darkest night of the year, when the
kolo (wheel) was turning to a new year, it was believed that a

347

window was opened to other realms for a brief time during which fortunes for the next year could be determined and set. Because these ancient people were so in tune and connected with nature, most fortunes and superstitions were related to weather. The association of the season to death, rebirth, and fertility also made health and matrimonial predictions particularly significant. Once people grew to accept Christianity, these *Koljada* superstitions carried over to Christmas.

Koljada — Christmas customs related to health

- Upon awakening *Koljada* morning, a person should never go back to sleep for it is certain to bring on illness.
- A dry crust of bread and a coin placed in a basin with cold water ensures plenty of food and physical strength for the following year.
- The first person entering the house on New Year's morning should be a man to guarantee health for the whole household; a woman entering would mean sickness.
- Christmas tree decorations: apples bring beauty and health, ornaments made out of straw bring wealth, and nuts bring happiness and love.
- A sneeze on *Koljada* guarantees health.
- Polishing teeth with garlic will guarantee strength (and few friends!).
- Eating apples at Christmas dinner will prevent throat infection, and nuts are eaten to ease a toothache.

• Feeding the animals the leftovers and a piece of the *oplatek* wafer after supper will ensure their health and strong offspring.
• Placing a piece of iron under the Christmas dinner table for everybody to touch will ensure strong and healthy legs.

Weather, wealth, and marriage were very important in the lives of the whole village, so some customs were strictly observed:

• A sunny Christmas Eve day guarantees lots of eggs from the chickens, as well as a marriage for young and poor people. A cloudy day means abundant milk from the cows and marriage of the old and wealthy villagers.
• When cleaning fish, scales should never be thrown away but instead put in a wallet to bring wealth. Scales placed in a red sack and nailed to the door will bring love.
• Sweeping floors should be done inward from the door so as not to sweep prospective suitors away.
• At the Christmas dinner, every dish must be tasted to ensure good harvests in the year to come.
• Placing straw under the tablecloth will bring wealth and good crops. Also, maidens will be able to tell the fortune of their future marriage — long, green straw indicates a speedy marriage, black blades mean a long wait, and yellow blades foretell spinsterhood.
• Everybody should have coins on them at supper to ensure wealth in the future.

- Christmas Eve supper must consist of 12 different dishes for each month of the year to ensure a wealthy year.
- Everyone should visit a neighbour and try to steal a small item — this will ensure wealth but only if the item is returned or replaced on St. Stephen's Day (December 26).
- An apple is eaten at the end of dinner and the seeds counted. They foretell love if the number is even, and more than six seeds means a wedding is guaranteed.
- Any unmarried girls at the dinner table are to place a piece of fish on the floor and then let the dog into the room. The first piece the dog eats indicates the first girl to get married.
- After a mass on St. Stephen's Day, people throw wheat or rice at each other as a fertility symbol to bring good harvest and wealth in the coming year.

Other superstitions:
- At midnight, animals speak in human voices, but it is bad luck to overhear them.
- Winning at a card game that day brings happiness for the whole year.
- In a region threatened by wolves, leftovers from Christmas Eve supper were placed outside the gate to invite the wolves who, when treated well, would not harm the host.
- One plate at the table should always be set for the dead relatives.
- Leaving the table during the meal will bring bad luck or even death.

- Mistletoe should be cut off, dipped in wax, and placed in a beehive to ensure lots of honey.
- Waking up early on Christmas Eve day will ensure punctuality throughout the year.
- After supper, all the dirty spoons should be tied together to ensure that the family will stay together.
- Children should not be spanked, as it will bring problems to them throughout the year.
- It is bad luck to lend anything at Christmas, as it will likely go missing all year.
- Laundry should not be left on the line overnight as this is guaranteed to carry problems over from one year to the next.
- Lit candles should always be included on the dinner table, as each person must see their shadow on the wall. No shadow or a headless shadow would foretell death in the coming year.
- The candles should be blown out after dinner, and if the smoke goes towards the window it foretells the birth of a baby, if it goes up it foretells a wedding, if it goes towards the door it foretells a death.
- When sitting down to dinner, one should blow on his chair first or else risk sitting on a ghost that came to join the festivities.
- On Christmas Eve, well water can turn into wine.
- Christmas Eve night was not quiet and calm. That night, after dead souls were fed, they were thrown out of the house by pot and table banging.

The traditions of the Festivals of Light, be they Winter Solstice, Christmas, Hanukkah, Diwali, or others, all offer opportunities to remember and honour those who came before and illuminated the way for those who follow. They offer a time to light the candles and reflect on what is important. They offer hope for a brighter tomorrow. The shared message of these festivals is that the light will return; life will go on and everyone has the opportunity for another chance. "I will live in the Past, the Present, and the Future." Ebenezer Scrooge and the true spirit of Christmas.

Notes

1. Kat Allison, "Solstice,"
   http://www.katallison.com/solstice.html

2. *The Real Story of Christmas*,
   http://www.historychannel.com/exhibits/holidays/
   christmas/real2.html (accessed 10 April 2005).

3. *Christianity or Mithraism*, http://members.aol.com/
   MercStG/ChriMithPage1.html (accessed 8 April 2005).

4. *Ibid.*

5. Tim Goldrick, *More Than You Need to Know About
   Christmas*, (Pre-publication manuscript, 2003). Used
   with permission.

6. Municipality of the District of Lunenburg, "Lunenburg
   County: The balsam fir Christmas tree capital of the
   world," (2002),
   http://www.modl.ca/CommunityChristmasTrees.html
   (accessed 29 April 2005).

7. "America's Best Holiday Cookies," *McCall's*, December
   1994, 85.

8. "Holiday Tradition With Spicy History," *Pittsburgh Post-Gazette*, 9 December 2001, N9.

9. Karen S. Edwards and Sharon Antle, "Gingerbread," *Americana*, December 1988, 49.

10. Linda Campbell Franklin, *300 Years of Kitchen Collectibles*, 4th ed., (New York: Books Americana, 1998), 183.

11. John Ayto, *An A-Z of Food and Drink*, (Oxford: Oxford University Press, 2002), 329.

12. Alan Davidson, *Oxford Companion to Food*, (Oxford: Oxford University Press, 1999), 208.

13. Webb Garrison, *Treasury of Christmas Stories*, (Nashville: Rutledge Hill Press, 1990).

14. "Mummers in Newfoundland," http://www.newfoundlandlabrador.com/history/mummering.asp (accessed 30 April 2005).

15. Jeffrey Vallance, "Santa is a Wildman!" *LA Weekly*, December 20-26, 2002,

16. *Ibid.*

17. Stephen Nissenbaum, *The Battle for Christmas*, (Vintage, 1997).

18. Stanley Frankel, "Rudolph that Amazing Reindeer," *Good Housekeeping*, December 1989, 126, http://www.frankel-y.com/append.htm (accessed 26 April 2005).

19. Tim Goldrick, *More Than You Need to Know About Christmas*, (Pre-publication manuscript, 2003). Used with permission.

20. Berit Haugen Keyes, "Christmas Reborn. The creation of a consumer Christmas — Professor Steven Nissenbaum in interview" (December 2004) http://www.threemonkeysonline.com/threemon_ printable.php?id=170 (accessed 23 Apr 2005).

21. "Grandfather Frost and Snow Maiden," http://www.christmas-treasures.com/duncan_royale/ Collection/SantaIII/GrandfatherFrost.htm (accessed 10 May 2005).

22. Douglas Anderson, "Candlemas,"
http://www.hymnsandcarolsofchristmas.com/History/
candlemas.htm (accessed 29 April 2005).

Bibliography

Baigent, M., Leigh, R., and Lincoln, H. *Holy Blood, Holy Grail.* London 1982.

Campbell, T.J. (transcribed by Thomas, Joseph P.) "Jean de Brébeuf," *The Catholic Encyclopedia, Volume II.*

Davidison, Alice Joyce. *The "J" Is For Jesus.* ZonderKidz; Board edition, October 1, 1998.

Garrison, Webb. *Treasury of Christmas Stories - Fascinating, Little-Known Stories of Christmas and How Some of Our Favorite Traditions Began.* Rutledge Hill Press; Book & CD edition August 1, 1998.

Haidel, David. *The Candymaker's Gift: The Legend of the Candy Cane.* Cook Communications, October 25, 1996.

Hole, Christina. *The Encyclopedia of Superstitions.* New York: Barnes & Noble, 1996.

Jones, Charles W. *Saint Nicholas of Myra, Bari, and Manhattan: Biography of a Legend.* University of Chicago Press, Chicago, 1978.

Karas, Sheryl Ann. *The Solstice Evergreen: The History, Folklore and Origins of the Christmas Tree* Rev. Ed. Fairfield: Aslan Publishing, 1998.

Miles, Clement A. *Christmas Customs and Traditions: Their History and Significance.* Dover: New York, 1976.

Nissenbaum, Stephen. *The Battle for Christmas.* Vintage, October 1997.

Opie, Iona and Moira Tatem. *A Dictionary of Superstitions.* Oxford: Oxford University Press.

Pickering, David. *Dictionary of Superstitions.* London: Cassell, 1995.

Sansom, William. *Book of Christmas,* McGraw-Hill:New York Society of American Florists. 2001. Society of American Florists DATELINE, Sept. 24, Vol. 14 (Number 16).

Studwell, William. *The Christmas Carol Reader.* Haworth Press, October 1, 1995.

Walburg, Lori. *The Legend of the Candy Cane.* ZonderKidz, October 19, 1997.

Bibliography

The Washington Post, Jan. 11, 1994, Corrections Roll In Like a Clap of Donder.

And various web sites.

Acknowledgments

This book was conceived as a part of an Old World Christmas Market concept I designed and created for Heritage Park Historical Village in Calgary, Alberta. The research I started for the project grew to take on a life of its own, eventually resulting in this book. So many people in one way or another contributed to this project and I apologize that sadly it is impossible to list them all.

Special thanks go to my friends and colleagues at Heritage Park for their inspiration and cheerleading. Thunderous rounds of applause go to my "elves": Jeanette, Denis, Carrie, and Ashley Pyle; Maureen Bedard, Joan Bedard; and, Karen Jennings, with eternal gratitude from your humble "Master and Commander from the far side of the world"! I would also like to thank the good people at Altitude Publishing and especially Kara Turner, Stephen Hutchings, and Cory Manning. I extend my sincere appreciation to Dr. B.K. Swartz, Douglas Anderson, and Tim Goldrick for generously sharing their bountiful knowledge of Christmas history and traditions. Infinite gratitude goes to my family for being endlessly fabulous, funny, loving, and supportive: to my parents, Orest and Mary Mandryk; to my sisters (and my Muses), Dr. Deborah Mater, Cathy Midzain, and Denise Moumos; to my "bro," George Moumos; and to my

Acknowledgments

aunt and uncle, Doreen and Jim Kirk. And last, but certainly not least, I wish to thank my husband, Thomas Andrejews, for his support, encouragement, understanding, and assistance, without whom this book would not have happened; and of course, for introducing me to the wonderful world of *Weihnachtsmärkte*, as well as *Lebkuchen, Glühwein*, and *Laugenbrötchen. Vielen Dank mein Schatz!*

DeeAnn Mandryk, exploring the origins of Christmas at the
Roman ruins, Villa Rustica, in Hechingen-Stein, Germany.

About the Authors

Born and raised in Calgary, DeeAnn Mandryk graduated from the University of Calgary with a degree in English Literature and Political Science. DeeAnn has carved an eclectic career path through the arts, advertising, investment, and tourism industries. Her work over the past decade as the Buyer and Merchandising Manager for Calgary's Heritage Park Historical Village has contributed to her interest in Canadian history and in particular to the origins and evolution of cultural traditions. DeeAnn lives wherever the German Air Force sends her husband, which currently is Geneva, Switzerland.

Born and raised in London, Ontario, Chef Jeff O'Neill ignited his love of Canada's cuisine in the world famous Rocky Mountain Resorts. Currently the Executive Chef at the Delta Lodge at Kananaskis, Jeff has had the opportunity to create and serve distinctly Canadian dishes featuring regional cuisine to millions of visitors, including kings and queens, political leaders, and the world's corporate elite.

Recipe Notes

Recipe Notes

Recipe Notes

Recipe Notes

Recipe Notes

Recipe Notes

Recipe Notes

Recipe Notes

Our Own Christmas Traditions

Our Own Christmas Traditions

Our Own Christmas Traditions

Our Own Christmas Traditions

Our Own Christmas Traditions

Our Own Christmas Traditions

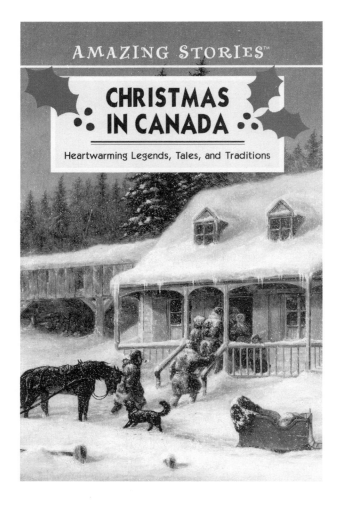

AMAZING STORIES™

∴ CHRISTMAS IN ∴
BRITISH COLUMBIA

Heartwarming Legends, Tales, and Traditions

HOLIDAY

by Rich Mole

ISBN 1-55153-786-9

AMAZING STORIES™

CHRISTMAS IN THE PRAIRIES

Heartwarming Legends, Tales, and Traditions

HOLIDAY

by Rich Mole

ISBN 1-55153-782-6

AMAZING STORIES

also available!

AMAZING STORIES™

CHRISTMAS IN QUEBEC

Heartwarming Legends, Tales, and Traditions

HOLIDAY

by Megan Durnford

ISBN 1-55153-784-2

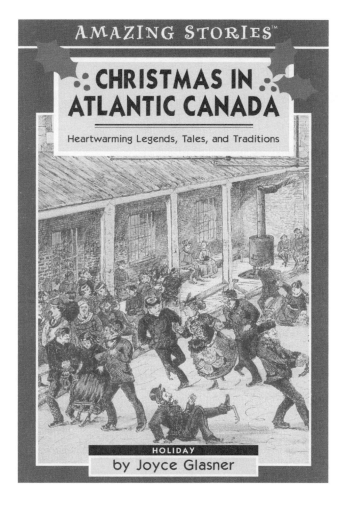

AMAZING STORIES™

∴ CHRISTMAS IN ∴
ATLANTIC CANADA

Heartwarming Legends, Tales, and Traditions

HOLIDAY

by Joyce Glasner

ISBN 1-55153-781-8

OTHER AMAZING STORIES

These titles are available wherever you buy books. If you have trouble finding the book you want, call the Altitude order desk at **1-800-957-6888**, e-mail your request to: **orderdesk@altitudepublishing.com** or visit our Web site at **www.amazingstories.ca**

New **AMAZING STORIES** titles are published every month.